QUEST FOR SHEBA

Few corners of the earth still remain shrouded in secrecy and mystery. Few places are left where Western feet have never trod and yet where glimmers and broods to this day the romance and glamour of a civilisation older than the Bible. Such a region--of unknown allurements, of strange and savage desert dwellers, of extraordinary sky-scraping cities rising like phantoms out of the sand, of shade-less glitter and thirst and wonderment, is the Hadhramut ("in the presence of death") in south-western Arabia.

Mr. Norman Pearn, a young Cornishman, risked his life to visit this unvisited Arabian wonderland, much of which is unmarked on any map. Odds of two thousand to one were laid against the possibility of his return. His remarkable and memorable travel commentary not only adds an important contribution to the romantic story of Arabia, but gives also the personal record of fascinating experiences and adventures while following in the steps of the Queen of Sheba who once ruled this land. Guided by instructions left to him by one of Lawrence of Arabia's lieutenants, Mr. Pearn found significant traces of Sheba's past--the only Queen in Arabian History

Norman Pearn was a traveller and explorer. **Vernon Barlow** was a successful writer in the subject and helped with the preparation of this exploration in book form.

T0347237

The Ageless Land

Quest for Sheba

NORMAN STONE PEARN
AND
VINCENT BARLOW

Routledge
Taylor & Francis Group

LONDON AND NEW YORK

First published in 1937 by
I Nicholson and Watson Ltd

This edition first published in 2009 by
Routledge
2 Park Square, Milton Park, Abingdon, Oxon, OX14 4RN

Simultaneously published in the USA and Canada
by Routledge
711 Third Avenue, New York, NY 10017

Routledge is an imprint of the Taylor & Francis Group, an informa business

© Kegan Paul, 2003

Transferred to Digital Printing 2009
First issued in paperback 2012

British Library Cataloguing in Publication Data
A catalogue record for this book is available from the British Library

ISBN13: 978-0-7103-0846-7 (hbk)

ISBN13: 978-0-415-65123-3 (pbk)

Publisher's Note
The publisher has gone to great lengths to ensure the quality of this reprint
but points out that some imperfections in the original copies may be
apparent. The publisher has made every effort to contact original copyright
holders and would welcome correspondence from those they have been
unable to trace.

PREFACE

MOST THINGS, WHETHER good or bad, are generally better
left unexplained, but there are always exceptions to every
rule. In this case, the collaboration of two names on the
title page in their relation to the first person used throughout the narrative, needs a brief explanation.

One day, in summer, a young man I had never met
before came to me out of the blue, and told me of his
burning desire to go in search of the lost cities of the Queen
of Sheba. Though unknown to me, he was not a complete
stranger to exploration, for he had traversed the Sahara
in the heat of midsummer, a feat which the Foreign Legion
had labelled impossible.

Could I help him with his new ambition? I rather
doubted it. But I tried. . . . Eventually we were able to
interest a publisher and a paper in the project. The young
man set out alone; there was not enough money for two,
and anyhow the idea was his and the search had been
entrusted to him. He slipped away quietly. No one saw
him off and no officials hurried to meet him at Aden. It
had been settled between us that he should do the exploration and I should write the book. He was to be responsible
for the important part, I for the writing and the research.

Fortunately I had been across a portion of Arabia and
knew something of the surroundings. In writing this book,
with Mr. Pearn periodically at my elbow, I have set out to
try and do justice to his travels, while at the same time
giving accurate details of little-known Southern Arabia,
and recapturing a few echoes of the splendour and the
wonder of those old Bible times when Sheba figured as
Queen.

We record with grateful thanks our indebtedness in particular to Commander Craufurd, many years advisor to the Imam of the Yemen, to the late Sir Wallis Budge and University College, Oxford, for expert translations on the Sheba period, and to the Aden authorities for their kindness and invaluable assistance on the spot.

VERNON BARLOW.

Author's Club,
    London.

CONTENTS

vii

ILLUSTRATIONS

INTRODUCTION

There is an old Arab description of the Queen of Sheba, handed down rather than written by people to whom books were unknown, and translated by a Frenchman, Dr. J. C. Mardus,[1] transcriber of the *Thousand and One Nights*. This word portrait depicts her at the height of her debutante days:

It is related in tradition and legend—but Allah knows all, He the exalted—that there lived in fortunate Saba, in the land of Yemen, during the time of Solomon son of David, a King's daughter, a child Queen, whose life was marvels and astonishment.

This Queen was the flower of Arabian flowers, a virgin of sixteen whom God had made in beauty. She was perfumed of herself and by nature amber. Her waist and colour knew no parallel except in Ban branches and Chinese tuberose. Her face was sorcery, as of an idol of Misraim; its cheeks were the shame of roses, the mouth was cut from a single ruby, the chin was marked by a forgotten smile.

And there were two long eyes upon it of black and white; antelope eyes where the black pastured upon the white, in the shadow of the curved sword of the lashes. And each was so long that it was seen in full even when she turned her face aside.

When she opened those Egyptian eyes, sighs were about her; and when she shut them the world grew dark before the faces of men.

This lily child breathed and reigned, white and undesirous, for she did not know what destiny of love was hers. But kept herself aloof, shaded by the bright pearl of her virginity, her mystery of thought.

Balkis was her name, a benediction; which the people of Yemen called Balkama. She was Megeda to the Ethiopians.

. . . It is clear enough that the young Queen must have been of outstanding beauty and personality, since otherwise she would never have gained the throne in

[1] English version by E. Powys Mathers, Casanova Society.

opposition to various male rivals. In all Arabian history there has never been such another, excepting Zenobia, Queen of Palmyra.

Matchless beauty and attraction in a woman, when recognised, becomes a beacon-fire to which many gather; it kindles, spreads, and turns into a blaze, setting alight the paths of history and causing men to stand at attention. Not more than a dozen names have possessed this universal power, in all the pageantry of the world, and they burn their way into memory and do not disappear.

The Queen of Sheba was the first of the beauties whose fame belongs not only to their own period, but to posterity as well; within two hundred years Helen of Troy had brought her blonder beauty to be a banner to armies, and she was followed by the sun-warmed allurements of Cleopatra, the Egyptian, who held in her arms the two greatest Romans of her day.

Of these three international beauties, the Queen of Sheba, by far the least known in the West, though not in the East, was the only one not to leave behind her a broad wake of strife and war, and for this reason alone is perhaps the most remarkable as well as the most beneficent of them all.

In the East, she lives not so much by virtue of her beauty as by accomplishments, causing her to be traditional and transcendent, for her very name has entered the loom of poetry. The Queen of Sheba! Queen of the South and of the morning! The beautiful Queen who worshipped the Evening Star and has been linked to the Wise Men! A Bible celebrity.

Out of one journey that turned into the most spectacular embassy of all time, developed the first monotheism of the South, besides the Abyssinian dynasty of the Negus, the Kingdom of the King of Kings. This one Queen overtopped the importance of kings and castles and knights on the chessboard of destiny.

It is not easy to resist the fascination of the great caravans linking Sheba to Solomon more firmly than ordinary ceremonial—a caravan journey whose fame walked into the Bible and the Quran.

"And the gifts of the Sabian were things of Yemen and of the countries of the South, borne by young beduin girls with forward breasts . . . powdered gold and ivory of the Soudan, with myrrh and cinnamon, nard and incense, benjoin and the tears of gum; there was Serendib nad, and ambergris with captive essences, and scented woods, with pearls from the Gulf and little bags of gems."

Solomon in return offered, "purple of Sur and gauze of Assur, silks of Liban and brocades of Sham, Khorasan garments and melons and green rose trees from Damascus. . . ."

In a sense the episodes between Sheba and Solomon represent, as nearly as may be in actual fact, a culmination of human romance, the caravan journey on which almost every man and woman at some period travels. They illustrate in far away focus the flowering of wide human aspirations and emotions. Woman seeks everlastingly for wisdom and strength in a man, and seldom rests content without the best; man, each according to his need, searches the faces of woman-kind for glowing, sympathetic beauty—a beauty that can reflect as well as shine, and if he finds it not, then it becomes for him a symbol of the unattainable beyond his personal horizon.

The Queen of Sheba has never been properly found or "placed" by posterity. Her country in its original condition has been beyond the reach of accurate history, and much of it lies in either forbidding or forbidden territory.

She has gained, no doubt, by being outside the bounds of everyday scrutiny and criticism. Yet she was a bringer of gifts to many besides Solomon the king.

It is more than possible that she was responsible for some of the famous irrigation works and dams that once made Arabia the parched and scorched into Arabia the happy. Her son started African civilisation. She is not forgotten in the East, and echoes of her meaning and her majesty have continued down nineteen centuries to us to-day—"from the Queen of the South and of the morning —Balkis—Megeda, daughter of kings."

QUEST FOR SHEBA

CHAPTER ONE

THE ROAD TO ADEN

MY JOURNEY TO the East started with a familiar P. & O. liner making its way through the cauldron of the Red Sea at a time of year when most people do their best to avoid it.

To Easterner and Westerner alike the Red Sea remains an unpopular and even fearful highway. This line of fracture in the ancient skull of the earth's surface was barred to the trading Indian for many sailing centuries at one end, and only opened to the white man at the other after Herculean efforts; but the brown borderland people, smearing themselves with indigo against the sun, have long ago found out the secrets of its fascinations, and trade on them: they sail their vessels quickly from Africa to Araby and back again, nosing out commerce and currents at night, rather than navigating the torrid lengths from Suez to Bab-el-Mandeb after the fashion set by steamships of the West.

The Red Sea is a funnel, and at times that funnel is a furnace. Europe, and especially Britain, holds the telescope of watchfulness to her eye at Port Said, gazing down the salt water rift, and Asia and Africa exchange visits in the darkness. Pearls and P. & O. liners, spice cargoes, sharks and slaves, pilgrims and flying-fish navigate the waterway between two primitive seaboards older than Noah. Beyond Perim two deep channel currents flow in contrary directions, like heated water in a test-tube, moving inward in the eastern surface channel, and outward in the western and much more salty channel, a hundred fathoms

13

below the surface, towards the Indian Ocean. During the monsoon winds the Red Sea sometimes sinks as much as two feet during the process of condensation and surface combustion.

I leaned over the rail of s.s. *Strathaird*, scanning the salmon-coloured sea, the cool, blue mountains of Africa, the hot, grey, humpy ranges of Arabia—naked, derelict and forgotten hills, huddled into shapelessness and giving the impression of an age-old loneliness and detachment. Somewhere over these mountains, in some place yet to be determined, dwelt, in Bible days, the greatest queen in Eastern history, the mother of Abyssinia, the face and form that launched a thousand caravans and caught the eye of Solomon—Balkis, Queen of Sheba, the Asiatic She-who-must-be-obeyed. A great name lingers unforgettably through the centuries, kept alive by transfusions of interest and attention from those who follow after.

Porpoises gambolled in ordered lines of leapfrog, keeping pace with the ship. Friendly fellows, they often followed us for hours on end before going about their own business. When in synchronised array they looked to be one great sea monster, a possible understudy and alternative for the sea-serpent.

Two sportsmen began throwing them rolls, but they paid not the slightest attention. An argument arose as to whether their swallowing arrangements were handicapped in the same manner as the whale. Tiny migrant birds would alight on our ship, accepting the hospitality of the rigging; they would flit about for days until the arrival of hawk or kestrel caused them to panic off in flight. With land on either side, the liner became a part of the age-old intercourse between Asia and Africa.

The second officer, a man who used his eyes, showed me where the deep water channel narrowed to a mere two miles.

"The Children of Israel may have crossed somewhere

here when fleeing from Pharaoh," he observed. "There are plenty of submerged islands and sand banks. A little less water running and it would have been easy. Perhaps the main channel had suddenly become blocked."

We discussed the question of plagues and miracles for some time, and I spoke of the theory of the Flood having been caused by the Atlantic breaking into the fertile Mediterranean basin through the Pillars of Hercules.

"And why not go back to the old days?" he inquired, his voice suddenly serious. "Engineers tell me that it would now be possible to dam the Mediterranean. A hundred miles of waterfall, as high as you like, between Atlantic and Mediterranean! Special locks for liners! With the power available you could generate free electric light for most of Europe."

Pharaoh or Solomon would no doubt have looked with favour on such a scheme promising a far richer return on expenditure than any war; but the modern Dictator, who prefers the sound of his own trumpet to the many voices of international plenty, hardens his heart and turns to self-interested financiers rather than to community-minded engineers.

The Red Sea funnel narrows here, and odours of the land drifted across the ship: the acrid, aromatic odours of antique regions which have slept and steamed for centuries in the sun: the incense of Arabia discussed by classical Pliny and colloquialized by Shakespeare with a gesture of Lady Macbeth's hand.

Hodeida, the only port of consequence in this region, has outlived all its rivals; the fast sailing Arab dhows, with hawk-wing sails and painted hulls, steal in here in their numbers, as they did ever since the days of the Periplus and the old navigators of Tarshish, Carthage, Saaba and Rome. Mocha, where the coffee brought from high Ethiopia, across the waterway, grew into opulence, is now a city of stranded pride, deserted by the waves and only alive to-day

by courtesy of the aqueduct running sixteen miles from
ancient Musa.

Soon we steamed past Perim Island, destined to be the
new Gibraltar guarding the far end of the funnel through
which West scrutinises East. I caught a glimpse of white
official buildings and rocks overtopped by wireless masts.
Since the Italians began to set themselves the imperial task
of reviving Rome, Perim is fast changing from an island into
a fortress: already the Arab trader, transporting his wares
of spice and mystery, may not touch there, but must sail
along the snout of Arabia until he reaches Aden. Perim is
twelve miles from the African coast, and Eritrea only three
flying hours from Aden.

Ocelis was the old Perim port, long ago abandoned to
silence and the encroaching sand. It was this forgotten
harbour that once marked the limit of the Indian traders
sailing across from Oman and Surat, eager for enrichment,
for none of their ships were allowed north of it, to
trespass on the precious grounds of the spice growers.
Cana, a little further west, mentioned by Greek historians,
was the sea port for the old Minean empire of Southern
Arabia.

As the voyage continued, my longing increased to wander
on these grounds of incense and coffee myself, to step upon
that wizened landscape where the world turns over in slow
simplicity and awareness, as do the waves on the beaches,
unheeding the profitless bustle of unquiet civilisation. For
how much does it not profit a man to make a start
from the very beginning of things; to forget the flux
and superiority of the present and gain refreshment and
contrast from the old wells of the past, time-honoured,
immutable and abiding, in a territory two thousand miles
and two thousand years away from London.

Once at Aden I hoped I should not have long to
wait.

There are long miles of Aden sweltering in the sun
from Tawahi, at Steamer Point, to Crater and Sheikh

Othman. The population is about the same as that of Hastings: among the traders, harnessed with pointed carpet-slippers to commercialism, is a large sprinkling of Jews. I landed in a native-run motor boat carrying a special awning so that the newcomer should not suffer sunstroke before setting foot on the Crescent front.

Avoiding, on my first day, officialdom and my fellow-men, I crossed the Maala plain to the old village port redolent with wharves, go-downs, and perhaps the oldest ship-building yard in the world. The Arabs said so, and though the Arab tongue is inventive, in this case, after a little investigation, I was inclined to believe them.

Old and salted as navigation and the ways of the sea are those Aden wharves. Here in aromatic sheds, shadowed and hazy after the brilliance outside, Arab women sort out and lade the incense merchandise. They did this grading in the first centuries of the Roman emperors and the times before them, before the days of Mohammed, before Christ, before Buddha, maybe. They do it still to-day, sorting out with stained fingers the gleaming gum-drops and spice nodules. Caspar, Melchior, and that dark king, Balthasar, came with offerings of frankincense and myrrh to sweeten the entry of Christianity into the world and make it of good savour. Sheba herself is said to have been the ancestor of the Wise Men. The perfumes of Arabia have tinctured the minds of poets and caused Southern Arabia, for all its sunstruck wastes, to be called Happy.

At Maala, the road branches, the right fork rising to Main Pass, the left fork to Khor Maksar and the R.A.F. Isthmus. Up in these blistered crags of rock-bound Aden, Cain is said to lie buried; perhaps it is his hell; I have seldom seen a district looking less like the Garden of Eden or where the physical earth is more scarred, scorched and abraised with the myriad wrinkles of a timeless fate.

The Arabs have a knack of adopting all the great ones of

the holy books, and if not naturalising them, at any rate claiming burial rights. Abraham lies away in the north beyond the great deserts. Eve has her tomb at Jiddah where the tamarisk sways its shade across the Mecca pilgrims. Adam is said to rest in the hills between Medina and Mecca; according to beduin tradition, Adam walked across the globe from India seeking out Arabian Eve, and wherever he stopped on his journey some village or oasis sprang into being to mark his progress.

A Ford tourer rushed me up the hill to Main Pass, for Ford has succeeded Alexander as the new conqueror of the East, and nothing stops his invading chariots.

Fortune was kind to me; the day was brazen hot and clear, exposing to view, beyond the camel-grey distances, the far foot-hills of the Yemen plateau, fifty miles northward, an escarpment not usually discernible from Aden. Sheer and towering, like the ramparts of some unthinkable city, the brown mountains of Yemen uprose beyond the broken ground of the middle distance, beyond the ancient Wadis: they were fanged and crenellated, light grey in the sunshine, darkly brooding in the shadow. Above them, the heavens were a dead, unchanging blue. No cloud sailed across that sky. No breath of wind stirred that parched landscape.

Somewhere out there beyond the ten thousand feet of mountains was to be found Sheba's lost city—either Mareb, the myrrh metropolis of the Sabaeans, or further west, beneath the glare of the sun, the capital of the frankincense trafficking—Shabwa, or perhaps some other.

It was naked, untamed, beckoning mountains such as these that had called forth Rudyard Kipling's "Explorer" into print:

> "Something hidden. Go and find it. Go and look
>   Behind the ranges,
> "Something lost beyond the ranges—lost and
>   Waiting for you. Go!"

The road from the pass drops down to Crater. Pock-marks hollowing into the walls of the upper crater are the famous Aden tanks, a system of water-control constructed of solid masonry or carved out of the rock. I am no engineer, but this gesture by man in answer to the inhospitality of the desert is nearly as old as Sheba and her caravans. Always, at all seasons and epochs, civilised man has recoiled from the desert as from an enemy; only the beduin Arabs, true descendants of Ishmael, treat the wilderness as friendly habitation, and they are simple folk who are happy living in tents and looking at nowhere.

The tanks, when full, contain 20,000 gallons of rain-water. These years of plenty only occur once or twice during each decade; lean times prevail for the rest of the period.

The mountains ramparting Aden are riddled in places with caves that are of extraordinary depth. I walked into one beyond the reach of daylight and almost of air. Ragged 'bedu' troglodytes of the twilight, had made their home here like the first cave-men, and like those of us whom the bombing aeroplane of the next wars, working its destruction upon civilisation, may force to creep out fearful days in burrows and caverns.

I walked past the 'bedu',[1] wondering why they cried to me to come back. They hooked their fingers at me. They seemed afraid of what might come out of the depths. Their terror took shape, for large birds, unsubstantial and ghostly, flitted out of the darkness and swooped about me. I had not a stick with me, and beat at them with my hands until I was forced to retreat. They were not bats I feel convinced, and they were not eagles, but without seeing them shaped by daylight, I am only prepared to be positive as to what they were not.

That evening the Crescent Hotel seemed a palace of pleasure and comfort by comparison with the caves. Running water and bedroom basins are a particular luxury in Aden. The manager of the hotel, known to everyone as "Albert," promised to find me a suitable guide as soon as

[1] badu is singular and bedu plural for beduin, as used locally.

I had mentioned my hope of going into the Hadhramaut and Yemen.

"How far will you wish to go—to get there?" Albert inquired.

"He must get there *and back*," I emphasised, while admitting the greater importance of the first half of the journey.

"Arab guides are no damned good," said Albert hopefully.

Albert is one of the personalities of Aden. He usually wears khaki shorts, featuring two of the most remarkably fat knees displayed by any man. He visits ships on arrival, and acts as news, fiction, gossip and stop press combined in one person; during the Italio-Abyssinian War he was invested with importance and gossip talked of him as a character in the John Buchan "thriller" tradition—an international mystery man with india-rubber actions, though in actual fact he is as innocuous as milk. Mules in Aden have doubtful antecedents, but Albert's birth, parentage, country of adoption and passport are almost zoological, covering between them, Spain, Portugal, Britain and Italy. He represented one other country, but I cannot accurately remember which it was.

Possibly the Latin side came uppermost in the evening, for the same six Southern records were played with un-varied regularity on the radiogram at dinner time. Their montony became almost fascinating, and taking into consideration that they could have some thousand varia-tions if played in different order, I found myself full of excitement each time the entertainment started afresh.

Aden boasts an open-air cinema and a "snobs'" night. On Thursdays everyone who is anyone changes their clothes and attends the Aden "first night" of the new film, whatever it may be.

I stayed in all the evening to interview guides, but no one materialised until early in the morning, when tea was

brought to my room with the announcement that an
applicant for the post was waiting outside. He came in
and I interviewed him in bed. He was short, sturdy, and
extremely ugly; he displayed an easy sort of bedside manner.
Evidently he was used to bedroom scenes.

"What is your name?" I inquired.

"Abdu Malek Noman," came the reply.

I noted it down. The name struck me as odd when I
reflected that it was no man's land that we should be going
to. He told me he was a Yemeni—not to be confused with
the average Aden native, who is generally a racial mixture
with an amalgamation of warring tendencies.

I asked his age. He told me he was forty-five, though
I suspected him of being ten years older, and I found
this to be the case soon afterwards. Guides older than
thirty-five are not considered to be good value at the back
of the desert beyond. Abdu, however, was a hardy rascal;
he could speak English a little; he had been a sailor, knew
the ways of Europeans, and could provide references. In
due course I leant from a naval officer staying in the hotel,
his previous master, that Abdu was embarrassingly honest,
worked well, but was inclined to be independent.

Had I taken more notice of the latter warning, I might
have saved myself much trouble in the future. But I had
been told about the difficulty of finding local guides, and
considered myself lucky to have come upon so good a chance
comer, more especially since the head boy at the hotel was a
relation, and willing to act as guarantor.

I asked Abdu whether he thought he would like working
for someone so young as myself. With a cold expression in
his luminous eyes he replied that he did not know; he must
wait several months before he could answer that question.
After a talk we agreed on forty rupees a month, food and
clothing to be provided for him.

So Abdu became my personal servant, and I was one
step nearer the hinterland beckoning beyond the Aden hills.

Eager to give me his confidence, he told me he had

B

been born in a small mountain village, fifty miles north of the Isthmus; he possessed a wife there and sent her money regularly, so he said, though he had not seen her for five years. In other words, he had become a typical sailor, and I found his blunt, straight-forward manner beguiling and disarming; he could be compared with Sinbad the Sailor, a man of unsinkable assurance, marvellous imagination and doubtful accomplishment.

My next objective was to make the acquaintance of officialdom. Wherever the traveller may go, either on or off the map, he cannot do more than delay the inevitable meeting with the particular uniformed official who represents local authority. Not even in the Sahara, I had found, can one escape the necessity for a check-up on the part of civilisation, and certainly not in Aden, the gateway to Southern Arabia.

Sir Bernard Reilly, now the Governor, was away in London in connection with the change over of the Aden administration from the India to the Colonial Office. The position has been extremely anomalous up to date. While the Aden protectorate, stretching from Bab-el-Mandeb to a point four hundred miles east of Aden, came under home jurisdiction, the seaport itself was an away proposition—administered from Delhi and Simla, and garrisoned by Indian troops. As from April, 1927, Whitehall does now control both.

Lieutenant-Colonel M. C. Lake greeted me at the Residency office with quiet sincerity. I saw before me a tall, very slim gentleman, with steady brown eyes that kept returning again and again to my face; they were the kind of eyes that could only belong to someone in whom sympathy, steadfastness and straight dealing were leading qualities. I doubt if Colonel Lake has made many enemies in all his twenty years of Arabian service.

I was received with sympathy, but this good-will was not extended to my project. I did not blame the Resident. To him, however courteously he disguised his inner feelings,

I must have appeared a portentous nuisance: the sort of irresponsible, will-o'-the-wisp wanderer, who seeks to reach the land of nowhere, who will probably succeed in tumbling into trouble, and who, at the best, during that process will be a source of official anxiety, and at the worst may occasion long, coded cablegrams, diplomatic representations and even a punitive expedition by way of rescue.

He talked sincerely and seriously about the delicacy of prevailing conditions in Southern Arabia. Whoever marched north-west, did so not only at his own hazard, but at the risk of the bowler hats in Whitehall. The Imam of Yemen, King Ibn Saud of Nejd, and Italy, were one and all arrayed against unauthorised and unlawful journeys such as mine promised to be. On my own admission I wanted to go in quest of Sheba's cities, to spy out the unknown, to cover ground unvisited by white men.

If go I must, it was necessary for me to separate possible places from the untouchables, those desert places open to hazardous inspection from those where trespassers would be politically prosecuted. Mareb was out of the question for political reasons; an international incident would be occasioned if I were to be found out. He asked me not even to consider entering the Yemen, and to lay temptation resolutely aside. A reconnaissance of Shabwa, in the Hadhramaut, and not Yemen territory, could be attempted, though no one so far had been successful, and he thought it tremendously unlikely that I should be the first fortunate one. "If you are bent on going," he exclaimed with a smile, "only you must be involved—this must be clear from the start if you want help from me."

In the traditional manner of the Greek Fates sitting back and enumerating human victims, we discussed the two attempts of the shadowy German—Dr. Helfritz, to unveil the interior (in which he had not been successful in reaching the outskirts of Shabwa) and, more recently, of that indomitable little lady, Freya Stark, who had travelled through a portion of the Hadhramaut, only to be brought back ill

in an aeroplane. To this list was added Maxwell Darling,
the locust hunter, from the Sudan; word had just come
through that he had been manhandled by beduins in the
interior, and Colonel Lake complained that a military
expedition would be assembled in all probability to put the
matter right. Southern Arabia was unlawful, untouched,
exciting—a half-heard, savage song to which words had
not yet been fully written. Uncertainty lingered there like a
haunting cry.

"You are bent on going?" the Colonel demanded.

"With your permission, if possible."

"You won't go near Mareb?"

"No."

"Very well."

"I shall have a try at the Hadhramaut."

"The difficulties are possibly worse. But only *you* will
get into trouble."

"I shall do my best to keep out of it."

"Very well. Go and see Seager."

"Thank you, sir."

"By the way, what sort of arms are you taking?"

"None. I feel safer without them."

The Resident threw up his hands in mock despair and
I departed in search of Captain Seager, political expert.
Actually Colonel Lake told me I was quite right and was
acting wisely. The idea of taking round ponderous arma-
ments and using fear as a weapon rather than the extended
hand in friendship, has never appealed to my mind.
One is not dealing with intractably savage animals; a
traveller is dependent on his luck, his tact, his character,
and his individual skill and sympathy in human contacts,
rather than on an experienced trigger finger and mass-
manufactured bullets. In the wilderness of the Hadhramaut
there are practically no animals or game for the pot, so
that even a sporting gun becomes no longer a necessity.

Colonel Blimp would no doubt object; hardy sportsmen,
who write their reminiscences to enliven the correspondence

pages of *The Times*, will entirely disagree with me; peaceful penetration is not for them. They dislike long expeditions without the possibility of measuring skins and skulls and brandishing something more lethal than a pipe.

The only excuse for rifles and automatics for me existed in the fact that in Southern Arabia, as in the equatorial desert of North Africa, their presence adds a certain quantity of prestige to the bearer. At the same time, I felt that if one is armed at all one must be strongly armed, and I had no money to spare for equipping bodyguards and warlike retainers. If I started, I had to trust to the immemorial hospitality of the desert and my own complete inconsequence and unimportance.

Captain Seager discussed the delicacy of the treaty now coming up for renewal between the Imam of Yemen and the Italians. Would it go through? Would the Imam, frightened by the fate of Abyssinia, turn back to the British? The answer to this question was of the greatest interest to political Aden, and might have consequences of wide importance. Nothing was to be done to discourage him. An unauthorised visit to the Yemen by even an unimportant person like myself might forfeit all chances of furtherance held by the British.

The Imam had already promised the Italians that they should be the first white people to see Mareb. Colonel Lake, however, considered he had as good a chance as anyone, while Seager himself rated his own odds at about evens. The Imam, like Queen Elizabeth, was playing off his suitors one against the other, while profiting from the competition; his chief excuse for delay was the necessity for constructing or, at any rate, improving the road. Political adviser to the Imam on these questions is a Turk, who is a virtual prisoner, with his wife and family, leave never being granted to him under any conditions; one of the Turk's daughters is now in residence in the royal harem.

When on his last visit to the Yemen, Seager told me that with great difficulty he had obtained permission to motor

twenty miles out of Sana and picnic there. His picnic had
come to an abrupt end when it had been discovered that
he had chosen the direction of Mareb—Mareb the unknown, the unvisited, a hundred miles and more to the
northward.

Besides the Arabs, a few Turks have found their way
to Mareb the mysterious, returning to Aden with certain
inscriptions. Old as Damascus, that emerald of the
northern wilderness, it was described in this wise to
Solomon nearly three thousand years ago:

"O excellent land of Saba! There are streams in her, with
eyelets of water in great abundance. There are figs and vines
in her, and many sweet lemons. There are melons whose flesh
is four hands thick, and apricots two by two in her. She has a
multitude of roses of sixty petals, and incense trees are set
about the east of her. . . . And we came down drunken
with odours into Mareb and entered her place with astonishment."

I remember asking Seager a point-blank question.
"Mareb is forbidden for me. What are my chances of
reaching Shabwa, the other untouched incense city?"
"Shabwa is more or less in no man's land. The Yemen
writ does not run there. Law and order are much worse."
"I know."
"Then why ask me about chances? There aren't any."
"You are an expert. I want to know."
"All about it?"
"Yes."
"Well, I put your chance of reaching Shabwa as .001
per cent. No more."
When he had heard I intended journeying in Arab dress
Seager outlined to me three possibilities of effective disguise:
to go as a badu (a beduin), as a holy man, or to impersonate
a woman—for the Arabs seldom, if ever, molest women.
The last two alternatives were out of the question where
I was concerned, for neither was I proficient enough in
Arabic, nor scholarly enough in Arab ways to pass off the

impersonation. Travelling as a woman had several points to recommend it, until the moment arrived when disguise failed and one was found out. A total loss of razor blades would be sufficient to attract disaster. In the end I decided to risk going as a badu, as being nearest to myself. This policy might present more dangers, but it would take less living up to.

CHAPTER TWO

OFFICIAL ADEN WAS very kind to me. Aerial photographs of the country I should be likely to traverse came my way; Captain Malcolm Sinclair allowed me to pore over the extensive reports of the Ingram's journey into the interior of the Hadhramaut on a semi-official expedition, two years previously; I was given the use of the best maps. In fact, I should like to place it on the tablets of gratitude that, contrary to the general opinion about brass hats and uniformed officialdom, there was never any reluctance shown to assist and help me in every possible way. Residents at Aden may be the exception that proves the rule, but they were a disarming exception and a charming lot of people.

Captain the Hon. R. A. B. Hamilton, third political officer—for Britain takes the gateway of Arabia seriously—was extraordinarily helpful to me. From him I gathered valuable hints about native tribes and how to deal with them suitably. I packed up packets of safety-pins, needles and coloured ribbons, which are the products of civilisation the beduin understands best and likes most. It is a little comic to consider how one's life may be preserved on occasions among the skirted followers of Mohammed by the use of a safety-pin or two, at the right time and in the right place; but such is the unadorned fact.

Captain Hamilton is a striking figure as he strides along the waterfront. His frame, which is powerful, and massive, ends in a battered nose—emblem of days spent in the ring,—but with all his power and physique, "Ham," as he is known, he-man of Aden, possesses the gentlest voice and eyes. He is a family friend to the natives, treating them with firmness, kindness and a liberal sprinkling of good Scotch understanding. He is the "Sanders of the River" of Southern Arabia, except that there is no river to liquidate his desert journeys and make paths smoother for him.

He was planning an expedition to Assaila, barely a dozen miles within the hinterland, and yet almost unknown territory, so veiled or forbidden still are portions of the surrounding territories, scorching ancient lives into unheeded dust and decay, while time fades into forgetfulness. The southern gateway of Arabia is being modernised with steamship, wireless and aeroplanes; but only a few miles inland, a very few miles, and Arabia looms still old and unheeded, an as-it-was-in-the-beginning land, sun-bathing starkly, peopled primitively, a slumbrous and shadeless landscape, lost in an age-old contemplation of space and sunshine, yet kept alive by the fierce vitality of its narrow-headed, hawk-nosed tribesmen.

Hamilton could not go with me to Assaila—he was called away on business—so I started alone on a trial trip with Abdu and two donkeys. I went unarmed, wearing shorts, a short-sleeved shirt, Arab sandals and a topee. That topee as good as saved my life and made me thankful I had not followed my usual custom of wearing the Arab cloth head-dress, which is cheaper, more comfortable and quite as cool, even if it looks less imposing.

Abdu and I motored to Shaikh Othman, where cars were changed for the journey to LeHej. The road across the desert was plainly marked, beaten down by churning centuries of travel, but some of the gradients were alarming —reminiscent of ski-ways in the Swiss mountains. The car would take a run at the hills and sometimes stick with a jerk. Going downhill on one roadway it stood on its head; once it went down backwards in reverse so as to maintain greater control over events. There were also ditches it had to jump in the cross-country steeplechase to LeHej, and once or

twice I should have been knocked out, or had my skull
cracked against the roof of the car, if the topee had not
intervened. Modern transport was up against an ancient
highway and did not know what to make of the situation;
it rattled out complaints and rebukes; sand got into everything, though the carburettor choked it up again. It was
all great fun. . . .

Abdl-Krim Fathl ben Ali, Sultan of LeHej, provided
Indian tea and British biscuits. His son, who could speak
English, in addition to Persian and Arabic, looks at life
through one real and one glass eye. The Sultan, an oldish,
wealthy man, living luxuriously, thanks to a large and
pompous retinue of slaves, was arrogant and lazy, with
suspicion lurking beneath his eyelids. According to report,
his son had lost an eye through attempted assassination on
the part of a cousin who wished to reign one day in his
stead. Possibly, as a consequence of this Eastern family
strife, the Sultan disliked young men, or at any rate viewed
them with disfavour. After the attack, the son was sent to
an eye specialist in Edinburgh, to be out of harm's way.
My visit to this powerful Sultan of the oasis, a figure that
might have almost stepped out of the Arabian Nights, was
like having tea with the vicar. The polite ceremonial was
much the same, and the tea was not too strong.

Next morning at sunrise I left the palace on my return
journey by way of Wahat. Donkey work for twenty-four
hours; possibly the oldest form of transport, since donkeys
helped to carry the loads of Islam before the camel shuffled
on to the Arabian sand, disdain permanently raising his
nostrils. But in return for discomfort, we had that sense of
progression and of getting somewhere so often gained when
travelling across wide spaces of the earth.

Gradually the sky turned from silver to gold and then to
a weak blue. The landscape stretched away in brown
ridges, and across the corrugated surface a breeze blew in
friendly puffs. A few withered trees showed skinny legs on
the sky-line. Abdu broke into a harsh, high-pitched noise,

a succession of shouts rather than song, meant to encourage the donkeys, so he said. Until the sun had climbed to its highest peak the journeying was open and pleasant. We did not mind the heat. We knew where we were going. The world seemed to be without worries.

We topped a ridge unexpectedly and came upon the ruins of a mostly buried city, covered by the sand. The top of a round tower and a few walls, greyer than the sand, stuck up and looked at me. Were they Sabaean? Were they Himyaritic? Or were they comparatively much more modern? Age is difficult to judge in the desert; probably these skeleton dwellings belonged to Bible days when the Semitic Himyarites, also called Homerites, overlapped the Sabaean kingdom. Looking at them, a longing to stay and unbare the old deathless bones of a dead civilisation, descended strongly upon me; for the thrill of treasure trove in the desert is an old allurement, surpassing the ordinary calls of antiquity, and carrying with it perhaps an atavistic touch of youthful spade-and-pail-work descended from infant days at the seaside.

At that moment I wanted above all else to dig and scrape at buried secrets, to unearth another sphinx, to join the learned ranks of archaeologists as pupil and excavator. It would be worth a hundred times attaining a stooping back and spectacles to have dug out Troy or Babylon or Ophir.

Curiously enough, Aden could tell me little of these ruins; it knew nothing about them, not even their bare existence.

Back again at the Crescent Hotel, plans for the main expedition came crowding, together with deputations of smiling guides, telling me how poor and totally inefficient was Abdu Noman, and how far superior were their splendid selves.

I had told only the Resident, Seager and Hamilton of my desire to reach either Shabwa or Mareb, those two capitals of ancient mystery and wisdom. For the rest, it was given out that I was about to make a journey into the Hadhramaut.

Even this announcement proved too much for some of the guides. The word "Hadhramaut" means "in the presence of death"; when I asked Abdu casually whether he had ever been to the neighbourhood of Shabwa he announced that any stranger, even Arab, in those parts was promptly shot at.

"Bad place," he said. "Very jealous people. Dislike very much see foreigner. All got guns. . . . They shoot."

He went off and cheered himself up with chewing Carte leaves, which he said had the same effects as whisky. He wanted to take a large quantity with him, but this idea I had to veto tactfully, telling him (what was true enough) that I had no whisky and he should not have the advantage of me in Carte leaves or Carte blanche or Carte anything.

"We not two men but one man?" he inquired. I agreed. I did not know in the least what he was talking about. . . .

Shabwa. The name had insinuated itself into my mind— perhaps partly owing to its resemblance to Sheba, though in the beginning the town was evidently Sabota, at the time of the Sabaean empire, when the incense trees grew thickly on the hills and their cultivation was the care of a privileged class.

Mareb, the old myrrh centre, was out of the question. The British officials at Aden had been so helpful and charming, so considerate to a novice that their request to me to keep out of Yemen territory had to be respected. One cannot injure the hand that has helped and fed one, however thickly encased with the leather of official protection.

Shabwa began to hold all my attention and thoughts. I turned up Craufurd's notes—Craufurd, friend of Lawrence and the Imam of Yemen, the man who had weathered seventeen years in Southern Arabia and whose work, at his own request, I was now trying to carry one step further. Craufurd had discovered Ophir; he had been privileged to carry out an extensive search of the Imam's library at Sana. He had become convinced, like Sir Wallis Budge, a curator of the British Museum, about the probability

Mr. Norman Stone Pearn in Arab Dress

Palace Interior at Mukalla. 'Ahmed bin Nasir Seated

of Mareb being the capital, or at any rate chief
trading town of the Sabaean Empire, the Saaba Kingdom,
rather than the more easterly and Himyaritic Shabwa. Sir
Wallis Budge has translated many of the ancient Ethiopian
and Arabian inscriptions belonging to the old dynasties;
Craufurd has combed all local records within his reach, yet
there is no mention of a Queen of Sheba or Saaba inscribed
on the tablets, as a ruler among these dynasties. This
may go towards proving that Balkis (the Queen of Sheba's
name in Arabic) belonged to Sabota and Shabwa, rather
than to Mareb, or, since records and inscriptions are not
complete, and Sheba evidently relinquished her dominion
at some period, in favour of a son, who became part of the
Axum and Ethiopian tradition, this lack of the earliest
recorded evidence may prove nothing. At one time the
Sabaean and Himyaritic realms were ruled by the same
king and it is beyond doubt that about the time of Solomon,
nine centuries before Christ, a Semitic influx into Ethiopia
occurred.

Craufurd firmly believes no European has ever entered
Mareb, the royal city of the Sabaeans, more withdrawn
and jealously guarded than either Mecca or Lhassa. He
should, however, make allowances for that thousand to one
chance. Reports of several white men penetrating to the
vicinity of the city can be rightly discounted; all efforts in
that direction have hitherto been repulsed by shooting—
with one exception. In the nineteenth century, Arnaud is
said to have reached the forbidden city, and taken a plan
of the ancient dam and wall, together with copies of fifty
inscriptions with which to occupy antiquarians.

Through the unfolding centuries, the rulers of Mareb
have suffered from a complex; they will not countenance
visitors of any kind, more especially infidels. Craufurd,
who has a deep knowledge of the Yemen, tells me Mareb
has lost not only much of its ancient importance, but also
most of its former architectural glories. He believes, however, that many of the old wonder buildings, erected to

the glories of the spice trade and frankincense highway, are still intact, buried beneath the desert. Towers have been seen protruding from the sand by the French airman, Mavraux, who flew over the spot. According to Craufurd, digging would be impossible, but a fully equipped expedition, having won the favour of the Imam, might reach the spot and "blow off" the concealing covering of sand.

The Sabaeans, dispensing with currency, built their palaces not on a foundation of beaten mud sand, but most wonderfully upon foundations of gold, silver, copper and other valuable ore. If and when the "blowing-off" operations revealed the top of palace or minaret, it would then be possible to decapitate the building and enter into its mysteries.

Craufurd is thought to be a romantic by some of his contemporaries, but he is a man of many labours, with a hard knowledge of the country in which he has spent so many of his years. For a time he was associated with Lawrence.

.   .   .   .   .

East of the Yemen territory, withdrawn from its volcanic mountains and more ordered realm, lay the Hadhramaut, the Promised Land for me—promised by Lake, Seager, and Hamilton, provided I started from Mukalla, not Aden.

The Residency officials had arranged for me to meet the Minister of the Sultan of Shihr and Mukalla, since he happened to be visiting Aden. Sa'id Hamid bin Bubaker bin Husein al Mah-dhar and I drank tea together; he promised to intercede for me with the Sultan, who was visiting Cairo to buy an electric light plant; I also met Shaikh Sa'id bin Aboukar el Azen, merchant of Shibam, whose hospitality proved a blessing to me when I eventually reached his town.

Seager warned me not to eat the exceedingly dirty native food unless I was driven to it; tinned food was to be my bill of fare for several months. I packed up my provisions in boxes and made preparations for the start. I went once more to the old shipping-yard at Aden to smell the odour of frankincense brought by gum-drops cut from the boles of the spice trees, the very breath of the queer, inhospitable, exciting land to which I was journeying. An old vendor shuffled out from the shadows and surveyed me with inscrutable eyes. I should be going back into the days of Genesis, travelling in a land that had altered not so very materially since the days of Moses, Abraham and Ishmael. The old dams of plenty, the irrigation system of the Wadis, the prosperous people and the incense highways would be gone, but the primary things of landscape, climate and custom would be unchanging in their continuity. Where Sheba's caravans had rested, I would go: where the unvisited cities lay beyond the sunburnt hills, I would quest into the timeless land.

Back at the hotel that same evening I was talking about my proposed trip to the Hadhramaut.

"You won't get far," an English trader told me. "It's the devil's own line in countries. Quite likely to get your throat cut."

I thanked him for his encouragement. "Places are seldom so bad as they are made out," I observed.

"What did they say up there?" He shrugged in the direction of the Residency.

"They gave me a thousand to one chance against getting away with it."

"Well, what did I tell you?"

I felt, nevertheless, singularly cheerful. I had been given my chance to visit Arabia Felix and did not wish for any better luck. The way lay open to me at last for an attempt, and that was what really mattered.

If I were to fail to get anywhere, it would not be without having made the attempt.

CHAPTER THREE

MUKALLA—THE GATEWAY OF THE SOUTH

ABDU NOMAN AND I set sail from Aden on July 27th in the
s.s. *Africa*, an old ship, 150 feet long and 450 tons, with a
tramp funnel aft; the vessel plied in the service of Bombay
merchants, Cowajee Dinshaw, between Aden, Mukalla,
Shihr, Hodeida, Jiddah and Djibouti, repeating in an
almost endless progression visits between the Arab ports
in Southern waters.

The moon rode low upon the sea as we slipped out into
the night. The s.s. *Africa* sounded her syren once, twice,
in the darkness like a voice that is repeated. We had
started, and the hot night looked down, unsleeping and
bright-eyed with stars. We had become a part of the
immemorial trafficking of Araby, old as the Saaba incense
highway, old as Solomon, sitting on his throne of ivory
and beaten gold, the twelve lions standing ranged beneath
him on the steps. . . .

The Authors are agreed that if the urge of travel and
its horizons can be said to be epitomized by a single note
of sound, it is the voice of the ship's syren bidding farewell
to the old encirclement of surroundings and reaching
out to new vibrations and wavelengths of living. Experience and expectation blend for an instant in a
sound that is a cry; the past merges into the future; then
the screws commence their mechanical routine while
the beyond is being bounded and localised into time and
place.

Starting points bind together a variety of emotions.
Awaiting release are expectancy, excitement, tension, hope,

activity, and usually an incipient desire to laugh at
oneself.

One has an uncomfortable and humbling glimpse of
personal perspective. One becomes in the moment of
starting as a man playing ping-pong on the Great Wall
of China or a traveller setting out to cross the Indian
Ocean in a Rob Roy canoe; one joins the special class of
fools whose eyes are in the ends of the earth and whose
efforts at the start appear ridiculous.

Captain Evans, the skipper, tended to increase this
diminutive feeling. He was a confirmed pessimist, though
he reads the Bible every morning as an Arab reads the
Quran. He said that you could not trust the Arabs and
were constantly being caught in webs of trickery and deceit,
and he thought I had as much chance of getting anywhere
in Arabia as a man has of crossing Piccadilly Circus with
his eyes shut. He had been nine years at his job without
a holiday, so his habit of running down everyone
and everything could be understood, together with his
relish for strong doses of swearing. It was not much
of a life being the Captain or the chief engineer of
the s.s. *Africa*, neither of them daring to take a day
off lest they should lose their posts amid the swarm of
seamen who perspire away their days in the Red Sea
funnel.

The only good cabin was shared out between myself,
a Javanese and an Arab; it was ten feet by five. I elected
to sleep on the Captain's bridge within sight and sound
of the motley crowd of deck passengers.

In a stuffy little room, even smaller than the one I
had vacated, an Arab beauty of high social standing passed
her time, never stirring, never appearing outside, her
meals served inside, the ports closed, the door only opened
to admit her husband. Whatever advantages the harem
system of feminine deportment may embody for Moslem
women on land, they are lost to sight at sea. Those women,
for whom deck accommodation was apportioned, existed,

c

stifled and veiled behind screens of bright cloth slung behind the aft wheel-house, corresponding roughly to a two-by-four bathing tent.

Our voyage was calm and mercifully the sun's breath was never brazen. Tuesday was cloudy and hazy over a sea flat as a mirror. On Wednesday when the sun had climbed the eastern sky, we came to Mukalla. We saw a line of houses dazzled in light with the cliff behind, and some white forts; we saw the white magnificence of a town, princely and parapeted in the distance, backed by a sweep of wrinkled hills; we caught once more the peculiar spicy aroma of the Arabian shore, and were soon surrounded by the friendly greetings of the brown men, busy in their boats upon the emerald water.

" *Ya hayya*," they cried in greeting, waving their oars.

We smiled and answered back.

I was met on the quayside by an imposing collection of sultanic officials with tarbooshes and parasols, and conducted in an ancient touring car to the house of the reigning Prime Minister. Seyyid Salim had been left in charge of affairs while his master and the Premier were away on business in Egypt, and I did not meet the last two until my return to Mukalla in the Autumn. The new Sultan had only been on the throne for nine months; since his first act had been to arrest some of the old ministers and throw them into prison, an atmosphere of unrest and sedition was agitating the ruling portions of the Hadhramaut kingdom.

Sitting with Seyyid Salim I found the Minister for Tribal Affairs, 'Ahmed bin Nasir, a magnificent, red-hearted specimen of an Arab, with a handsome, smiling face, brilliant brown eyes, and around him the gay, plaided skirt or kilt of the tribal chieftain. We became good friends at once. 'Ahmed bin Nasir would spring up and shake me by both hands simultaneously when he thought I needed encouragement. He had quick, smiling ways and the ready tongue of his nation. The Arabs down south are the true descendants of Shem when they have not inter-married with Somaliland negroes, the type running to dark hair, narrow heads, full lips and straightish noses; many of the men wear small beards.

The ministers and I limited our first talk to the subject of England, since this was their wish.

"Is it true that your people can travel fast below the surface of the ground and that your women serve in the shops?" they asked me.

"It is true," I replied, wondering what they might say next.

"Sights such as these must be astonishing."

"But you have many wonderful things in your own country. I am anxious to see them. I have heard much of your Sultan, of your caravans, and your ancient cities, older than any of ours."

They seemed pleased, but they wished to know more details about London, so I produced picture postcards I happened to have brought out with me and they looked at these with enormous interest, and not the polite indifference of acquaintances when confronted with snapshots to supplement a lagging conversation.

St. Paul's Cathedral impressed them most; I suppose it reminded them a little of their own mosques. They were also visibly moved to wonder by the Houses of Parliament and the glitter of the Life Guards in Whitehall; but Buckingham Palace they considered disappointing and unworthy of so great a King.

They hoped to visit England one day in the company of the Sultan, but feared they would not have enough money for so grand a country.

After the ministerial tea I was taken for a long drive through a swelter of shops displaying a minimum of hygiene and a maximum of flies. We visited the bazaar and revisited the port, with its nodding dhows gazing down at their own reflections in the water, restless even when at anchorage in harbour. The side streets branch at right-angles, finishing abruptly and with a full stop against the red hills; but the houses do not always end; some climb, one above the other, clinging to the side of the cliff in delightful and undismayed stages of dilapidation.

The boats in the harbour are largely concerned with the industries of the town—dried fish in various stages, an odorous food for camels, together with sharks' fins and sea-slugs for the Chinese. Watching the ebony slaves at work lading dhows, one could think of those fearsome banquets in far away China, starting with shark fins and steamed sea-slugs, and proceeding with leisurely courage through thirty or forty courses to the climax of live mice dipped in treacle.

My quarters in the Guest house, which was the Sultan's old palace, adjoined the Western Gate of the town, through which proceeded the daily traffic to Shihr. The Palace stares at the world through coloured glass windows; in the vicinity are grouped a block of barracks and official buildings. The Guest house is an architectural achievement, for it is built as part of the city wall, and from its shaded balcony you can be an onlooker of life within and without. In its interior, I found a comfortable bed, plush chairs, and a stone bathroom with a long bath ornamented by unexpected running water. I was like St. Paul in the city wall at Damascus, and morning and evening the balcony called me out to see the ebb and flow of life below me, both in the street and on the sands of the estuary.

The view from the Guest house, unrolling day by day, was a microcosm of southern Arabia. From here you could watch a procession of living illustrations to the old tales of Caliph and carpet and caravan. You could see Arabia shuffling, walking or riding by—at Arabia's pace. Nobody could have wished for a better introduction to the most fascinating peninsular on earth.

Hot, luminous waves lapping on the sands, the fore-shore duned and dazzling, the hills behind, almost belonged

to a seaside resort on the Riviera; but not the black caravans and bedu of the estuary beyond the West Gate, nor
the kites circling the sky with their strange, sweet
cries, as though the monsoon wind had become full of
voices.

Beduins, camping apart along the estuary, run the caravans and the merchandise from town to town. They
despise city quarters, and their little brown, naked children disport themselves in the surf, regardless of sharks
or warnings of danger.

A caravan at Mukalla may consist of a hundred camels.
With one or two exceptions I had never seen such large
caravans in the Sahara. In the distance a camel has a
peculiar, unhurried dignity, matching well with the
immensity he traverses; a hundred camels strung into a
moving necklace give a sense of journeying to the outer
limits, in a way that cannot be captured by a succession
of railway carriages or a fleet of motor-cars, and although
the pack camel goes no faster than three miles an hour,
the racing camel can beat the average train or the urban
speed limits imposed upon wheel traffic by a Hore Belisha,
keeping up their speed over long distances.

The camel wears a supercilious smile, the Arabs say,
for the reason that the Moslem knows ninety-nine names for
Allah, but the camel a hundred.

To watch a line of camels diminishing into a distance
only limited by the natural curve of the earth, to see
them going on and on until they step over the top of
the world that lies beyond vanishing point on the horizon,
is to witness something both satisfying and legendary,
something that symbolises perhaps better than anything
else the progression of travel and the linked movement
that stirs the wandering races of mankind.

An eastern caravan, wise in day and night, the sky and
the stars, binding together man and beast collectively in
a common purpose for ends which yet lie beyond the
reach of sight, is the beduin's only traffic with civilisation.

It is travel, timeless and tameless—on legs, and not an unfeeling, upholstered movement made possible by petrol.

When the badu women were not holding a mothers' meeting interspersed by cries and excited shouts, I watched them sitting timelessly below me, beside the Western Gate, awaiting in silence a gift beyond words—a free distribution of water from the Sultan, their men-folk meantime bringing in unpleasant-looking sharks for supper. They took their water jars to the bazaar, selling the contents to merchants who did not wish for the labour of providing for themselves. Half an anna buys a canful; in this way, the bedu women earn perhaps six annas a day (about eightpence). But they are well content, and think themselves rich if they obtain any money at all in hard cash. To see them shoulder a six gallon can and move beautifully down the street matched well with the spectacle of a Covent Garden salesman, in London, balancing with ease a minaret of vegetable baskets on his head.

Watching these primitives, like Freya Stark I wondered at their grace and vigour of movement—more especially the women, until I noticed that none of them wore shoes of any kind. People who go habitually without shoes and stockings either walk like gutter-urchins or gods. The absence of unnecessary clothes, particularly shoes, had made many of those bedu women of Mukalla develop a carriage descending in lineal descent from the proud-footed handmaidens of Sheba and Semiramis. How much the daughters of England might gain from a course of walking barefoot, the fulcrum of their feet unrestricted and poised for forward momentum!

When sunset changed the sea to pink coral, the people of the estuary, putting aside their outer garments, would turn towards Mecca and go through the motions of evening prayer. Thousands upon thousands of gulls wheeling towards the west turned for a few minutes into bird-clouds the colour of flamingos.

According to the Quran, the faithful must pay worship to God five times a day. King Ibn Saud, Keeper of the Holy Places and the most powerful ruler in Arabia, breaks off from a Cabinet meeting if the call to prayer circles the housetops; while he prays, two Nubians of his bodyguard protect his back.

The proscribed times for Moslem prayer are as follows:

1. In the early dawn before sunrise.
2. In the early afternoon when the sun has left the meridian.
3. Later, when the sun is midway towards setting.
4. Immediately after sunset.
5. Between the disappearance of the sunset glow, and bedtime.

Arabs are fortunate in having the sunshine to play so prominent a part in the ritual observance of their worship. The sky is their pulpit, the sun their pastor. In the simplicity of their worship, they have no need of priests, and individuals take on the departmental duties of religion, turn and turn about. Moslem prayer is supposed to be preceded by an ablution, including washing of hands, cleansing of mouth, nose and face and of the right and left arm up to the elbow. Wet hands pass over the head, and the feet as far as the ankles, first right, then left, socks and boots being included when necessary.

The worshipper first turns towards Mecca, declaring his intention of prayer, and, putting hands to his ears, he repeats the words, "God is great." He then stands erect, places his hands in front of him, gradually bending his head until the palms of his hands rest upon the knees. Standing erect once more, he lets the arms fall to the side. Next, dropping on his knees, he touches the ground first with his nose, then with the forehead; finally, raising both head and body, he sinks backwards upon his heels and repeats: "God is great—single and without partner."

This series of devotional physical exercises, coupled with the repetition of Versicles from the Quran, make up what is called "one bowing." For each separate period prayer of the day, a certain number (from two to four) of these bowings are performed by the devout.

Sir Richard Burton, when on pilgrimage to Mecca, noted that certain of the pilgrims, when forgetting their prayers or breaking some observance, bought and sacrificed a sheep by way of penalty for misconduct. Moslems apparently believe that if they slip when crossing the knife edge to Paradise, the souls of the sheep they have slaughtered sacrificially will support them and prevent them falling into the abyss. Burton also noticed that the cooing of pigeons in Mecca and other holy cities was taken to be the intoning of prayers to Allah.

.   .   .   .   .

I was taken one afternoon to inspect one of the chief industries of the town--sesame oil ground by blindfold camels. The camels walk round in slow circles throughout the day, pulling the weights controlling thirty-one mill-stones which grind the seed into pulp. The whitish-yellow sesame plants grow in abundance in Arabia, opening in the daytime and shutting at night; it was this flower in season that brought forth the remark made by Ali Baba. Sesame, I was told by Seyyid Salim, is more important than olive oil; the soot obtained from burning the oil is used as one of the compounds of Indian ink.

We visited Ras Mukalla, where the Sultan owns a country palace. Between Ras Mukalla and Mukalla I saw Khalf, the local centre of the fish-drying industry for camel food, and also a depot for R.A.F. oil fuel.

The greenest spot in Mukalla is the Sultan's garden clustering around the present guest house. It is a strange sort of garden stocked with palm trees, decayed banyans, and coconuts for the Sultan's table. The gardeners, brown as the earth, work with their feet rather than with their hands, side-stepping the soil into place.

At Gheil ba Wazir I was shown round the tobacco-growing industry—a good Arabian mixture. We drove out to Kherba to see some ruins attributed to the Portuguese. They consisted of an aqueduct and a boulder called "Hazar Ferenji," under which the architect lies buried; in Mukalla there is a well called "Boi Ferenji," to which, some say, the Kherba aqueduct, fourteen miles away, once ran. Nobody knows much about it, and the ruins are another of those unexplained antiquities of a still remote country.

Seyyid Salim ridiculed the Portuguese theory: "Anything old on the coast is at once put down to the Portuguese," he told me, "while in the interior such things are put down to the children of 'Ad."

We climbed the frowning perpendicular heights behind Mukalla, the mountain called "Quara." On the top sprawled ruins of an old fortified settlement, marking the spot where the first tribesmen lived when they founded Mukalla. Their position at the start must have been starkly insecure, for them to have perched so feudally eleven hundred feet above the shore, with a correspondingly difficult water supply.

Seyyids, in Southern Arabia, form a fairly numerous aristocracy or noble class in the old tradition, avoiding trade and agriculture, but being persons of education, property and authority. They trace their descent from Hosain, grandson of Mohammed. Deriving great sanctity from the family tree, the heads are called Munsabs, and become important religious leaders. Among others in this list are the Sheikh of Ainat, the el-Aidrus of Shihr and the Sakkaf of Saiyu. The Seyyids called in the Kaiti tribesmen to protect their interests from the plundering beduins, sweeping down on the cultural valleys from the desert tablelands, and as so often occurs in history, mercenary soon became master. The Kaiti tribe is now the most powerful in the Hadhramaut, governing not only the sea coast towns, but also Hegerain, Haura and Shibam in the interior, and banishing the Kathiris to a secondary status

of importance. The strife between tribes such as these over
the arid body of Southern Arabia can almost be compared
to those old troubled combats between Guelf and Ghibelline,
Montagu and Capulet in medieval Italy.

Kaiti tribesmen form a firm link with India, for the
soldiers take service among the irregular troops of the
Nizam of Hyderabad; the Kaiti Sultan is now hereditary
commander of the Nizam's bodyguard, dividing his time
between the Hadhramaut and Hyderabad.

.   .   .   .   .

'Ahmed bin Nasir, the Sultan's Minister for Tribal
Affairs, insisted that I should see a parade of the local
troops in the palace grounds; and I was forced into the
position of taking the salute while 600 regulars marched by
in solemn display.

The Sultan's brown army consisted of 600 regulars in
khaki puttees, bare feet and shorts: 2,000 irregulars, skirted
and turbaned, clad in the colours of the rainbow, and a
small number of slave cadets; all these were paid by the
possession of a rifle and ammunition—Arabia's most
cherished gift. Parades took place on Tuesday and Saturday.
Two antiquated field guns were treated with the same
veneration as Field Marshals, and the climax was reached
when the soldiers, in order to celebrate my presence, were
allowed to signal with flags. 'Ahmed told me that the Sultan
had asked the British for machine guns; whether in this
case request would precede delivery was a question on which
I refused to express an opinion.

The commander-in-chief of the regulars, a martial figure
in a red tarboosh, held the rank of lieutenant in the Aden
forces; he was extremely proud of both honours, and is
the only Arab, so far as I know, to be granted a British
commission.

At the conclusion of the ceremony the band halted
opposite to where I stood with 'Ahmed, and broke into a

loud, gay tune, smiles of joyful anticipation on their faces. They continued to smile and nod at me as though expecting some special applause for their ungrudging efforts, so I turned to 'Ahmed to ask what tune they were playing. Suddenly I understood and snatched off my hat. The day was hot enough already, and I was thankful the parade ground was still in shadow, while the band started to play through "God Save the King" a second time.

"Your anthem turns all Englishmen into Hazzis," said 'Ahmed approvingly, referring no doubt to the fact that Arab pilgrims to Mecca never wear anything on their heads, though in recent years they have been allowed to shelter under umbrellas.

By the time Saturday was over, my plans for leaving Mukalla and going north had nearly been completed. Introductions to one or two leading figures in the interior had been given me, and warnings were once more distributed by authority. No foreigner had ever succeeded in reaching Shabwa, the Seyyids said, and I was not likely to enter this ancient metropolis marking the spot where two incense highways met. I must leave Yemen unvisited: on that point Mukalla was as emphatic as Aden. Italy and the Yemen were in a state of dangerous equilibrium, and no one knew what might cause an upset. Italy, during the Abyssinian war, had tried to land 800 troops at Hodeida— by mistake for Africa, according to the excuse given for their surprisingly unlawful presence.

As for Mareb, capital of the Sabaean empire, Captain Seager had given me his opinion that an armoured car and cavalry escort would be necessary to get there.

After talking with the various authorities, I came to the conclusion that only two methods of travel were possible on the caravan routes of Southern Arabia: the journey must either be made in a big way with dominance, or in quite a simple one, without guards or superiority of anything, by relying on the hospitality and kindliness of the local people. I had found the latter course to prove

successful among the tribes in the depths of the Sahara
to whom I had been prepared to trust myself, and saw no
reason why it should not work again. Hospitality and
simplicity are two keynotes of life in Moslem countries;
to my mind, no two opinions can exist as to the choice,
from the point of view of the wanderer, between a show of
force and a show of friendliness; it becomes necessary to
share the way of life of the simple bedu and tribesmen
to get the best out of them. A traveller is seldom left long
without human companionship of some kind, and in the
inner Hadhramaut, where strangers are unmistakable,
one white man in Arab dress is just an accident, while two
begin to make an expedition.

But at the start I knew I must be guided by local conditions and not plan too far ahead. The Hadhramaut,
as I spread the maps out on the floor, here, on the spot,
appeared even more unlimited than when distance across
Europe had added its enchantment to the view. To the
north-east, Shabwa, the unvisited, beckoned with her sixty
temples, but many other forms of wonderment and surprise
in addition to the incense metropolis, awaited more ample
delineation or discovery: Shibam, a wadi city of fantastic
skyscrapers before New York existed; the Wadi Hadhramaut, a Methusaleh among highways of civilisation, old
and sunken between the desert tablelands; the Rub el Kali,
most desolate of deserts, crossed by Thomas and St. John
Philby a few years previously, and said to contain the bones
of incredible cities; and Warbar, the legendary, its whereabouts marked on no map; Warbar, the will-o'-the-wisp
which no explorer has yet been able to find, much less
approach.

I talked over the preliminary stages of the journey with
Abdu, collecting all the details possible.

"You must go with a caravan," the guide declared,
holding his swarthy head in his hands.

"I would rather travel alone."

"Then you will be killed."

"*We*," I corrected him.

Abdu rose from his heels, expectorating carefully. He believed in being frank about the future.

"It will cost more. You will want camels—donkeys—slaves, doubtless."

"How much are—well, slaves, for instance?"

"You would wish to buy them, of course?"

I suggested to Abdu that perhaps hiring would be a better plan, and even inquired whether such a thing as the hire purchase system existed in Arabia.

Before leaving, I compiled, with the aid of Abdu and one or two visitors to the guest house, approximate prices of current merchandise in Mukalla. The list worked out on the following lines:

A good camel	150 M.T. dollars
A good donkey	50 ,,
A chicken	5 annas.
A slave (adult)	100 dollars
A slave girl	500 ,,
A slave boy	300 ,,
A jug of water	½ an anna.
A rifle	150 dollars

At the suggestion of the Seyyids we joined forces with a tobacco caravan, the bedu contracting for the transport of my luggage.

The stage was set for the next step forward.

We would be caravanning across the wilderness to Wadi Du'an, using tracks created thousands of years ago by nature in evolution—natural connections between plateaux and valleys made by the forces of water, fire and storm, and left untouched by men. We would be renewing that old physical compact of well-being made by Adam in the Garden when man loved the untamed earth, and found it good. Discarding civilisation as a man strips off his coat, we would soon be breathing the energy of new horizons in an antique land where each day was bounded by its own sufficiency and purpose.

For almost the last time, I surveyed Mukalla from my balcony, a town of placid occupations and unhurrying deportment, whose only enemy was where, beyond the sunburnt houses, forbidding mountains, black in shadow, threatened to push the little seaport into the foam of perilous, shark-infested seas.

CHAPTER FOUR

THE CARAVAN SETS OUT

THE EVENING BEFORE the military parade at Mukalla, and the day before departure, beduins arrived at the guest house to take away my luggage to join the tobacco caravan assembling at T-hila for the journey across the wilderness to Du'an.

They were wild little men, climbing everywhere like cats and smiling through their teeth. They wore nothing on their lithe, burnt bodies, except a loin-cloth, deeply stained in indigo. All were armed with their beloved, if ancient rifles, and the curved knife in its U-shaped sheath, as useful as the Ghurka Kukri, fastened to the front of their loin-cloths. Two of them, acting in the position of advance guard to the growing caravan, had come earlier in the day to inspect my loads, and, after a weight-testing interlude carried out between them, had ordered me to cut two of my boxes into halves. This sounds in the style of an Old Testament judgment, but my boxes consisted mostly of wooden cases, so that the alteration brought a carpenter and not a crisis.

In the morning I was awakened from a fitful slumber by the upraised voice of the military band struggling to play "Rule Britannia" under my window. After I had dressed and gone out, another and larger band was working up the emotions of an assembled crowd to boiling point. Arab music is entirely oriental when judged by European standards; instead of four tones it possesses fourteen, and these queer, inhuman quarter tones not only make a virtue out of repetition and monotony, but also characterise to some extent the great void of Islam, the middle distance between Europe and Asia, spacious and yet simple, threaded through with wars and wonderings and wanderings. To an ordinary Arab listener a Western wireless programme of music appears infantile, and a prima-donna circulating lofty echoes in the Albert Hall, no more than an angry child. To me the Arab music was without melody, counter-point and point.

At ten minutes to eight, the cool of the morning still fresh upon Mukalla, the Sultan's motor-car arrived to take me as far as T-hila. 'Ahmed bin Nasir, hospitable and helpful to the last, took his seat beside the chauffeur, who wore a red tarboosh and a banana stuck behind his ear. 'Ahmed carried a rifle at the ready across his knees, while Abdu and I shared the rear seats with the more precious part of my baggage.

No visa for my passport had been issued, nor any special permit or licence to travel in the Hadhramaut. I had not any official papers nor was I cross-examined by officialdom before starting as would have happened in most countries. I was equipped voluntarily with letters of introduction, and it was I who was asked if I would be good enough to keep an eye on the caravan and attendant bedu, sending back reports to 'Ahmed if necessary. I was warned that Hadhramaut beduins are inclined to be independent, hasty and short memoried; therefore likely to misbehave if they think they have anything to gain.

To add to the story-book atmosphere of my departure, 'Ahmed himself, I noticed, was exactly typical of what the Arab Sheikh is supposed to resemble in popular Western literature. His slimness made him appear tremendously tall; he had a hawk-nose set between remarkable brown eyes; his walk varied between the upright stride of the horseman and the cat-like tread of the people of the hills. He was frank and jovial and dominant.

The car swung out of the western gate of Mukalla accom-panied by the salutes of the guards and beduins assembled around the massive carved-wood doors. We flashed past the Sultan's summer palace set back a mile behind both mountains and town, leaving them behind us. Sharp bends in the road were taken with the same speed as when traversing the straight, only with incessant bleatings of the bulb horn, in order to avoid the massacre of wayfaring sheep or goats. Apart from the glimpse of palm trees in the Sultan's garden, foreground and mountains alike showed a dull buff or grey. The rippled plain, scored with rain gullies like wrinkles, fell back behind our wheels, swallowing our dust.

A little over two miles from Mukalla, we climbed steeply into a defile, hooted a small caravan off the track, and flung ourselves down an incline with an impetus that made me hold my breath. 'Ahmed sat nonchalantly beside the driver, one arm flung back, viewing the flashes of scenery with a leisurely approval. He was evidently armed with the fatalistic trustfulness of the Arab who hands on his misgivings into the merciful keeping of Allah. Wave upon wave of crumbling, stony hills hurried towards us, and then, when my watch showed twenty minutes to nine, 'Ahmed flung forward a graceful long arm and sensitive finger, beyond the wind-screen. "T-hila!"

We had arrived.

He was soon greeting the Sheikh of T-hila; I was introduced and we repaired to the second floor of the Chief's house. T-hila is the home of the two tribes, Akbari and Bene Hassan, Sheikh Muhammed bin 'Ahmed bar Omar, their leader, informed me. Tobacco and dates are the local industries, and it was this tobacco that my badu, belonging to the Ba Brahim tribe of the Du'an Valley, would be taking home with them. Travelling with them, 'Ahmed and Muhammed agreed, would cause less suspicion than if I went alone.

Soon we were all seated on reed mats, cushions separating our backs from the mud walls. Hookahs passed from hand to hand, even Abdu being pressed to join the smoking party,

D

much to his evident embarrassment. He was not used to such high society and preferred spitting to smoking. Seated between 'Ahmed and the Sheikh of T-hila, he looked as uncomfortable as a small boy at his first grown-up party.

The Sheikh was an old, grey-bearded man, willowy with age, but mentally upright and alert. Years had seamed his face until a hundred wrinkles creased the thin parchment of his two cheeks; but these same years had caused the old Chief to look kindly on the present-day world, as his watery-blue eyes clearly showed. A turban and a beard streaked with grey can add a look of dignity and wisdom to an old man, attributes befitting the accumulated years. 'Ahmed wore his short skirt, very like the Highland kilt in style, colour, pattern and general appearance. In his waistband showed the inevitable dagger without which no nomad is considered dressed. The Sheikh wore a one-piece dress of white, rather reminiscent of a nightshirt.

The four of us sat in a circle round a mat covered with various delicacies—dates, nuts, Turkish delight, pancakes made of batter, and native biscuits. In order to make some conversation 'Ahmed politely asked me if I was married. I had been handed two bowls of gingered coffee, so I took the sip demanded by etiquette before replying, and then answered in the negative.

At this remark there was a general raising of eyebrows—the hairless ones of the old Sheikh, besides the bushy black ones belonging to 'Ahmed. Abdu kept his eyes discreetly lowered.

As my statement had clearly caused an unexpected shock, I felt I must try to offer some explanation. I remarked that men marry at an advanced age in Europe.

"That is so," the old Chief agreed, "but you—you are twenty, no, twenty-three or twenty-four, maybe?"

"I am twenty-five," I said.

"Twenty-five, and not married!" the old man exclaimed, in some horror. "What can we do for you?"

Nothing I could say, no excuse I offered about the marrying age so often being delayed in Europe, appeared to have the slightest weight with 'Ahmed or the Sheikh, who regarded me with increasing wonder and perturbation.

"But you have somebody," the old man persisted, "someone you will marry when you return to your own country? Surely this must be so."

"I have no intention of marrying at once when I return to England," I declared, shaking my head to show the negative.

"Then," exclaimed 'Ahmed, clearly in his excitement about to make some important observation, "then why not marry one of the girls of T-hila or the neighbourhood? We could find you a most attractive and well-desired wife. You would not be obliged to marry more than one, since you are a Christian."

I thanked him without enthusiasm, hoping the subject would be dropped. Unfortunately the Sheikh seized upon the advantage gained by the Sultan's minister and pressed home the desirability of marrying on the spot and settling down.

Cornered between their hospitality and curiosity, I made haste to shift the conversation to a different and safer angle.

"I have come out here to seek a woman—a very beautiful and famous one," I declared.

They grasped the idea a little too soon.

"Does not every man look for a beautiful woman?" Sheikh Muhammed Bar Omar declared. "Some search all their lives. In your country is it not the same? Here it does not matter to the same extent, for the Moslem is told he will find beautiful women in Paradise."

"The woman I seek is a princess, a queen," I said. "She has been dead three thousand years."

'Ahmed and the Sheikh looked at each other in some perplexity. Of course they did not understand me, though I did what I could to explain. They had heard of Balkis, for they had read about the most famous Queen of the South in the thirty-fourth Sura of the Quran; I outlined to them as well as I could my wish to visit one of the great cities, perhaps the chief city, belonging to Sheba, and to find if possible some traces of her empire in this timeless land.

"It is bad when men do not marry," said 'Ahmed, shaking his head and puffing hard at the hookah. "Here in Arabia we have no bachelors, and with our harems, there are no lonely women—all are provided for and find a home. . . ." Thus spoke the typical family man, and in Arabia variations practically do not exist. . . .

Luncheon arrived to interrupt the conversation. First a slave appeared with a piece of soap and a spittoon; after my hands had been washed we sat round an enormous bowl of rice from which protruded the legs of chickens and goats, spiced with a nut that gave them an appearance of mildew.

It did not seem possible to refuse to eat the food hospitably set before me. I nibbled a chunk of meat handed to me by my host, dipped unleavened bread into a bowlful of green soup of unknown ingredients, and poured some fiercely hot curry sauce on the portion of rice stacked in front of me. I am afraid I made a sorry show, my lack of appetite calling forth real concern, and I longed for the tomato soup, corned beef and fruit at present somewhere on the road with the beduin caravan!

The repast ended, my hosts showed their appreciation of the food by suitable belching accompanied by the word Hum'd'llah. Their hiccoughs were loud and continuous and at intervals they thanked Allah.

A siesta occupied the afternoon, the two Arabs retiring to another room to give me more space. The caravan made a noisy entry into the sleepy little town, flies buzzed incessantly round my head, some youths below gambled with cards and dice. Abdu occurred suddenly; he told me the old Sheikh had hoped for the benefit of an Englishman residing in his town, and had been serious enough when he exhorted me to stop in T-hila and settle down. Abdu had a habit of occurring rather than arriving, for he generally entered without warning. He was a hardy rascal, far from impressive, yet with character written large across his ugly face, and with a kind of amusement I had begun to think of his sudden entries as descending from those beings who magically arrived upon the scenes when Aladdin rubbed his lamp instead of raising his voice or ringing a bell.

I asked Abdu to translate into English the introduction given to me by official Aden for the eye of the Sultan of Mukalla. This is how the letter read when he had done his work.—

"Will give you salaam from me to you, to looking after Mr. Norman Pearn, English boy. He want to go to Hadhramaut. I am very quite well and if you give Mr. Norman Stone Pearn, think what he want and help him since he live in your country. Salaam. I hope see you. All well."

I passed the time resting, a target of objective interest to thousands of flies who had evidently never seen or sampled a white man before. The decorations of the room consisted chiefly of cigarette cards, and so many portraits of Ronald Colman adorned the walls that I wondered whether T-hila thought they represented different men. For some reason or other, the only two men film stars in this picture gallery were Ronald Colman and Jack Hulbert.

When it was cooler my hosts arrived to take me round the old Sheikh's garden, where a mango and a cotton tree from India, among other things, showed what could be accomplished by patient and insistent cultivation. Walking round this desert garden 'Ahmed and the old Sheikh confided to me that in the summer no more than two or three hundred people resided at T-hila, though these numbers more than doubled when the tobacco harvesting came along.

To my astonishment, while taking the air, I was asked several questions about European history, past and present.

What was the situation in the Irish Free State? Had the Irish cut the last cord binding them to England? What sort of tea had been thrown into the sea at Boston when Britain lost her American Colonies? Apparently the answer to this riddle of strange up-country knowledge and learning lay in the fact that history, particularly English military and political history, was a special subject in the Mukalla schools.

'Ahmed warned me about travelling in the Humami country where the tribesmen were truculent. "They been fighting the Government," he said, "until just fifteen days before, when a peace was concluded, or so it is thought."

A delightful uncertainty hung over the interior, like a muslin veil draping a harem beauty. The Minister for Tribal Affairs, himself, knew little, if anything, of what was happening, and anyone who ventured up-country would not be journeying into regions dulled or denuded of the elements of danger and surprise. I was also put on my guard about the state of affairs in the Wadi el Ain, near my proposed route along the Wadi Himam. A tribe called the "Outbathani" were intent at the moment on killing themselves and any others who got in the way, this tribe having spasmodically fought against itself since the Dark Ages.

Entering the house of a T-hila merchant, I kicked off my sandals in the approved fashion, this action bringing cries of delight from 'Ahmed. "Now it is clear you must be one of us," he said, "live as the Arab!"

I was introduced to T-hila's oldest inhabitant—a man well over ninety, to judge by the reports I received in answer to my queries. There was not much of the old man left, and but for his clothes, I had a feeling I should have seen nothing but a mass of protruding bones. He was hairless, almost blind, and his legs were like cricket stumps burnt black; his hands to touch were cool and knobbly, and unpleasantly twisted.

The ancient was curious about me, and 'Ahmed sang my

praises, hastening to follow up his earlier remarks about marrying me off in the neighbourhood. The old man (who seemed to be somewhat of a celebrity about the place) was told that I really ought to marry an Arab girl and become a famous man, because no one had done such a thing in Arabia! When I pleaded I could not afford to marry, 'Ahmed, not to be beaten, slapped his thigh and exclaimed: "But if you marry in Arabia you *will* be able to afford it. Wives are cheaper here than in England."

A large basket of local dates was brought in for us to eat and the old man mumbled toothlessly a story explaining why the Arabs call dates 'the fruit of Mary'. Apparently Moslems are told that when the Virgin was about to conceive, she asked God for a special kind of fruit which she might eat, and a date palm began to grow so as to satisfy her need. The Bible and the Quran are still alive in Arabia, nourished on the sustenance of locality and patriarchal descent; they are part of the family and not legends or lessons.

In the weary mud house of the ancient, curious nests clustered among the rafters in the ceiling, and 'Ahmed told me they belonged to blue-bottles. The room buzzed with a loud monotonous hum of sound and in a high-pitched, quavering voice, to which was added a lisp my host warned me of snakes, tarantulas and scorpions, though he himself seemed to be impervious to flies and winged things.

'Ahmed and I left him to his croaking, and went down to the north-west corner of T-hila, where the camel track—one of three routes for Du'an—stretched away out of sight behind the hills. My caravan was making ready for the march, the donkeys were being prodded into line, and I took careful stock of those carrying my paraphernalia of travel, especially the one bearing the five thousand Maria Theresa dollars packed in boxes.

In my hearing 'Ahmed impressed upon the beduins that they would be answerable for my safe conduct; to me he said by way of farewell: "Next time you come to Mukalla may it be as an officer of the British Government—a high officer." We shook hands heartily, then the caravan crawled across the last of the narrow valley and began to climb up and over hillsides leading to a long, descending plain reaching to far mountains. Chattering happily to himself, Muhammed, leader of our thirteen donkeys and ten men, rushed up to me, skipping the sharp rocks with bare feet. He paused a second, smiled, touched my hand in friendliness and sped after our caravan.

Short, indigo-dyed, almost black, naked but for his blue-stained, once-white loin-cloth, in which his treasured dagger lay sheathed at a horizontal angle, an amulet around his thick, powerful neck, and wisps of camel-wool string tied around his sinewy legs a little below the knee—for defence against weariness, so he said; around his forehead a similar strand of black string for preventing headaches; this was Muhammed. A rascal, yes, but a friendly one. Approaching forty, but having lost none of his youth or the fun that a youth can have. A black beard making a final effort, just straggled across his chin, and the long, jet hair, well greased, that curled unruly about his forehead and ears, completed the picture of a typical Hadhramaut beduin.

He was one of the most agile men I have ever seen, and a born mountaineer. He was thick-set, the muscles rolling over his arms, but without suggestion of over-development, and not an ounce of surplus flesh. Invariably he was to be seen happily tramping (or skipping if the ground was at all rocky) after the donkeys, his ancient rifle, the pride of his heart, slung over his shoulder, or nursed across the back of his neck with his two black, but well-shaped hands resting for support at muzzle and butt respectively. Sometimes gun barrels turned so hot in the sun that my fingers would not have been able to touch them, but Muhammed still nursed his treasured rifle round the back of his neck. When we were traversing waves of rocky hills, he would some-times beckon me and we would set off together, leaving the caravan to wind its way painfully and slowly along the defined tracks, while we took a short cut. Out of breath in the heat, I would strain to leap up an almost perpendicular slope after a guide who never slackened his pace when he was with me, and since I was not going to call for an easier rate of progress, I was forced to follow hard on his footsteps.

Downhill it was a different proposition. Muhammed would leap from crag to crag, often selecting the steepest section of the descent for his route, his legs and feet seeming to contain elastic as he sped down to the gorge below. In my sandalled feet I sometimes slipped, and once I thought I should not be able to save myself from a six hundred feet fall over granite boulders; but in such times of absolute necessity I feel one can be given superhuman aid, and I was able to slow up and come to a stop just in time, my legs trembling with fright. Muhammed, seeing my plight, came back a little way to me and pointed out the route to take. Often we went off together, and having reached the point where we encountered the recognised caravan routes, we would lay ourselves down in whatever shade we could find, dozing or chatting away the intervening minutes or hours until our caravan laboriously reached us.

We had left T-hila at 4.15, and having hurried the donkeys over rocky ground, unsuited to speed of any kind, through ravines and up to the top again, we came to the small village of Wadi Lusson, situated on a hillside under a cloudy sky. Here we made camp. We made a small fire in the moonlight and our cheerful conversation interrupted for a time the silence of the sky.

I slept moderately well for my first night in the open, on hard ground, but was awakened at midnight by two very hungry mosquitoes. With the arrival of dawn we breakfasted, and I surveyed my surroundings with fresh interest. Round, smooth-faced boulders caught the eye everywhere, for they had turned pink in the early morning light. A youth of about fourteen was prominent among the badus, since he was dressed in smart robes with a rich turban. He was the son of a rich Seyyid, so I was told, travelling by way of Du'an to see his mother at Behran. He had a special badu attendant, and evidently corresponded in social importance to something rather higher than the old-school-tie status.

At six o'clock the donkey caravan struck the trail again, real Himyar (donkeys) travelling through the ancient Himyaritic kingdom. Muhammed announced a four-hour trek lay in front of us. He exhorted us all to hurry. A high and difficult mountain had to be surmounted before the midday camp could be reached with shelter from the sun. Out of the East a tiny wind, felt, rather than seen by any movement, played along the shiny boulders before being lulled by the burden and heat of another day.

CHAPTER FIVE

LITTLE BLUE MEN

FROM MUKALLA TO Wadi Du'an takes six days of hard travel, plodding steadily into the highlands, morning and evening, using the cooler night for forward progress when and if a full moon, flood-lighting the difficult country, happens to make this possible.

Immediately Mukalla is left behind, the mountains begin, piling up in height and difficulty, tortuous and tortured, seared with gorges and gullies through which, at rare intervals only, there flows the cooling grace of water. North-west, in the Yemen, the Arab word for "right hand" (Arabia being judged geographically in the Arab mind from the point of view of Mecca and looking east), the upland mountain regions, touched by the moist monsoon winds, are green and fertile enough—especially round Sana and Jauf, cultivated with the coffee bush, date palm and incense tree, and, compared to the rest of Arabia, a comparatively green and pleasant land for man to inhabit. But the Hadhramaut, especially in the heat of midsummer, is a stony wilderness, skin-brown and scorched: a stark, uncovered display by mineral powers rather than any beauty on the part of the animal and vegetable kingdom. The camel-coloured mountains consist of a granite base, convulsively thrown upmost in places, with higher stratas of sandstone broken and falling into landslides of shale and scist. Progress over these Djebels and Djols is painful and arduous—a succession of interminable ups and downs, a visual imprisonment without the satisfaction of the wide, less smothered vistas of Northern Africa and Arabia.

Travelling in August, I saw practically no signs of trees, shrubs or any living green thing. If trees were there, they did not exist to the eye in the brown and frizzled wilderness. We did sometimes encounter ilb trees (the local acacias) but they were more or less without leaves, and only when looking up from the bed of some Wadi, could one occasionally glimpse skeleton branches patterned or twisted against the sky. So stiff were the leaves on these trees that they did not move with the wind; they had become rock trees, sunstruck and almost petrified, and it would be only after a rainstorm that they would turn again to greenness.

No flowers changed the colour of the landscape, no grass grew, and no butterflies danced in the air. The general effect was an unrelieved grey and buff, an active Service uniform, with lighter tones unrolling most curiously in the shadows at the bottom of the valleys where the white stones of the Wadis showed up.

When possible we rested at midday, sheltering, except for the last halt before Du'an, beneath the deep shadows of hillsides. We would lie up under the rocks, slinging my tent to increase the shade. I never used the tent for sleeping in at night: it was protection against daylight rather than the darkness.

The caravan, the donkeys advancing nose to tail, ate up the distances like a caterpillar crawling along with fifty-two legs. We kept on the march as a rule from six a.m. to six p.m. with a siesta during the noonday heat; it was wickedly inhospitable country, the boulders and precipices and the heated stones mocked at travel, and frustrated speed.

The route taken by our tobacco caravan was too bad for camels; travel became donkey-work for man and beast alike; the polished limestone pebbles sprawled at the bases of the wadis, making marching difficult, and as we went along the noise of our footsteps sounded like dominoes being interminably shuffled.

The donkeys were good ones, inured to back-breaking hardships, but they began to slip when tired; their loads

Muhammed and the Tobacco Caravan from T-hila

In the Desert of Stone

had to be readjusted and they themselves navigated round some of the worst boulders. The badu gave the donkeys frequent stick, although when they showed signs of collapse they would help to pull and push them, exchanging a beating for a wise if also unavoidable assistance. On the two occasions when a donkey completely collapsed, Muhammed and his assistants stretched it out and slit its nostril with a knife. This bleeding operation proved successful, but for some reason the badu were exceedingly secretive about the whole business, and they would neither allow me to ask questions nor take a photograph.

It is startling what these Hadhramaut donkeys can do; they keep going heavily loaded all day; for much of that time a human being is added to the weight on their backs; yet at night they seldom if ever lie down, preferring to sleep standing upright under the stars.

When the badu wanted the caravan to go faster, they began to sing encouragment to the donkeys. Muhammed gave the word and they sang in chorus, an almost endless chant with a headlong swing about it. The song was all about rain, which donkeys hate, telling them to hurry or the heavens would open and pour down water on their backs. The donkeys would invariably prick their ears and break into a jogtrot, doing a steady six miles an hour instead of four. This daily chant, a river of sound threatening the little donkeys with rain, reminded me of a sea shanty, though more full of gutturals; perhaps only sailors and nomads understand why people need to wander, and how to use to the best advantage the choral arts of repetition.

.   .   .   .   .

Passing up the Wadid Himen, we came, on the second evening, to the dusty village of Rowan where dejected date-palms and some coarse blue-green grass looked cool and refreshing to the eye. Shrinking figures crept out of mud hovels, slinking from door to door. The people were horribly dirty and poor, and the guest house, which Abdu showed me, was so filthy that I chose to sleep within a walled-in enclosure among the caravan.

Abdu told me that the inhabitants of Rowan were mostly ex-slaves who had escaped from the coast. Slaves in Southern Arabia, if dissatisfied with their masters, can put themselves on the transfer market like footballers. If no exchange is made, they can, in some cases, take the law into their own legs, and run away. But such a course is rare in the Hadhramaut, Abdu assured me, for Arabs as a rule treat their slaves with kindness and indulgence, and they become in time "one of the family." Children of well-to-do parents are given a slave child as companion and servant, the two growing up contentedly together.

Wolves howled round Rowan that night. The donkeys huddled together, hee-hawing almost continuously to register their fear, while the badu sat round the fire, un-sleeping black shadows, their rifles across their knees.

Towards dawn I was awakened by a sudden hubbub of noise and excitement. Shouts reached a sudden crescendo with the report of a rifle.

"Wolf! wolf!" Abdu called out. "They saw his eyes flash in the firelight. The silent one had come to investigate."

My first thought proved wrong; the wolves apparently had not jumped the high wall of the enclosure, but had found a convenient gap, and one of them, probably their leader, had ventured inside. We never shared camp with wolves again, although we heard them one night of moonlight, howling in the hills. My last glimpse of the troubled midnight at Rowan before falling asleep again, was of the badu—who always seemed cold at night—shivering dis-tressingly round the fire, covered with nothing more than a meagre loin-cloth and with a thin strip of indigo cloak round their shoulders. I did not wonder at their need of constant coffee and conversation to comfort them through the hours of darkness.

I slept on a reed mat, on top of which I spread a prayer carpet; my burnous cloak was eiderdown and blanket.

On two nights of heavy rain, my tent came in useful, used as a tarpaulin sheet, and Abdu shared it once when he was not feeling well. But the badu got wet and cold, and when thoroughly chilled they just shivered—they were creatures of the wilds, and like wild animals would make no compromise with civilisation.

Since the genesis of travel, almost every caravan must have suffered from some member who shirks his share of work and proves a passenger in the most modern sense of the word. Our caravan was no exception to the rule, for the young Seyyid constantly traded on his position. Although only fourteen, he ordered the badu about and made them wait on him. He was first to go to bed and last to rise in the morning; sometimes he might not have got up at all if Abdullah, his acting servant, had not pulled the reed mat from under him, forcing him to bestir himself. He sulked if ever crossed, he was constantly demanding that I should take photographs of him, and he took his meals apart.

The badu ate rice, bread and dates. They took possession of my saucepan from the start of the journey and used it as a common bowl for food, fingers and dirt. They never washed or cleaned the saucepan, much to the annoyance of Abdu, who was a Yemeni and looked down on Hadrami cookery.

"They very dirty men," he said to me one morning, after watching with an expression of disgust, the badu packing up the well-encrusted saucepan without tipping it up first.

"They are not used to water," I pointed out to him.

"The bowl is not their own. They do not think of others."

"They have not had the advantages of going to sea, like you," I said, half jestingly.

"Ah! the sea," Abdu echoed, rubbing his blunt nose vigorously, "—the sea and the desert—they are both places for men, and the Arab knows both, though he loves the desert best—he has grown up with it."

He watched me take some meteorological readings with great interest.

"To tell whether the day is hot or cold is very wonderful," he observed, "but only Allah decides which it shall be. In my country it is not very difficult, yet away beyond the seas it must not be an easy matter."

I agreed with Abdu, and we went on to discuss the thermometer in connection with illness.

"The Arab usually does not know when he is ill," Abdu commented. "What does it profit him since death or recovery is ordained beforehand?"

I could agree with my guide's vocal measurements of Moslem fatalism, for in Mukalla I had seen a man drop dead in the street, and the crowd that gathered testified shrilly to the fact that the dead man had been in robust health only that morning. Most Arabs, when stricken with illness, either recover naturally without thinking about it or die quickly; long invalidism or courses of treatment are not for them since God alone knows when they are ill and when their time has come.

On the third day out an amusing incident descended on the caravan from out of the stark and staring hills. Toiling along the wadi, we were approaching the village of Loo-bayb, situated above us on the mountainside, when a village woman rushed down towards us with a baby in her arms. She was evidently not unknown to Muhammed, for he began waving violently at her, dislodging in his efforts, a tin of biscuits carried on his back, which crashed to the ground, scattering into fragments. The accident sounds harmless enough, and the badu enjoyed themselves picking up the bits—a task in which the Loo-bayb mother helped with the rest, slinging the baby across her hip and quieting his cries with a shake—but more was to follow.

The tin had contained my favourite dry biscuits, and Muhammed had insisted on transporting them under his own care, rather than trust them to any of the donkeys. Now he felt he had lost dignity in public. At the evening halt he had evidently got as far as deciding how his prestige, scattered like the biscuits, could be recovered, for he stepped forward with the demand for goats' meat.

My contract with the caravan had expressly stipulated that the bedu were to supply their own food. I pointed out the fact to Muhammed, adding that if they felt they needed meat, I would help them to buy the necessary goat, paying my share, but not providing more than this.

For the first time Muhammed began to lose his usual smiling ways, threatening me with words and calling up the others. They talked of Colonel Boscawen, who had actually reached the gates of Shabwa only to be fired upon and forced into retreat: Colonel Boscawen, apparently, had given freely, never grudging goats to his beduins and they had providentially arrived to order when required.

I stood my ground, shaking my head. They could have my share of the goat, I told them, but not my money to pay the whole sum. When Muhammed produced a dagger I thought it was time to be firm. The situation struck me as interesting rather than alarming; I could not take these little blue men quite seriously; they had seemed too friendly and unaffected, too much like imaginary inhabitants of Barrie's *Never Never Land*.

Summoning Abdu, I told them that if the quarrel continued I should make a point of reporting them all to 'Ahmed on my arrival at Du'an; also that if Muhammed did not return at once to the fire I should no longer consider him leader of the caravan.

Muhammed took the hint and left me, making the best of the old cooking pot and the old stew. Quite soon he was back again at my side like a dog that needs forgiveness; if he had possessed a tail he would certainly have wagged it.

"Muhammed not bad," he exclaimed. "His head run away sometimes. But his heart is good."

This concluded the incident, and no goat was roasted, though a good, gluttonous meal of meat is unmistakably a

E

badu's chief delight and his nearest approach to heaven on earth.

Soon after passing Loo-bayb, Abdu was thrown from a donkey, the latter hurting its leg, the former his dignity. Donkey-back travelling in the Hadhramaut is an uncomfortable method of transport, not to be compared with riding a horse or even walking. We sat on the front of the donkey when going uphill, on his rump when descending. We would usually walk for an hour, then ride for a time, continuing the march for five hours before making a halt.

Our caravan was led by a white donkey who knew his way almost perfectly, following with unerring instinct and complete modesty mere tracks that often faded happily away into complete nothingness. A Boy Scout would have been brought to a standstill, and possibly even a Red Indian tracker, since, unlike earth or sand, passers-by leave no marks of footsteps on the surface of shiny white stones.

Priced at anything between £2 and £5, but worth more than a motor-car to the tribesmen, the meek donkeys of Arabia have walked their way through history, geography and religion. I always think of the camel in connection with Northern Africa; but if Arabia is mentioned, one of the first things to step into mind is usually the little, uncomplaining donkey—the modest maid-of-all-work in the Near East. You can see them walking in their hundreds up the streets of the towns, an Arab seated on their hind quarters, legs swinging, bundle in front of him. You can start out, knowing they are going to take all the ups and downs of Hadhramaut travel in their stride, eating no more than a few wisps of hay curled into a dry rope for the uses of transport. Somehow the black cross for ever marking their backs and shoulders takes on added meaning in the Bible land of Joseph and Mary, and Jesus of Nazareth. The only reason I have ever discovered why a donkey should be thought foolish, is that he is unselfish enough to eat thistles; I noticed that donkeys get up like a horse, forelegs first, while the camel rising on his hind legs, behaves like a cow.

The third morning among the tangled wilderness of mountains, grimly forbidding, radiating the phantasy of fairy tales, the badu for the first time suddenly appeared to have had enough of it. As though some queer negation had taken possession of them all at once, they slackened visibly, dragging wearily behind the donkeys; the sap and spring had left their bodies and run dry; at 8 a.m. they made camp and refused to go on. Nothing Abdu or I could say would move them; finally in despair, we decided to let the badu have it their own way, hoping they would regret this strange and unaccountable inertia that had affected them almost as though their will-power had melted in the glaring day.

To distract their attention to other things, we began a discussion on knives. I showed them the knife used by beduins in the Sahara. It was straight, not curved, with a lip to it, and one badu tested its balance with interest, deciding, I think rightly, that it was an inferior weapon to their own. Afterwards, gathering a little energy, they went through the pantomimic of killing, thrusting at throat and heart, but never at the stomach, like Malays.

Tested by this violent arm exertion, one or two of the badu, who were wearing silver armlets, passed pieces of string between metal and flesh to ease the strangle hold of adornments put on when children and never removed. One badu had a cord tied round his leg, and a silver ring set with a ruby, glittered in the sunlight. The ruby he had picked up on one of his journeys: the ring was tied round his leg since it is considered an insult to manhood, if worn as women do, on the finger.

"I not woman," the badu explained to me indignantly. "I much better—look!"—and he spat to a distance certainly unattainable by any woman, brown, black or white. . . .

They are strangely inexplicable, these little blue nomads of the Hadhramaut, and it is difficult to account for them, or fit them into any racial compartment. They are certainly not real Arabs, although Southern Arabia is the ancient

home of the Arab peoples; they do not use the black tents
of the beduin, nor are they whole-hearted wanderers.
Like the Bhutiyas in the Himalayas, they take charge of
caravans and transport, keeping generally on the move,
but their wives and families do not go with them, and stay
in fixed districts. In a sense they are the sailors and traffickers
of the southern wilderness, but though the phrase may
delineate, it does not explain them.

To me these little blue men out of nowhere, seemed
animal men, belonging to the higher animal world rather
than to the races of human beings. They belonged to the
earth when it was younger, unclothed, unexploited, untouched by the collar of education or the coat of civilisation. They might have skipped out of the Stone Age,
except that they carried knives instead of clubs and slept
under the rocks rather than in caves. They lived in an
untutored world of their own, grown-up children, their
chief joys in movement and in eating—men without minds
or traditions, but nevertheless intelligent enough through
the proper use of instincts. They were clannish, however,
always protecting me from alien tribes or caravans, and only
allowing me to be bothered by their own people.

I remember asking them if they had any gods? No.
Did they ever pray? No. Were they Moslems? Yes, they
were Moslems, but did not know what they had to do about
it. They disliked the Nazranis, but again they did not know
why. What did they like best in life? A sheep or goat cooked
in broth for dinner.

Soap they regarded as unclean: water seldom came
within their reach. I watched them pour grease and melted
fat over their heads—their method of cleaning—until it
ran down their bodies in thick streams. Afterwards when
they sweated in the sunshine, the indigo would run from
their clothes, turning them into blue instead of brown men,
acting as they did on the principle that if the skin is not
kept open it must be securely sealed and shut.

The next village our caravan passed was Kevar, where

every one suffers from swollen stomachs. Children with enormous stomachs, befitting at least a mayor or alderman, ran out to greet us. It was a painful sight to see them hurrying with short, uncertain lurches. The bodies of these unfortunate people swell more and more, I was told, until death descends; no one at Kevar lives after the age of thirty-five.

"Can nothing be done for them?" I asked Abdu.

"It is the water," he said.

"But why do they stay?"

"They have always been here. They do not think of going away."

.   .   .   .   .

At Zimam and Unkerdun an ex-slave with two donkeys joined our caravan. His grandfather had pleased the Sultan of Mukalla in some way and he had been freed. The negro was a fine specimen and an example to all by his good nature and unvaried unselfishness.

He had travelled with the Ingram's caravan two years before and, more mysteriously, with some Japanese. He recognised Philby from the cover of a book I was reading. He called him Sheikh Abdullah Ibn Saud.

At Zimam, on Sunday, we passed a woman sitting by the roadside. As soon as she saw us she became very wild, rushing after the caravan and trying to lay hands on me. She wanted money; she talked of slaves to sell for seven hundred dollars, this price comparing oddly with the three hundred and fifty demanded in the Yemen and the five hundred on the coast. Abyssinian girls can actually be bought for twenty-five to forty dollars, boys costing a little less. Until the Abyssinian War plenty of slaves were available from Ethiopia and Mombasa; the supply is not likely to fail for at least ten years, unless the British Navy were given permission to search all ships plying between Africa and Arabia.

Soon after the ex-slave joined our caravan, a fight broke out for the first time, the Seyyid youth with his beautiful turban, and his badu, Abdullah, coming to blows. The Seyyid ordered Abdullah to throw away the stew he had left and cook himself a fresh dinner. This waste of good food proved too much for the long-suffering badu, and the two Arabs aimed blows at each other. Abdullah, who had flung the cooking pot at the Seyyid's thin legs in a sudden graceful gesture of annoyance, would have made mincemeat of the youth if we had not hurriedly intervened.

All the time that we were moving forward into the mountains we climbed more than we descended, for the land sloped upwards towards a higher and wider un-inhabited emptiness. The furrows of the valleys were like frowns in this waterless land. The Wadis were shuttered and pressed upon by grim and stony hillsides, the entire landscape giving the appearance of having been stoned. But the world was free of man and his works.

I sang with the badu and browned my body to the wide freedom of the wilderness. . . .

The primary annoyance all through the journey were the ants; the small black ones were the worst, but there occurred also a larger brown variety, and a few red. They moved in long columns of one-way traffic. Sometimes the parallel ranks would approach too close, meet round a boulder, and fight; the brown ones could carry loads many times their weight, working with their hind legs grasshopper-fashion, if they found portage becoming difficult.

Of birds there were few. One bird, however, left notice-able tracks, and, hidden mysteriously from view, practised a sweet and plaintive call at intervals. When questioned, Abdu told me it was one of the oldest inhabitants of Arabia, connected in legend with Sheba and the Sabaeans. I wrote it down in my diary as being either a stone curlew or plover. I saw signs of deer or gazelle, but little cover for track-ing existed, and the colouring of the quarry toned with the rocks; once or twice, higher up, we heard a leopard cough in the darkness.

There were spiders of the tarantula variety, grey and obscene-looking, not so numerous as in the Sahara, but feared by the Arabs more than snakes, since the camp fire sometimes attracts them. Several times while on the march a shadow moved on the brown stone, the badu flashed their knives and a serpent the less existed in Arabia.

We went on and slightly up, the donkeys shuffling across the stones, the little dark men singing their rain song. We had escaped altogether from time and its mechanical insistence. We had come into a land so old, so scarred as to appear ageless, and in existence from the beginning. Somehow or other we seemed to be coming to the uttermost parts of the earth, unvisited by civilisation even in an aeroplane—a no man's land, and certainly a no woman's land.

And yet the very withdrawn and antediluvian aspect of this region in which we had come to grips with physical nature, unadorned and unavoidable, seemed to me to hold within its wrinkled hand the promise of the past. The Hadhramaut was becoming to me like an ugly and unwanted character, left unexplored by the majority, and yet holding deep down within it, rare redeeming qualities or secrets well worth excavating.

Looking up as we rode along, I beheld Muhammed, who never "bossed," and believed in waving aside disobedience and disorder, instead of concentrating attention on them, rush up and touch my hand. He pointed to the brown ridges ahead of us, a little higher than any we had passed.

"The highlands! The Djol!"

The leader of the caravan ran on again and I watched his strong legs and thick ankles advancing with the short, powerful steps of the mountaineer, climbing upwards, above the cities of the plain, into the desert of stone.

CHAPTER SIX

THE DESERT OF STONE

IN THE WONDERFUL TALES of the Arabian nights, it is recounted how Sindbad the Sailor when travelling in the region of the Gulf of Oman and becoming lost in just such valleys as we had been traversing, was transported to safer and less imprisoned levels of country, by sitting on the back of the Roc bird; no such magical succour was at hand for the assistance of our toiling caravan, and we climbed out of a dead land of catastrophic imprisonments into a higher world, horizontal and more expansive, yet extending in front of our eyes an unbroken desolation whose limits were mercifully shrouded by the cloak of night or the heat haze that quivered on the horizon.

Soon after leaving Wadi Himem we ascended the mountains for the best part of a day until we reached the flat highland summits, the desert of stone, that forms the prostrate thorax of Arabia. These tablelands of Djebel and Djol attain their maximum height in the Yemen, a mountainous zone fifty miles in width rising steeply on the sea side to 9,000, and then forming a plateau zone of more than a hundred miles sloping gradually to the great Jahna desert, or Rub el Kali. In the Hadhramaut the zone is less wide and high, but is still part of the mountain chain buttressing the interior and shutting it off from the sea.

There are undulations with half-formed indentations, where water, gathering from the rains, has worn away the limestone, seeking to find its own level, but for the most

part these tablelands are extraordinarily flat and undeviating. They represent, more than the sand desert of Rub 'el
'Kali or the sand dunes of Oman, the real flesh and bone
of Arabia, much as the green moist lowlands of bog best
typify Ireland, the prairie grasslands Canada, and the
brown veldt South Africa. They appear so old and primitive as to have forgotten Nature's more ordinary and more
pointed convulsions, their volcanic past rubbed by immemorial processes of time. Bold and bare, they look to
belong to the days of dead sea bottoms, and the first fossils,
and the upthrown excitements from the flood waters of
long ago.

At intervals we walked over perfectly flat layers of stone,
consisting of huge irregular slabs—nature's paving stones
of granite or marble. These extraordinary escarpments
over which our caravan walked with smooth contentment
gave the impressions of gigantic causeways, and sometimes
lasted for many miles on end. They were straight and undeviating, almost as if man-made out of the stress of relent-
less slave labour, or else as though some subterranean
wadi had been heaved up solid by incalculable forces of
fire and steam at work deep down in the earth.

Charles Doughty travelling in North-West Arabia
describes how he saw "stones of granite in a row and flag-
stones set edgewise."

The probable explanation is that over granite base and
tertiary deposits of limestone, beds of larva have been
poured by volcanic convulsions, protecting the softer layers
from disruption and decay and forming in places this
uplifted crystalline floor.

No dust troubled us amid the desert of rock, and the
sun, as though abashed by its own pitiless reflection,
receded for a portion of each day behind a noon-tide veil
of haze and vapour. Often a cold wind blew and at times
mist-clouds rolled and billowed across the landscape.

The effect produced of journeying across a route convulsively carved by nature, but also implemented at some

period in the dim past by the hand of man, was increased when we reached places where boulders had been shifted and high-piled, giving the appearance of work done deliberately on very ancient traffic highways.

When I questioned the badu about these stony mysteries, they looked at me and shook their heads.

"It has been like this always," they said.

Talk about the antiquity of roads! That caravan route across the Djol to Wadi Du'an must have belonged to old Testament times. Much has been written of Roman roads and their triumphal march across the crests of Europe, but the ageless caravan routes traversing Djebel and Djol put them into sun-struck second place. They do not belong in substance or in spirit to Cæsar, Alexander and Saladin, but rather to Nebuchadnezzar, Sargon and Sennacherib. They are not so much pre-historical in their attributions, as pre-Flood.

Sabaean footsteps must have touched these highways, and the dagger prints of camel caravans bearing the incense of Yemen and the Hadhramaut northwards to the marts of the Nabataeans. If soldiers in their thousands ever passed this way across the Djol, they were barbarians, with the sinews of wild animals, nature-worshippers, sun and moon dancing on their metal breastplate and a sea of spear heads.

These scorched tablelands, more than any rockfastnesses near Quebec, are the heights of Abraham.

Backwards and forwards, summer and winter, across this strange uplifted rock structure, come the beduins of the tobacco and salt caravans, little wild men still journeying in their stone age. They sing to help their footsteps forward and to kill monotony, as do all mountaineers, Semites, Hamites, and the first Aryans singing their songs to Pushan the Pathfinder away up in Asia on the roof of the world. We passed other caravans singing their way into the night; my badu would judge numbers and distance by the volume of sound, remaining quiet themselves in case of hostility or a surprise attack. One tribe would be their friends, another their foe, so that they took no chances.

Occasionally we came unexpectedly upon stone rest houses. A wealthy Sharif or Seyyid, who had experienced some painful hardships, no doubt decided he would make the way easier for those who came after, and therefore sent slaves to construct a shelter for wayfarers on the spot where he had suffered. There were also some artificial wells, " bir," the water in them, being the colour of beer.

I made a record of the temperature, which was not as high as I had expected. At T-hila the shade temperature was 84° in the early morning, 79° in the evening. At Mukalla the mean temperature was much the same. On the plateaux, on a cloudy day, my thermometer mounted to 105° at 11 a.m. The days tended to grow hotter later when I approached Shibam and Shabwa. Near the last named, the sun heat reached about 120° at midday. Whilst talking of scientific instruments, I should like to mention the assistance I derived from the Rolex Oyster watches which survived the strain and stress of sand and rain storm, and told the truth about Time at the close of the journey.

No flowers of any kind broke the monotony of stone and rock. I did not notice a single drin bush—grey-blue in colour, like an air-force uniform—good for camels, and nearly always on active service somewhere. Down in the walled-in valleys or alongside the village, my badu would discover a bush about four feet high with blue-green leaves, which they picked and chewed to keep the throat moist. But up here there was nothing. Not so much as a butterfly flitted into view until I reached Henan, and even beetles were black or dun in colour, not gay.

I suppose that flowers and rock plants do exist on the Djol, but in hiding, called into sudden visibility after the October rains. The traveller remembers with gratitude the flower-drenched hills of Palestine in mid-spring, and the sudden unworn carpet of crimson anemones, the untoiling lilier of the field. Palestine itself is no more than the largest oasis, about the size of Wales, saved and cut off from the dead fingers of the desert by the Jordan river. Even the sand blossoms without difficulty after spring rainstorms, and for ten days in the month of snap-dragon and mignonette, the desert by a miracle changes to a paradise of sweet-smelling bloom, a wonder to behold. In the deserts of North Africa, too, the butterfly bush supplies sanctuary for the winged insects of summer, pro-vided they never leave the shelter of its shade, resting con-tent with diminutive days and not scorching their wings with freedom. Oranges, in Samaria half as big as foot-balls, are the real tree of life in the tillage zones of Arabia, date palms take their place at shady intervals in the desert, but the Djol in high midsummer is an uninhabited, un-relieved emptiness—a dead, dried-up world, suffering from sun-stroke.

Time has forgotten these tablelands of Arabia, and its passage from age to age is marked by the dead weight of unnumbered stones. Up here, far from the mechanical hurry of civilisation and its clocks, time is measureless, slipping along effortlessly in sandled feet from unimagined times.

The start of the day is best and early morning more forceful than sunset. The sky awakening with the dawn, silver-lidded if clouds are about, turns slowly to indigo and darkest blue, to cobalt, grey-blue and finally to an impalp-able shimmer of heat haze when the sun has climbed into power.

The earth rolls into another day.

By noon the air is quivering and dazzled and the ground seems unsubstantial, unsolid underfoot; yet mirages occur but rarely. The periphery of the horizon shortens, until sometimes the eye cannot penetrate the powdery haze of atmosphere beyond a distance of two miles.

There is no brazen expanse of sky as is often the case in the desert, for heaven and earth merge and become nebulous; the sun, like Aaron striking fiercely upon rock, precipitates not water but a veil of heat vapour slow drawn and lingering. The hour of sunrise is the best hour in the day, unleashing over everything a sudden burst of gold. It is then for a brief interval that the Djol becomes beautiful, for the grey tablelands turn into the golden road that has illuminated the fancy of the east and tinted the thought of Elroy Flecker, the latest poet of Islam. The resplendent pathway of the sun stretches out undiluted, uninterrupted, and in imagination endlessly—to Samarkand, to Sheba, to Timbuktu, to any of those other far-off, echoing places which seem to embody in their own keeping the goal of travel.

I tried to paint the golden hour on the Djol, but although I could get the colouring, I could not infuse into the picture the effect of early morning, rather than sunset.

Towards evening any clouds that hung in the sky always gathered round the sun in the west; they tended to form a cloak over the face of sunset, and the sun, thwarted of his last splendours, turned to crimson rage before disappearing. For a few minutes, too, the mountains kindled to an angry reflection before fading their fires through green and mauve into the violet gloom of an Arabian night.

The glow of sunset passed, life departs from the Djol. The change is not a fancy, but an actual feeling of cosmic change when the world rolls over into darkness. Distant objects appear closer, yet journeying is more tedious and longer.

At night the quietness became absolute: no cock crow, no dog barking, not the sound of a streamlet, not so much as the croaking of a frog. Silence stretched in all directions until it created a spell that bound the tongue and linked one across the abyss to starlight and the spheres.

During the day the Djol is harsh geography, but at night it becomes pure astronomy.

I had only one perfectly fine night on the Djol—the others were interrupted by cloud and drizzle, and I shall always remember it, for these flat dessicated heights, unlike most mountainous regions are rewarded with a spectacular sight of the heavens.

I saw the sky so brilliant with stars that no man could hope to count their number unless he had a squared ceiling. Moonlight was strangely exciting and phosphorescent. One was forced to look up and marvel at the burning faces of the constellations.

I could pick out Pegasus, the winged horse of the East, Hercules with his club, the Waterman following upon the heels of the Horned Goat, and close to the horizon the Archer shooting up at Altair, and I had seen Venus rising and setting—the sun's hand maiden, his pale and beautiful daughter worshipped by the Sabaeans and ancient peoples of Arabia, as Astarte, goddess of moon and evening star.

A little distance removed across the unyielding ground, the camp fire, kept alive with difficulty, had died into ashes. Muhammed, leader of caravans, stood upright but undimensional in the gloom; I felt rather than saw the other badu shivering in their rags, the chill of the heights striking at their bones. Abdu lay prone and fast asleep, wrapped within the folds of my tent, for perhaps it is true after all that sailors don't care.

The sky was thoughtful and tremendous. The door of the night was wide open. A million worlds looked down at me. Low down in the West a star fell down, and a sudden little wind blew out of to-morrow.

I felt completely happy. I could understand why Jaafer the Barmecide, had said to Haroun al Raschid, one night in Baghdad, without the assistance of champagne or a dance band:

> " Let us go on the roof of the palace
> And watch the myriad of stars; How
> Beautiful and how lofty they are, the
> Moon rising like the face of one we
> Love, O commander of the Faithful."

CHAPTER SEVEN

STARLIGHT

DURING DAYLIGHT LITTLE romance or attraction can be found in the Arabian highlands of the south, which, from the point of view of the traveller, are often tedious and wearisome almost beyond the limits of sufferance. But when night has fallen like a curtain this is changed and transformed into an unearthly beauty.

Nobody can throw stones at the Arabian night. If they did so, and picked up the rocks over which they had just passed, the stones would vanish into the dusk, and in their place would hang stars, the first of the uncounted multitudes of stars that make beautiful these high nights of the south.

Nobody who has camped on these flat mountain tops in summer time can forget the purple patch of an Arabian night. The stars are gold not silver, as though they had been minted into sovereigns scattered from a purple cloth. The night transmutes and transfuses, lifting up squalor and monotony to the levels of its own high mystery and magnificence, and relieving eyes unrested by green vistas in the daytime.

The night mesmerises. The silence becomes incommunicable. You almost hold your breath. You travel out into the immensity of starlight. You see the universe in a new unclouded relationship.

Not for nothing did Arabia nurture the Chaldeans and Babylonians,—stargazers and astrologers of antiquity, men who mapped the secret courses of the moon, made charts of destiny, and sometimes followed the stars as moderns follow a new leader or the compulsion of some fresh social phase. The wise men of Arabia! The royal astronomers of the East!

To this day certain Arabs believe that a star comes into the sky whenever a soul is born, a register and individual beacon on the heavenly chart. Since we are told that there are some 15,000 million stars revolving in the Gallactic system, they could not be disproved by the quotation of numbers.

In the times of the Queen of Sheba, the Arab shepherds and nomads, simple men, worshipped the beauty of the stars, and the Evening Star, which was the most beautiful of all, they conceived to be the goddess Astarte, and because the stars were friendly and close above their heads, they sometimes thought of their goddess as a shepherdess of sheep walking the hills, and they put up horns in her honour.

In three thousand years the purple cloth has changed but little, and you can experience the same brilliance, the same cool beauty of the night that surrounded Sheba and her caravans. These things are unchanging and unfading in their wonder.

At the point when the evening star shows at its brightest, when she keeps company with the Earth on the same side of the sun, she outshines the other planets in the heavens and can occasionally be seen in Arabia with the naked eye during the daylight. Some believe it was this star in an unusually bright phase that the Wise Men observed glittering in the East, and that they sang for joy when they saw the morning star.

Three Wise men brought their gifts to Bethlehem. The Arabs, schooled in the enquiry and computation of the stars, brought three gifts to civilisation—Astronomy, Algebra and Aristotle. Night and her mysteries has done more for Arabia than the hot sequences of the days.

Standing on the Djol you can gain a faint perception, if the night is immense enough, of the reasons three of the great religions were born in Arabia, and of how to shepherds and psalmists destiny and divinity seemed very close at hand. You can understand how heaven and earth came nearer to each other and how Arabs and Israelites, seeing a little farther than others into the sky and beyond, glimpsed, in inspired moments, the unutterable and the ultimate that lies beyond daylight and beyond contradiction.

You can imagine, too, caravans of stars and the creation fires of the stellar nebulæ. The stars are the great wanderers, unending in their courses, and bearing their commerce between worlds ; like Lucifer they are light-bearers, alone in movements that touch the shores beyond the boundaries of our universe and the waves of worldly intercourse.

In some curious way on the high ground of Arabia they become closer, almost personal, and no longer aloof and pitilessly remote in space. You do not think that out in the ether the sun is really blue, or that Betelguice may be many millions of sizes larger than the sun; you think how on certain times on the hills above Nazareth, on the cedared ridge of Lebanon or on the tablelands of stone, the stars glow so large and close it looks as if you could follow almost any of them to some splendid and illumined objective beyond the dark.

You can say, as did Flecker: "I will go, where the fleet of stars is anchored and the young star captains glow. . . ."

During the nights of most tropical or semi-tropical countries, an emanation of evil sometimes walks abroad, oppressing the quiet: nature feeding upon herself, the moon rising white and hungry, the vegetation stretching luxuriously—but this is not the case in these high desert places of space and burning starlight, where men are not moved to buy motor cars or to explore cultured avenues of sport and amusement, but rather to study the wanderings of the heavenly bodies and to look up into the calm face of eternity.

F

CHAPTER EIGHT

THE FURY OF THE HEAVENS—OUR CARAVAN IS WASHED DOWN FROM THE DJOL

WANDERING BADU COME up to the tablelands of stone during the winter months when the nights are cool and the sun tempered by the haze; they visit them for the sake of their healths, otherwise this region is inhospitable and wearisome to a degree not easily describable; our caravan stayed apart as possible from others; once we all remained quiet after a detour while Muhammed whispered to me that roving or marauding bands sometimes came up here, and the caravan that we could hear approaching faintly in the distance might be up to no good.

Since we could travel during the night on the crystalline causeways, the midday siesta became the time when our caravan rested. We camped about 10.30 and started again at 2.30 if we had marched by moonlight.

By this time, to the outward eye, I had gone almost completely native, except that I was brown not blue-black; identical colouring was suggested by the blue shirt and shorts that I wore, which were hailed with satisfaction by Abdu and Muhammed. I found the rough and ready life suiting me; I never feel the heat much and the tinned food I had brought with me kept my digestion in good order. Whether I should have felt the same if I had eaten the rather doubtful food cooked by the badu, I do not know, but I felt fortified by not taking the risk.

The outstanding worry harassing me on the trek were my feet. I did not go barefoot like the others; I wore the shoe of Arabia, the sandal, which affords protection underfoot while at the same time allowing stones and grit picked up while walking to fall out again.

Everything proceeded according to plan, save for my big toes, which stuck out and struck things—yes, there was the rub At night they kept me awake, in the daytime, do what I might, they insisted on coming in hard contact with the stones. Looking at the big toes of the badu, I came to the conclusion that mine were unsuitable for this kind of work.

The Arabs of the Sahara, I had carefully noted, possess big toes that are shorter than the middle ones, evolution having fitted their feet to their environment. The badu of Arabia were not quite so well equipped for walking in the wilderness, but at any rate their great toe did not stick out and hit things, like mine. The skin on badu feet, tested and coarsened by a million stones and rocks, is thicker than most hides; it is almost as if nature had shod them with rubber soles. I saw Muhammed who had surprisingly developed a corn, quietly sit down and carve a chunk the size of half-a-crown, from the bottom of his right foot, jesting with Abdullah while doing so.

We passed few wells on the Djol and carried with us two goatskins of water. These skins could never be placed on the ground, since apart from the heat of the rock, they soon become objects of interest for ants and beetles with excavating instincts. At first I used to boil the water for drinking, but I soon became tired of this precaution and worried no longer.

The donkeys were uncomfortable to ride and had never been taught to walk properly. They seldom managed to keep their backs level even when travelling across horizontal ground, and they began to remind me of the pantomime ass whose forequarters never agree with the hind. Possibly they were so used to going up and down hill that they continued the necessary movements when no longer necessary.

Abdu was most scornful of the Hadhramaut donkeys, and said they did things better in Yemen. He carried about with him a black umbrella, to keep away the sun. Muhammed would borrow it occasionally, holding it out in front of him, in a cheerful, ceremonious manner; everyone thought it was a great joke, and Abdu had his umbrella open as much as possible except when it was raining.

The umbrella had escorted Abdu safely to Mecca—at least this was the sailor's story and he stuck to it. He told me in a burst of midday confidence how he had disembarked at Jiddah, spent the night at Eve's tomb, and gone on the twenty-five miles to Mecca, the next day, arriving at last before the great black Kaaba stone temple that is the focal point of Islam. He had not known which way to face when praying, now that he had reached the exact geographical centre of his faith; some, he said, looked to the East, others faced the West.

"And what did you do, Abdu?" I asked.

"I looked up."

"That was well done."

"No, Nazrani."

"How was that?"

"It was raining!"

He talked to me about the Kiswat cloth that covers the stone. In the old days pilgrims used often to strive to secure a small piece of Kiswat, not in the vulgar souvenir-hunting spirit of the West, but because they believed it supplied a passport to Paradise. At the present time some of the more fanatical Wahhabi warriors wear, attached round their neck, a special piece of paper which it is believed will transport them into Paradise, if they die in battle, without any examination at the hands of the recording angel. I learnt from Abdu that pilgrims do not pay board or lodging when they reach Mecca; the city entertains and treats its visitors as guests, each man paying what he can on departure, as a free-will offering for having reached the end of his ambition. . . .

I asked Abdu whether he possessed any children.

He said "No." He had three daughters, but naturally they hardly counted. Was it the same in my country?

"Not at all," I replied. "Some people go as far as prizing them more than boys."

"How can that be? The Prophet himself said they are inferior."

"Girls are often less difficult, and they cost less to bring up."

Abdu could not understand my reasoning at all, coming as he did from a race that has believed man came first, from the day Adam walked in the Garden until the present. He shuffled off to try and fix my tent in an acacia tree in place of an awning, for the sun was scorching too fiercely to discuss anything so inflaming as the relative merits of boys and girls.

. . . . .

For our last midday camp on the highlands we sheltered under two large and unexpected acacia trees, seemingly almost miraculous in appearance after the unending corrugated-iron roofing of the Djol over which we had passed.

Unfortunately camels had rested there recently, and they had carried with them enough insects and bugs to keep everything on the move: not until we had attempted in vain to lie relaxed under those trees did I appreciate to the full the superiority in cleanliness as well as willingness possessed by the desert donkey in comparison to the cynical and superior beast of burden that has a hump.

I sent on a badu ahead with a message for Du'an. The young Seyyid wished Abdullah to go in advance, too, to announce his arrival, but without a present of money. "He must go for nothing," he said. "Is it not an honour to serve me? No other reward is necessary." Actually neither of the messengers reached Du'an; Abdullah never started and the badu I chose took the money and disappeared soon afterwards.

Shortly after one o'clock clouds began to gather, rolling up across the horizon, thick and menacing, overcasting the day with shadow. Soon it became apparent that this was no mist haze of unusual density, but a summer storm advancing unexpectedly from out of a blue sky that had looked until now as though no clouds could ever trouble it.

The badu loaded the caravan with extreme haste. "Hurry, hurry," they cried, using their sticks on the donkeys' flanks. They showed signs of alarm, which, at the time, I did not share or take seriously.

Our donkeys did not need to be urged forward because they knew better than anyone that the rain they disliked so much was close at hand. All that morning the day had been unusually hot, working up at midday to the brazen breathlessness that is supposed to precede an earthquake, though the sky was not copper-plated in warning, and danger did not seem to threaten.

For my part, I suggested the wisest course was to stay where we were, sheltering as best we might behind some rocks, and manipulating a breastwork to try and shut out the storm. But the badu insisted on starting at once, saying that if we hurried sufficiently we should reach Du'an and safety before the tempest grew into alarming proportions: to be caught on the Djol, by a full-grown storm was worse than being attacked by robbers—so they said—possibly the thoughts of the comforts and goat's meat of Wadi Du'an worked more powerfully in their imaginations than any other consideration.

Hardly had we started on, hurrying at top speed, when great heavy nimbus clouds began rolling up from two sides; they rushed at each other thunderously yet noiselessly, two sides of a heavy curtain stretching the width of the heavens, joining together in mid air the material of storm that turned from the grey of cygnets' feathers to the gloom of cormorants in flight.

A wind, Biblical in its association, rushed down at us from out of the obscurity of sky and earth; the donkeys laid back flattened ears, men bowed their heads, Abdu's umbrella blew inside out with a bang. The caravan broke into a fast trot; from the fallen sky the rain song was flung around the terrified donkeys by a hundred elemental voices. Before we had gone very far, the gloom turned to semi-darkness, daylight shut its eyes; the tempest, gathering its powers, swept forward to the main attack. . . .

In my mistaken enthusiasm for recording some of the more startling moods of the sky, I had loitered behind taking hurried photographs. My companions were about a mile ahead of me, when they were suddenly blotted out by the blackness. Not only had they become lost to sight but I was not sure even of their direction. I rode on alone, hurrying to catch people I could not see. I think I realised at that moment something of the meaning of the plague of darkness.

A gash of light rent the skies and ahead of me, all at once, I saw an awe inspiring sight—rain moving in spirals, cyclonic fashion, sweeping the earth with a solid beam of water. The wind screamed madly as I buffeted my way towards the caravan; it yelled derision at my poor efforts, lifting stones like leaves from its path. At last I struggled to the others. At the moment when I reached Abdu the rain came down; not the sort of rain that falls headlong, like you expect from the skies, but horizontal rain flooding sideways more in the manner of a burst water main.

It broke the caravan into pieces, sundered ropes and links, threw the donkeys into the disorder of panic. One minute the caravan was there, toiling forward, the next almost all trace of it had been swept away into Egyptian darkness. I could only find one guide—Abdu, holding on to two donkeys.

I attempted to shelter behind the second donkey, clutching the rope as though I was drowning. Abdu had loaned me his best red turban, which I had put on to celebrate our entry into Du'an. The dye turned me into a red man—my

hair was a striking shade of colour for several days afterwards. The downpour lasted for two hours of fury, the
rain lashing, the wind scourging; then the storm suddenly
stopped. The sky was no longer liquid and hissing.

Our broken column began to piece itself together again;
we inspected the tale of damage. Luggage had become a
mess; maps, notebooks, clothes had turned into a pulp—
nothing could have protected them from rain that ran as
well as fell; only a tin box or two had escaped from total
immersion.

We started off again. Muhammed was shivering with
fever; his teeth were occupied in a kind of involuntary tap
dance. We were drenched and there was no fuel available
for fire, so we kept moving. Some of the badu began
singing the rain song, an extraordinarily plucky exhibition
for stone age men, I thought—and the rain started
again.

For nearly an hour we struggled along as best we might,
and then we arrived at the edge of the cliff where the Djol
dips perpendicularly nearly two thousand feet into Wadi
Du'an.

Should we go on or should we stay on the tableland?
Should we descend the precipice or should we stay and
shiver on top? No question of retreat entered into a problem
consisting of a choice between the evil we knew and the
evil which we could look down upon and guess.

Had I known by the comparison of any previous experience exactly what lay ahead of us and what the descent
would mean, I doubt if all the badu and all the badu's
donkeys could have dragged me down into Du'an. Why we
ever attempted anything so hazardous and unnecessary
and how we succeeded in reaching the bottom intact is a
mystery I do not find easy to explain. The gravitating of
our caravan down the rampart of cliff to the Wadi below
was worse than any nightmare, for it was a nightmare come
true, and a fall meant death.

The edge of the plateau resembled a wall in places; no

camel could have descended from the cliff edge on which we stood, and the donkeys had to be led in single file. The badu, Muhammed acting as spokesman, refused to spend another night on the Djol at the mercy of horizontal rain, when the palm trees of Du'an were beckoning to them from below. I had a horrible suspicion, I remember, that they were comparable to children who saw some desirable apples across a river and started rolling up their stockings, without considering for a second whether the water was deep enough to drown them.

The badu clambered down. The caravan took the plunge, and I could not control what followed. Water gushed and streamed and fell everywhere, so that at first we appeared to be walking in the heart of a river. Mostly we never saw the path at all, for it had become transformed into a mixture of slipping mud and tumbling water. At the best of times the descent to Du'an must be unpleasant, for the track is a mere ledge, with a sheer drop on one side of several hundred feet across bare rock; after the deluge, the feat, worthy of acrobats, seemed principally to depend on the right mixture of luck and instinct. Acrobats never fall, but I gained no comfort from the thought.

I took off my sandals in order to gain a better grip of the slippery mud, yet I believe that I should never have walked out of my nightmare into Wadi Du'an if it had not been for the practice in dangerous descents I had already gained following the flying heels of Muhammed at the start of the journey.

The caravan slipped and stumbled and drew breath, panting. Once we arrived at a horrid ledge creeping along the face of a small precipice. Cloaking this ledge from the daylight, a waterfall had thrown a foaming curtain of water that thundered into the valley below. The noise was terrific. The fall was about two hundred feet in height and sounded, as we passed behind it, like an outlet from the heavens above, the earth beneath, and all the waters under the earth.

No beauty gleamed back at us as we crept along in the gloom, the fall of water acting as an almost solid handrail, for we were on the inner side of the opaque flood, walking behind the torrent. The wall of water helped us to regain momentary equilibrium, though two or three of the donkeys tried to jump straight through it.

I have always wished to walk behind a waterfall, where rainbows play and flash in the sun, or better still to live in concealment in a cave behind one, as happened to occasional pioneers in Red Indian story-books of the Fennimore Cooper variety. The overlap of water was so discoloured, however, with the red soil of Arabia, and the noise so deafening, that we came out the other end, stunned and shaken for the task that still lay ahead.

To go back was worse than going on. No one had either time or breath to ask advice from the others.

In many places rock tracks had become water tracks and the torrent, sweeping down the cliff, sucked greedily at our knees. I learnt afterwards that under ordinary conditions the path down the sides of the Wadi is bad enough to necessitate steps cut carefully in the rock; in olden days these staircases were both the care and the despair of ruling monarchs anxious for freer and less difficult circulation within their realm and they are still a tall problem.

Twice, donkeys stumbled on the edges of precipices and I thought they were going over. Once a donkey fell sprawling and could not regain his feet for several minutes while the caravan behind him halted, shivering.

The rain stopped and we could see a little better. We came, at this point in the descent, to one of these flat and glistening crystalline causeways we had encountered so often on the Djol. I think the sight of firm and more level ground caused me to relax vigilance for an instant or two which nearly proved my last.

I was walking along the narrow ledge, Abdu close behind me, when I slipped—and slid over the edge. Abdu throwing out his hand like lightning, saved me. He happened to seize me by the only piece of clothing I was then wearing—my shorts, and with this good English flannel between his fingers, hauled and steadied me back to safety.

The marble path left behind, the descent grew more difficult and tortuous. The donkeys were almost standing on their heads; the luggage hung about them in queer bunches and festoons. I admired the calm deportment of the ex-slave from Zimam, coolest among us, quiet and unselfish, always ready to help when needed, finding happiness in service—a lesson to us all.

Just when I feared my legs and ankles could stand no more, and I must suffer disgrace by halting for rest, thus holding up the half of the caravan behind me—for no man could pass another in that storm on those narrow ledges—I saw the bottom of the cliff wall close at hand.

The clouds had heightened by the time we had come down to earth. The wind no longer blew out of the Bible. We were no longer struggling with plagues and powers of darkness; a peacefulness of shelter and quieter breathing came upon us and the little steaming donkeys raised their heads.

We reached a path, broader and of gentle incline, presenting few difficulties either for two feet or four. Soon we had arrived at the beginning of Wadi Du'an and saw a crowd gathering to greet us—clusters of little woolly-haired children, screaming and shouting, and spreading advance tidings of the arrival of a caravan, bringing an unexpected white man out of the clouds.

CHAPTER NINE

THE ARAB CHILDREN greeted us with shrill cries, but their elders remained silent, motionless with the uncertainty of wisdom, until the first of our donkeys touched foot upon one of the little mud viaducts that link village to village along the Du'an valley.

The bottom of the valley was hidden beneath surging brown water, hurrying towards the wider reaches of the wadi where it could fling itself to right and left and be free to settle down and refresh the thirsty earth.

I had lost my sandals, and with bare feet I took a flying jump to the first of the viaducts within leap, while the rest of the caravan followed more sedately, scrambling down into the water-logged gully and then heaving themselves up again to solid earth by holding on to the donkeys' tails.

The viaducts are the streets of the towns and villages in the Wadi Du'an. They give the landscape the appearance of being ribbed and corrugated, but the centuries have found them necessary for safety, since otherwise water after the storms would sweep the traveller away. The high road between the various villages is really a water course, so that progress is slow and at night risky. Two people can pass abreast on the viaducts, and in certain places, where they have been widened for donkey transport, three can pass each other by.

We were met by a deputation from the Governor Princes of the district—the brothers Ba Surrha. Our descent had been noticed by the guards on the watch towers, so that

Descending from the Djol

Admitted Within the Ba Surrha Fortress

during the two hours we had taken coming down from the Djol, preparations had been made to receive us.

On every side, Arab children, pleased by the approach of new arrivals, jumped high into the air to express their delight, clapping their hands in a rough, expressive rhythm. A slave, representing the Governor Princes received me with a gentle air, and at the same time a deputation from the richest of the chiefs took me solemnly by the hand and asked after my health. What I was doing there seemed not to concern them at all; it was my state of health and well-being after the storm that exercised them, surely a testimony to the fadeless hospitality of Arabia.

Wading and climbing through the honeycomb of streets we left the caravan and the badu behind, Abdu and I mounting a slope that was part of the mountain side; above us loomed a strange fortress-like building made of mud six feet thick, square, and not rounded and towered like the castles of Europe, dwarfed for all its six stories of exalted mud, by the ramparts of the Du'an cliffs.

High up in the featureless wall, a head peered out in the gathering dusk and surveyed us closely. Satisfied we were not enemies, but friends of the Ba Surrha, the guard gave a tug at a long connecting rope which pulled a chain that in its turn lifted a latch to allow the massive gateway to swing inwards. Our entry looked to have been effected by Heath Robinson in person, but with the portcullis raised, the freedom of the castle and its mysteries stretched invitingly before us. We now found ourselves in a courtyard with a further slope to climb and another massive door appeared in one of the main buildings. Unseen people were watching us from the depths of these walls. A signal was given and a peep-hole was disclosed ; a sudden, fierce, bearded face looked down with suspicion. Satisfied by what he saw, the guard allowed us to pass through into a second courtyard; we walked across this for the ceremony of peep-hole and face to be repeated once again, only now it was a younger man who surveyed us, this time an African slave whose face darkened the aperture through which he looked. At last we were in the inner sanctuaries of the castle, and I found our escort had been increased by seven or eight patriarchal figures robed in white, royal blue, and one in a long nightgown of green and yellow.

We fumbled our way along passages sleeping in the half light; to my disquiet, I was now pressed into the front of the procession, and, in silence, our skirted procession followed slowly into a more magnificent courtyard than any we had yet passed, roofed in, and supported by pillars, square like the castle itself, decorated by barbaric carvings, embossed and coloured crudely.

Robed and semi-robed figures squatted on carpets and cushions, motionless as statues, their backs to the wall. A medley of strange colour and personality encircled three sides of the room in excitement, leaving the remaining space for ourselves; everyone who was anyone must have been present in that vaulted room in the ruling palace of this forgotten valley. It was easy to pick out the two Princes of Du'an, not on account of spectacular clothes, but because of the added dignity of their deportment. They were plainly dressed in tailored duck jackets and plaided skirts; their heads were shaven close, but they resettled their turbans of red and yellow patterned cloth like a man putting on his hat again; rising in one motion to their feet they approached me with an indescribable air of courtesy, their lean brown fingers closed over my cold hands, communicating a warmth of welcome that I have never experienced before, so that in that moment I knew I had fallen among friends.

I took up a squatting position beside one of the Princes, feeling thankful that I was able to cover my muddy legs and feet, though my appearance, bedraggled after the battle with the storm, must have left much to be desired. I was a tramp being presented to royalty. My only clothing— a blue, silk sports shirt and blue shorts, the dye running or already run, seemed a poor apparel in which to meet with

Princes in this castle which can have no counterpart except in story books.

Before formalities commenced, hookahs were handed round, a ritual in itself more expressive than most of our Western hyperbole, for the pipes vary in quality and importance, naming at once the relative values and merits of tribesmen, chieftain and visitor. A very ornate pipe became the immediate business of the brother Princes, a second hookah of less magnificence, but still shapely with its curves and glass mouth piece and bowl of bubbling water, was provided for the use of the most important chieftains, and lesser pipes without the advantages of quality or cool smoking satisfied the needs of the tribesmen and beduins. Looking round the room I could accurately guess at a man's importance by the turban he wore and the pipe he smoked. A fine Arab with a bearded, kindly face and a pair of twinkling, restless blue eyes, patriarchal and benevolent, caught my attention; he could be described as one of those mighty men of the Bible—a warrior, a law-giver, a Prince who possessed the only unwalled village in the valley, and whose possessions had never been attacked. This was the Munsab of el Meshed.

The brothers Ba Surrha acted in unison, echoing each other's conversation, one never standing up without the other, and behaving as though they were united by invisible strings. I think this dual role, carried out in friendly and perfect agreement, undivided and unquarrelsome, must provide something of a record in the annals of ruling princes anywhere in the world.

The brothers talked idly of my journey and its prospects. Soon we were discussing Freya Stark, and the brothers showed, with pride, a postcard she had sent to them when recuperating in Italy, depicting her in native dress supplied to her when she stayed in the palace. She had tactfully worded a message on her postcard in Arabic, a polite touch that had not failed to find its mark in the appreciative minds of my hosts. Freya Stark had had the

misfortune to develop measles, an illness that is more
or less endemic in the Du'an valley, babies catching
it at an early age and either dying or becoming immune.
According to the Arab inhabitants of the Wadi Du'an,
particularly the women, Freya Stark is thought to have
contracted the illness owing to the fact that she insisted
on washing herself, and with scented soap.

The courtyard grew dim, and the gathering gloom distilled
drop upon drop of darkness until the arrival of paraffin
lamps, standing in rows upon the ground, attracted the
visits of numberless, brown winged moths that flitted about
the room in noiseless activity. Acting upon the hint of the
evening lighting, many of the tribal chieftains rose to their
feet, saluted the Princes, touched my hand in parting and
faded into the darkness of arched doorways.

Not until the next day was my business to be transacted
or the badu of the caravan to receive their rewards.

I was told a room was ready for me on the floor above:
a room, carpeted and cushioned, with kitchen, bathroom,
and terrace all in one. Everything I wished for in the way
of food and drink was mine. I had but to clap my hands to
attain the services of willing slaves. Rising to my feet I
followed a dark and silent servitor, feeling once again that
I had strayed into some fairy-tale whose existence had
managed in some secret fashion to outlive the bounds of
paper and print.

I was about to depart, when Abdu reminded me of my
letters of introduction from the Sultan of Mukalla; I told
him to apologize for my lapse while I handed over a very
sodden foolscap envelope. The Princes opened it, glanced
hurriedly over the scrawl, one brother reading a passage
to the other in undertones. They gave me smiling acknow-
ledgment and nothing more was said. I followed my servant
from the room and we went upstairs. Not for a long time did
I discover that the Ba Surrha hold little love for the Sultan
of Mukalla, and do not acknowledge his friends, but so
perfect is Arab courtesy, so delicate the treatment of the

stranger, that I received no hint of this during the whole of my visit. . . .

I steamed in the luxury of a hot stand-up bath and Abdu prepared a meal for me. We were allowed to do our own catering since I had told the Princes that in England I was used to certain foods and my stomach took a long time to get accustomed to changes of diet; an assertion to which they agreed, declaring that if they ever came to England they would need no doubt their hottest rice and curries to keep them comfortable. I composed myself for sleep on the terrace, but Abdu preferred the stifling heat of the room, ventilated through the archways of narrow medieval windows, cut in the lower part of the mud wall.

Standing for a few moments on the terrace, looking out across a valley of velvet darkness, the sky vitalised by uncountable stars, the villages lit by ghostly flickering lights, I was carried out beyond the borders of daylight. The night was not quiet, but alive with unseen forces: the shrill cries of homecoming revellers, a sudden feminine voice upraised near by from the harem, a sound of singing mournful and far away, an occasional rhythmic beating, swelling at intervals, that I hoped was someone beating a drum and unconnected with the harem.

Punctuation marks in these drawn-out sequencies, were an occasional cry of a jackal or a bark from some wild animal which would be taken up and challenged by the dogs of the villages, their chorus of reply, echoing from one rock wall of the wadi to another and upwards towards the stars. These dogs in the Moslem villages have no master, yet somehow contrive to keep alive, and are preserved for the protection of the flocks at night; ill-treated, uncared for, despised in the Quran, these outcasts of Arabia defend civilization at night from the attacks of their wild kindred descending in search of food from the wilderness of the highlands, where no man lives.

A light rain started during the night, but not sufficient to send me indoors to join Abdu whom I could hear groaning

G

frequently, wrapt in his own imaginary troubles. No doubt he was missing his Carte chewing, and instead, had to content himself with puffing at a filthy European pipe stuffed with Arab tobacco. Yet Abdu and his pipe between them were not sufficient to keep away the mosquitoes of Maasna and their incessant hum of activity, although where the Arabs were concerned, mosquitoes did not seem to worry them or interrupt their slumbers.

Breakfast at sunrise on a diet of grape-nuts and condensed milk introduced our first day in the Du'an valley. Grape-nuts, I found to be one of the most useful of all the stores I had brought from Aden, being in texture and colour not unlike some of the Arab food, especially by the time it has been hidden by the dye of red sauce, and in this way un-offending to the susceptibilities of hosts, accustomed to having their hospitality appreciated. Grape-nuts too, I could eat with my fingers, and this again was more friendly than taking knife and fork to corned beef or tins of sardines.

Sunshine had not yet guilded Maasna, being still withdrawn behind the cliff bastions that made the town of the two Princes a citadel moated within a greater citadel. Downstairs, I found the Ba Surrha sitting at their morning council, sucking at the morning pipe and puffing cloudy, grey smoke into the broad back of the Munsab of el Meshed —a mighty man, judged by almost any standard, wearing a resplendent ribbon across his chest; a medal dangling on its end, was a gift, I was told later, from the Nizam of Hyderabad, by far the richest Moslem in the world, his private fortune worth, so it is confidently stated by Moslem and Hindu, more than five hundred millions. Two bowls of coffee, steaming and comforting, one for each hand, were presented on brass trays to the councillors, and letters were written on tablecloths and handed round to the various chieftains. The elder brother dictated letters while the younger one read them aloud in a gentle, clear voice. Quietly, without hurry, yet with more dispatch than is

usual in the timeless East, the Ba Surrha dispensed justice
to their skirted followers.

On this morning, my badu from Mukalla were due to
present themselves before authority in order to give an
account of their stewardship; with tactful courtesy the
Arab Princes, insisting that I should be able to hear what
transpired, had brought in an interpreter from a neighbouring village, an Arab whose home had once been in
Addis Ababa, in distant Abyssinia. In a moment or two
Muhammed arrived, leader of the caravan, rendered self-
conscious by the glances of civilised faces, shyly touching
first the hands of the brother Princes and then my own. I
smiled at the humble air of this nomad of the wilderness,
and folded hands in patience while the audience overflowed
into the centre of the floor, all the wall seats having been taken
by the inflowing tide of Du'an authorities. Time seemed of
no particular importance once everyone had sat down
in readiness for proceedings to be opened. A courier
arrived with a letter from a tribal headman, his cloak
dusty with travel, and spoke of the rebellious actions of a
certain chieftain—a man suffering from a grudge, if the
stories that circulated about him were to be believed.
The court room was packed to the point of suffocation,
for it was not every day that Du'an had the chance of
seeing their governors hand out justice to the servants
of a Christian.

Muhammed was asked whether he had discharged his
duties towards me and obeyed the instructions given to
him by the Sultan's minister before leaving T'hila.

"Na-am," Muhammed replied briefly. He had done his
duty. He had performed all that had been asked of him.
Muhammed looked towards me a little doubtfully when he
spoke, fidgeting with his fingers and twisting his toes.

The Princes now turned towards me, demanding if I
was satisfied with the way in which the caravan had been
conducted. When I replied that where guidance and accur-
acy were concerned the badu left nothing to be desired, I

saw Muhammed rub his hands together, his eyes darting pleasure at my words.

"Then there is nothing to do but distribute the rewards of money," spoke the two Princes, while the attention of those present brightened, the slaves at the door standing upright and no longer leaning huddled against the door-post.

Into this crowd, ears bent forward to hear words of silver or perhaps even gold, I was about to throw nothing short of verbal bomb shells, upsetting the age-old currency of placid Moslem jurisdiction, faithful to precedent.

I told the interpreter from Addis Ababa to repeat the exact conditions under which the caravan had been assembled for the trek from Mukalla to Du'an, bidding him expressly state that I did not have to feed the badu, who had been made responsible for their own transport. Passing through the country, however, Muhammed and some of the others had asked for my food and had demanded it under threat when met by a refusal. They had followed this up by doing what they could to force me into buying a goat for their meal; finally several of the articles carried among my luggage were missing—unaccountably. Did it seem right that members of a caravan should try to intimidate a visitor to their country?

A look of dismay went round the room as though a cloud had passed over the sun; the gloom increased when I told how the badu had bought a goat at a very high price, without my permission, and had then asked me to pay for it.

'Ahmed and Muhammed Ba Surrha looked at each other in perplexity, seeking words to please their own people while at the same time defending the rights of the stranger within their city.

"But," said the Ba Surrha at last, "these badu—they are but children." By way of argument little could be said against this defence. They went on to please the other side.

"You should have bought the goat and finished with the badu," the brothers continued, "it is the custom to give them meat."

"But would you buy your followers anything if they demanded it and threatened desertion otherwise?" I asked.

"But the badu are such children," persisted the brothers.

"If this is the way badu treat travellers entrusted to their charge," I said to them without changing the tone of my voice or letting them see I was not taking the council so seriously as the Arabs, "then it is time someone came along to put a stop to it. You say that the badu are children, but children have to be educated, is this not so?"

The brothers beckoned mysteriously to the Munsab of el Meshid and the trio talked to each other with the language of glances and nods which is older than any words of legal procedure. One of the brothers took off his turban, resting it on his knee; he looked worried. A buzz of conversation broke out in the room, exciting the moths and other winged creatures to fresh activity, and I thought rather foolishly of a crowd at a contest where the referee has made a doubtful decision.

"Well," said 'Ahmed and Muhammed, voicing their decision together, "the badu have been punished, they had no meat. Let us return to the question of payment."

I sipped my coffee and explained my position. I intended making a present to the members of the caravan until I had discovered that practically nothing was left of all my provisions except the tins of meat and fruit; every bit of rice I possessed, not to mention one or two other stores, had vanished. I applied to Abdu to confirm my story, so that no doubt was left in the minds of those present that my goods had been stolen. Until these were returned to me, I said, with a smile, I could not see my way to giving money presents.

Tradition must die hard in the Arab's heart, a sort of ancient conservatism holds them in thrall, for, looking round the room at the curious faces directed in my direction, I had no doubt at all but that right or wrong, they could have wished me to make the customary present to the beduins.

Muhammed, when summoned to stand up and come forward, mumbled out a few words of explanation to which few people listened, more concerned by his looks than his words. Muhammed and 'Ahmed took up judgment again. The stolen goods must be returned to the Ingleezi, then no doubt he would give a money present: in their minds busy working out justice on the problem of stranger versus servant, traditional remuneration probably counted with them of more value than the return of the articles stolen from me. I nodded my head several times to convey my approval of the Princes' decision; Muhammed was sent from the room to see that my luggage was recovered; Abdu followed him. Muhammed had made a shamefaced exit from the assembly, a favourite dog slinking off after a beating; silently, but with their usual elastic vigour, three of his caravan fellows rose upon their bare feet and padded across the tiled floor to share disgrace with their leader.

Tension flowed away with them, cups of coffee were replenished, smiles returned to the room. Half an hour later Abdu came back with the badu, doubt struggling with embarrassment on his countenance.

"Sir," he said to me, "about half the things taken have been returned."

In this room where food was plentiful and where the whole day might well be spent in listening with Arab courtesy and calm to differences that might almost be described as a test case, I finally asked the caravan leader myself whether he would prefer me to tell the truth in full in a letter to the minister of Mukalla and at the same time to give him his money, or instead to hand over a letter proclaiming his abilities as guide but leaving out of account both the trouble and the money.

Muhammed leapt to his feet, a current of joy shooting through him; he shook my hand vigorously while eagerly accepting the second alternative.

To the three other badu of the caravan I gave small presents of Maria Theresa thalers, and so the meeting broke up cheerfully. The brothers had listened to the whole affair with a dignity suitable to kings; though they knew I had justice on my side in principle, they had their own people to consider in practice. Before closing the inquiry with a wave of their hands, they took the trouble specially to thank the Arab from Addis Ababa for his arduous services as interpreter which had lasted many hours.

.   .   .   .   .

During the days that I was a guest of the hospitable Ba Surrha, the weather was brilliant, making me thankful for the protection given by the immense cliff face which plunged the narrow valley into shade for much of the day. Every morning the sky was an unfreckled blue, but after the midday siesta clouds blew up and distant thunder would be heard rumbling its passion away to the west and north. Scissor gashes of lightning tore apart the clouds, competing with sheet lightning which flickered the whole sky into fitful brilliance, dusk fluttering into sudden daylight. The hot fury of the desert was behind the storms. The thunder magnified itself into awesome majesty when recoiling from rock wall to rock wall along the blistered sides of the Wadi Du'an.

The interpreter from Addis Ababa invited me to inspect a village, sleeping in the sunshine a little way along the valley. He took me to see the intellectual club of the neighbourhood where twelve patriarchs and three younger members sit in simple dignity upon the mountain side to discuss news and problems that concern the lives of the men of the valleys. The club premises were in the open air, surrounded by fields of vegetables, no papers were written or books read; all argument became a personal matter, depending upon the vitality and texture of the individual mind.

"Have you news to bring us, O Traveller?" the patriarchs of the Du'an club demanded on my approach.

"News from where and of what?"

"The tales from the hills above," they said, "and from the town whose feet rest in the sea."

I told them of Mukalla and of my delight at visiting the

wadi about which I had heard so much. A debate started
between one of the younger men and a grey beard who
talked with calm deliberation and without the slightest
emphasis or excitement. I sat down, wishful to gather
what these imprisoned inhabitants thought of the wide earth
that stretched outside, and of the human rumblings which
shook the world; but a shower of rain, increasing to sudden
violence, broke up the meeting better than any human
interruption could have done, sending us hastening to the
sheltering village of Rubat.

Rubat entertained me with bags of Huntley & Palmer
biscuits, but it was a most unpleasant place, the sanitary
arrangements making me shorten my visit. The streets
were narrow, sewage shot down the sides of houses in shafts,
then ran along the middle of the street; wherever one
walked was dangerous, for one could not look both up and
down at the same time. Here at Rubat I was shown the
curious hornet-like bees that make honey in artificial honey-
combs fitted into eighteen inch diameter holes in the walls
of terraces high above the valley bottom. The honey was
thick, heavy, of the consistency of treacle, the taste in
some way sour; the Du'an honey is famous all over Arabia,
but the one or two tins I brought home to England were
not appreciated. What the bees of the valley collected for
honey was a mystery to me, since flowers only grow scantily,
for a short spring, and problematically after the autumn
rains: possibly the date palms give the clue to the riddle of
how bees manage to store honey though denied shrubs
or flowers or any possibility of garden parties.

The young merchant from Addis Ababa, who had inter-
preted at the badu court scene, happened to live at Rubat.
I asked him how it was that the Sultan was little liked and
respected in Du'an, while the Ba Surrha had only to lift
their fingers to be obeyed. I was informed that the Ba
Surrha are a large tribe, easily the largest and most powerful
section in the territory. The merchant in his turn asked me
what would be the likely result should a revolt break out

against the Kaiti Government. Would the British stand aside? Would they help the Sultan of Mukalla? Or would it be possible that they might throw their weight into the scales already weighted down by grievances of the inhabitants of Du'an valley? Evidently he took me to be some sort of secret agent, and he was quite unsatisfied with evasive replies, so that at last I told him that I believed, if the Du'an people had a real grievance the British might sponsor it to the extent of asking the Sultan to incline his ear, provided everything was done peacefully.

The weather became vindictive on our return to Maasna, the wind had turned Abdu's umbrella into a queer shape, of no use any longer for protection against sun or rain; Abdu kept his head well down, charging the wind as though he was a bull, while our slave-guide hopped along, bird fashion, in jerks, making me run and walk alternatively to keep him in view. Once we sidled past a donkey standing on the viaduct, at least the slave and I did so, but a different fate lay in store for Abdu struggling dismally in the rear; head down, eyes and ears shut, he did not catch the slave's yell of warning, neither could he see through the tangle of umbrella held in front of him, with the result that he charged the donkey full tilt. It was the end of the umbrella, and nearly the finish of Abdu as well: the shock of the collision threw him back on to the edge of the viaduct, where, losing his balance he fell over the edge, to crash into the muddy red stream swirling violently down the valley. Fortunately he could swim, though I doubt if the water was deep enough to drown him. In any case, neither his clothes nor temper were improved by his ducking, and the next day when I went off exploring down the valley he stayed at home wrapped in his own thoughts.

There was a ditch—a sort of chocolate-coloured swimming pool, caused by the removal of boulders and material for building purposes, and full with about fifteen feet of flood water: it had just happened, but like other unexpected offerings was joyfully acceptable to simple people. I watched Arab boys, naked as the day they were born, climb thirty feet above this enormous dyke, throw their arms towards heaven, and then fall headlong, always feet first, into the brown flood water below. None of them ever dived, but they sometimes jumped off in groups together, their splashes synchronising musically before woolly heads appeared on the surface, water and faces almost indistinguishable one from the others.

Women dressed like nurses in dark blue, with veils, some on donkeys, some on foot, passed, perambulating the viaducts. All the gardens of the Du'an valley are cultivated by slaves or women, who also fetch wood and water. Hewers of wood, come lower in the social scale of the Hadhramaut than drawers of water. A single standard of wealth distinguishes the status of women in these out-of-the-world regions: women of position all possess a donkey, otherwise necessity forces them to walk in the dust and make the best of it

Little girls approached me to stare and wonder, their skirts short in front, no more than knee level, but long at the back, almost trailing the ground; they wore their dresses slipping over one shoulder, and their painted faces stared up at me. Girls of the Du'an valley paint their faces yellow since light skins are considered beautiful and becoming; their lips are bedaubed in blue paint and often a tattoo mark runs from cheek to forehead. To me the general effect of this feminine make-up gave the impression of a population of invalids struck by jaundice.

The Munsab of el Meshed lent me one of his two horses, last survivals of the royal stables of the old Sultan—bony animals they were, pathetic and miserable-looking, tormented by flies who kept their sores open and raw, and to my consternation I was asked to suggest a treatment. All I could think of was the use of adhesive tape, but the old Prince was delighted and accepted a roll. The black horse, stuck all over with dirty sticky-tape looked a bit patched up, but my treatment was hailed as miraculous by the inhabitants, and certainly brought some relief to the horses.

A slave-boy, of miserable demeanour, although possessed of the figure of a god clad in a dirty loin-cloth, was brought to me one day. His body was perfect, his life happy except for one ever-growing trouble that weighed him down with shame. Although twenty-five years old, his feet were still growing and were already twice my size; that I could suggest nothing to alleviate his extraordinary case proved a bitter disappointment to the boy. I told him the most hopeful thing was for him never to look down, for then he would not be reminded every minute of his misfortunes. I am afraid it was not much of a prescription. An Arab who pretended to a slight knowledge of medicine told the boy he must iron his back and eat a beetle at breakfast time.

There was excitement whenever I ventured abroad, especially on the occasion when I rode the Munsab's black horse. The slave runner was a fine-looking fellow, but he was soon panting hard, and I began to slow down thinking he was unable to keep up; divining my intention he smiled and urged me to continue, saying he was used to following a horse, and had not yet got his first wind. We cantered on faster than before along innumerable narrow twisting viaducts. Sometimes I came face to face with groups of women carrying firewood, veiled and frocked in dull indigo cloth; they would fly before me, or scramble into a muddy ditch, screaming "nazrani, nazrani," in chorus, and as I, and my scraggy steed charged along, we approached a large group of women and donkeys who were blocking our way and either could not or would not move. The Munsab's horse was excited and refused to stop, it was an impossibility to pass, so we took off, and with a leap and scramble clawed up a crumbling viaduct slope to land on another causeway. Although immediate danger was past we still galloped on, for my dismal-looking mount was out of control and enjoying itself. Overhead branches flashed by perilously near my head, but at last the horse tired, and looking back I saw the slave runner, a gallant pursuing speck in the distance, symbolising to some purpose the lasting faithfulness of Africa in Arabia.

CHAPTER TEN

AN INCIDENT IN THE HAREM

AFTER LUNCH AND the usual Arabian siesta, I went down to take my farewell of the brother Princes. To my surprise, they tried to dissuade me from setting out for Shibam, telling me of a route across the mountains from the Du'an valley leading, as they said, to Shabwa by a quicker and more direct route. I got out my maps and showed them the lost city marked in a very different place from where the track they advised seemed to lead; I thought the two Princes probably had their own pet route and did not understand the advantages of a map. How sadly wrong I was, I did not realise until many days later, when it was too late. If I had taken the advice of the Ba Surrha and gone west, directly across the unmapped mountains, I should have reached Shabwa in all probability before Philby's arrival there, or at any rate have met him in the town itself. But I was tired of being side-tracked by authority, and as I had been forbidden entry into Yemen territory, I was now resolved to have my own way where the ancient Sabaean city was concerned.

At that time, no one from outside so far as I knew had ever succeeded in reaching Shabwa, the traditional approach to which was by way of Shibam and the Wadi Hadhramaut. I shook my head at the suggestion of the people on the spot. I thought I knew better. I thought at any rate that the centuries knew better than the brother Princes of Du'an.

They looked at each other smilingly, it was as if they had a secret code of communication between themselves before expressing their joint opinion, usually in perfect unison. One of them had on red slippers, the other blue, otherwise they were dressed identically.

"Well then," they said, "if you must depart, we shall be pleased to send couriers to Sif where the Sheikh will supply you with armed guards. The country beyond Sif is a dangerous land with roving bands of ill-meaning men. Between here and Sif our writ runs and you will find only peace and friendliness. But we would much rather you stayed a little longer here."

I explained to them that time was most important, and they nodded their heads incredulously. Being Arabs of the Hadhramaut, they must have considered this to be a joke. They pressed tins of honey on me, each about ten pounds in weight, decorated with a soldered strip; and they gave me English biscuits. Abdu was presented with enough flour to last him for many days' travel in the wilderness; one of the brothers pulled out an embroidered bag and presented it to him. Abdu lost all at once the air of suffering martyrdom that had been his favourite expression ever since the storm on the Djol; it was not until long afterwards that I found out the bag had contained twelve dollars—a rich tribute to the hospitality and generosity of this ageless land.

We were a cheerful party as we stumbled down through the puzzling system of viaducts from the stony slopes surrounding the Ba Surrha fortress, the citadel of fancy and fairy-tale, where we had been transported back a thousand years. Five laden donkeys stepped daintily through the palm-groves in a heat that seemed to press upon us physically, and we set our faces northwards towards Sif, and to el Hedgerain, that fortress owned by a slave, situated where the Wadi Hadhramaut meets the beyond.

Soon we were picking our way across an unending carpet of sharp stones, broken in places by huge boulders blocking the path; here and there glimmered sections of river, cut into segments by the fierce heat of the sun, and called into fluid being by the turbulent floods of the recent storm.

Abdu put up his Aden umbrella to prevent himself faltering. After a time he insisted on riding a donkey, since, as he said, the donkey must in any case pass over the ground so why not allow it to do the work for two people? We had set our minds on reaching Sif that night, so that our pace was a hurried one, and the little donkeys trotted miraculously through the stones, until we had to call a brief halt to re-adjust their loads.

Deep down in the valley, without a soothing breeze or even the freedom of distance, the day was brazen hot, and we walked along in a kind of half-swoon, unconscious of events until they had actually happened. Two of the donkeys had to be stopped so often on account of their shifting loads that part of the caravan lost patience and went on ahead at a better pace; Abdu, Abdullah (who was guide Number One) and I, dragged wearily along behind, acting as rearguard.

Without letting us know of their change of course, those who had gone ahead branched off on a track that led across a doubtful no-man's land where the risk of ambush and robbery was greater, but the day less fierce and distances shorter; by this means they hoped to save themselves an hour or two of purgatory. About one o'clock I called a halt. Animals and men alike were reeling in the heat; Abdu was in a bad condition, for he had been rocked mercilessly on top of the baggage, adding the discomforts of a sea voyage to those of a desert journey. Discovering to my disappointment that our provisions were on the caravan ahead of us, I sent Abdullah to overtake it and bring back some refreshment. We were languishing for want of a drink and lay back with mouths open. Abdullah could not catch the caravan, for the simple reason that it was not there, and he sat under the barren branches of an unexpected tree waiting for us to catch up with him and glean the news.

"We must go on," he said, "and we shall rest and eat in Sif."

As a gesture against circumstances this sounded all right, but I felt certain Abdu could not reach shelter without food besides rest, and I felt utterly tired myself, even breathing having become painful. An argument developed as to whether we should go or stay; finally I sent a slave-boy—a piece of animated ebony—to go the way we now knew the caravan had gone.

"This will take two hours if the others are to return," Abdullah complained, "we shall not reach Sif until dark."

"Then it must be so," I said, "we will not move from here until we have eaten; the fault is not mine, but belongs to the men of the caravan who have deserted us; it will be a punishment for them to return. This is a wild country, and we are left here without guards or possibility of defending our property."

Abdullah, apparently, had set his mind on getting quickly to Sif, avoiding further delay, and Abdu, talking in bursts, and muttering as a man does when at the end of his strength, surprisingly backed him up. It was a case of the wills of two Arabs against one white man, but I meant to win, and after a time Abdullah went off reluctantly in search of the others. His speed was less than that of a donkey, and if there had been any point in taking such a course I was sure he would have gone neither backwards nor forwards but run away somewhere on his own.

Tempers were shortened by the time the slave-boy returned with the other half of the caravan. Abdu by now was in a torpor, his mouth wide, his face a terrible colour. The badu flung the goods in silence from donkey back to the floor of the wadi; if the donkeys, covered with sweat and dust, proved troublesome for a moment, they turned upon them in a way that was horrible to see and impossible to describe. The cruelty they practised on these long-suffering donkeys made me wish for Muhammed and the

little men out of the stone age, who had taken me across the
Djol—primitives perhaps, but not a case crying out for
humane intervention.

After the first mouthfuls of food, however, the temper
of the beduins changed, passing from scowls to smiles;
one could almost see the food altering acids into the juices
of contentment, and all at once they started to sing. . . .
so great, so unaccountable is the fortifying action of food
upon an Arab.

Lunch over, we rode away into the hot afternoon, the
loads of the donkeys properly fastened, for I had insisted
on merciful treatment of the baggage animals. The
sun disappeared behind a haze; a shade of coolness
descended upon the parched valley; annoyance and disquiet seemed to have dissolved, when, without much warning, the sky suggested storm. Huge flake-white and black
clouds bore down from the north and the north-west;
wind sprang up from nowhere, and it was a cold wind
blowing at our backs, though the clouds were rolling in the
opposite direction.

Abdu shook his head, "It always means storm," he said,
"when clouds and wind do not move together."

At intervals I had my first sight of the phenomenon called
"sand devils"—a sight in the desert equivalent to water
spouts out at sea. I could well realise how it was that in
the old days of the Arabian Nights story, when the Caliphs
ruled Islam, Djinns and Afrites and other terrible spirits
were supposed sometimes to take shape and manifest themselves from sand spouts. As we watched, some of them
grew to such alarming heights that they appeared to touch
the ceiling of the sky revealed all at once between patches
of colourless cloud. They whirled round and round, so
fast that once or twice they looked to be solid, and they did
not disappear until they came into conflict with the rocks on
the sides of the wadi. Once we encountered a small whirl-
wind which formed in our path. For the space of perhaps
twenty seconds, the caravan found itself helpless, men and

beasts caught up by an invisible hand, lifted from the ground, turned round several times and set down again. Levitation by Yogis could not have done it better, or in more startling fashion. I saw the Arabs feeling themselves to find out whether they were hurt, and whether this magical removal had actually happened. They took it calmly enough, the donkeys, however, were terrified, at first refusing to go on; but with the passing of minutes the gale at our backs increased, hurrying us willy-nilly northward along the valley bed.

A camel caravan which we had seen weaving its way in our direction before the coming of the "sand devils," was now brought to a complete halt, head down against the screaming wind, it could not move at all, and it was as much as anyone could do to keep his feet. The caravan humped together in a lump, and camel and camelier gained precarious shelter crouching behind a clump of ilb trees.

Our badu cried out to them, but we could not exchange greetings, for their voices were torn away and hurled like sand into the distance down the valley.

We wondered whether we could reach Sif before the rain; the pace of the donkeys, driven before the wind, became almost equal to horses, but we lost the race, the rain beating down upon us three miles out of Sif, so that we straggled into shelter wearily, and in disorder, and we waited with longing for someone to kindle a fire.

.   .   .   .   .

The settlement of Sif clung to the hills on the western side of the valley, the headman's house being built at the top of the town in order to be able to raise its head a storey higher than any of its neighbours. The son of the headman came out to greet us; he was a young man of perhaps twenty-six, big, powerful, the muscles bulging on his arms, for he worked in the fields, baring as much of his body as possible to the air. The headman himself was absent, but

H

I had a strong suspicion that he was purposely avoiding us. The handsome young Arab, gesturing with hands and head at the same time to make certain we understood him, told us there was no accommodation for travellers in the town, but that he would have a room made ready for me in his own house, and another for Abdu. I asked him whether I could sleep out on a terrace, should the storm subside, explaining my preference for staying in the open by saying that I always had bad dreams if I slept within doors.

The storm was loud enough to make conversation difficult. We had to shout at one another to be heard above the thunder and the grumbling heavens; that thunderstorm in Sif was the most spectacular I have ever seen. One minute the sky appeared to have caught fire and the next to be disrupted and torn apart by uncontrollable convulsions of earthquake.

The passion of the heavens worked off after three hours, or little more, dissolving into distant mutterings and gloom over the lower stretches of the Wadi Du'an. The valley by this time was glistening with flood-water promising a rough passage for the camel caravan we had passed.

The Sheikh's son, Abdu, myself, and seven others, squatted around the fire late that evening, dipping our hands into a rather fearful bowl of unsavoury stew, the others tearing away with their teeth at the crinkly pancake bread. But the strain of the day had for once caused my stomach to set up a revolt, and I asked to be excused. The elders of the village were at first offended by what they took to be a display of bad manners, until Abdu, coming to my assistance, began to go through the motions of vomiting. I left the diners scraping away unsavoury scraps on a reed dish; afterwards I heard them spitting hard into the roadway.

Up in my room Abdu curled over and went to sleep, cat fashion, on a pile of richly-coloured rugs, while I watched lighting-up-time stellar in the sky, by lying full length and peering through the carved-wood windows on the floor level.

Usually the coming of storm leaves the air clear and cool in the Hadhramaut and this thunderous example had been no exception, but an Arab room as a rule is impervious to refreshment, being invariably constructed with the smallest convenient windows in order to shut out the sun; fresh air is banished beyond hope of recall and the Arab soon gets used to it. Stifled by the atmosphere in the room I took up a petrol lamp and found my way out on to the starlit terrace once more; bending over the parapet, I saw a balcony above, the street shuttered below, and houses that had become part of the night. I stole some rugs from Abdu's pile, and, rolling up on the terrace fell asleep, only to be awakened again and again by the pangs of hunger.

About midnight I could stand the sensation no longer. Breakfast was still six hours away. Fumbling for some matches and lighting a lamp, I started to go downstairs, remembering my stores and provisions were on the ground floor, near the main entrance. The light of the lantern seemed to dazzle the darkness and, though I had every right to help myself to my own food, I wondered whether an innocent construction would be put on my actions by anyone who happened to be awake. I decided, I remember, to put out the lantern and trust myself to the light of a weak moon, feeling my way down the mud-built stairs, narrow and uneven and dark as the inside of some monster. The staircases of Hadhramaut houses are puzzling to a stranger, particularly at night, since the landings are little bigger than the irregular-shaped stones which form the stairs, and can only be distinguished by the feel of adjacent bed-room doors or the sound of heavy breathing behind those doors.

I have never discovered any form of basement in these houses, so it was not difficult to know when the ground floor was reached; with arms outstretched in front of me like a sleep-walker, I traversed the main passage to find my packing cases of sardines, tomato soup and tinned fruits for which I had been hungering; even cold soup is delicious when hunger clamours. Since sound travels with difficulty in mud-walled buildings I smashed some of tins with a hammer when I could not find a tin-opener, the contents losing nothing by their knocked-about condition.

With renewed strength I groped my way upstairs again, wishing I had had the foresight to count the stairs coming down, for I had little idea which landing I had left. Blissfully unaware that I had climbed high enough, I stumbled past the door leading to my terrace and went on up to the floor above, approaching a door which I felt instinctively to be mine. Perhaps I should have been warned by this door being shut, but I thought little about it. Sliding back the wooden lock I pressed forward, emerging, as was the case on my own floor, on an archway leading to a terrace with the stars twinkling beyond.

I was in the middle of the room when the first hint came to me that something was wrong. I heard a movement, a queer, unexpected rustling sound that involuntarily stiffened my feet. Then I heard other things: a girlish giggle spluttered like a match in the darkness and the giggle woke others and those in turn changed to exclamations and screams. I don't know how many people there were in that room around me, but they knew very well without a word passing my lips, that a man had blundered into the harem at dead of night.

The rustling took shape into an unseen commotion, and women were all about me.

I turned and fled.

Instinct rather than reason pointed the path to safety, and within a few seconds I had flung myself on my couch of rugs on the terrace immediately below the harem. I strove my hardest to lose consciousness, feigning sleep, but the noises from the harem quarters pursued me like a bad conscience; hurrying footsteps passed my door, making their way upstairs, shouts filled the house, but it was a large one and they lost themselves in empty rooms. The next thing was the unshaven face of Abdu leaning over me, consternation plain to be read on it, even in the dim light.

"What is all this disturbance?" he asked, "people running hither and thither."

I pretended to have been aroused from a deep sleep, and sent Abdu away. But he was not to be banished and returned within a few minutes, this time squatting beside me.

"Up there," he jerked his shaven head towards the upper terrace and the babel of sounds, " . . . up there they say it was a Ferengi who disturbed them."

"Well, what are we going to do about it?" I said, pretending innocence no longer.

He shook his head solemnly from side to side and then up and down; his eyes, tightly closed seemed to epitomise the gloom of his thoughts.

"You have insulted the headman," he said, "the more so since you are a Nazrani. We must leave at dawn. No, we must leave at once."

"Is this hurry necessary?" I asked, "could no explanation or redress be offered to the headman?"

"Nothing would take away the insult," Abdu declared. "You have seen his women, if you stay, I go."

Go we did, after this unfortunate indiscretion. A hurried glass of tea, some dry dates, a few morsels of bread, and Abdu went off to summon the badu for an immediate departure.

The sun had not yet topped the mountains; the false dawn showed a half light of rather mournful promise, when we hurried off, watched at even this early hour by a few curious onlookers—members of the sheikh's household, early astir, who tried to delay us.

"You will wait for the sheikh's son?" they enquired, "he will wish to see you before you take your leave."

"We seek to miss the heat of the sun," I volunteered. "We felt unwell yesterday. I have left messages for your master and his son."

We departed at last, hurrying at a pace that made some of the Arabs rub sleepy eyes and wonder. It was clear our badu did not like the turn of events, since, so far as they could see, there was no purpose in this unreasonable haste. But we went forward into the morning as though driven by the storm of the evening before.

CHAPTER ELEVEN

THE CARAVAN HASTENS FROM SIF

OUR ESCORT WAS now reinforced by four soldiers, lithe beduins, more ornately dressed than any I had seen hitherto: they wore skirts of fanciful material, they were well armed, and they were acting under orders of the Ba Surrha to defend us against the attacks of possible roving bands.

Salim, their leader, was a jovial young man of twenty-eight—friendly, unmercenary, a finger missing from his left hand. From him I learnt that the headman of Sif was not trusted by the brother governors of Du'an, who kept ascaris at the town to keep an eye on him. El Meshed, the city of the Munsab, marked the limit of their patrol and they had hastened back to Sif to follow out orders from Du'an. An even taller, skinnier soldier than Salim solemnly marched in the rear of our party, about three hundred yards away. On a closer inspection he looked to have had little enough to eat before joining the Ba Surrha soldiery, for his chest was starvation thin, his ribs showing their pattern through his blue-brown skin; he was an old man, nearly sixty, but agile as a goat; white-grey hair around his seamed face, with a little rabbity-tail tuft of white beard low down upon his chin, gave him somehow a spectral appearance, and I was almost expecting him to disintegrate into a skeleton if worked too hard. The other ascaris remained so far ahead that they could seldom be seen and had to be taken for granted. Salim explained to me that they were scouting, and that if they discovered suspicious-looking badu they would come back and report. The whole business of keeping watch and ward seemed to be a delightfully haphazard affair, with two men beyond reach of recall in front, and an ancient who might have understudied Father Time bringing up the rear.

"What would happen supposing we were attacked?" I asked Salim.

"My soldiers would shoot," he replied proudly.

"But the others might be sheltering behind rocks where they could not be hit. And they might shoot better."

"Then we should trust in Allah that their guns were old ones—very old."

I gathered that if efficient modern rifles made their way into the ancient domain of Wadi Du'an, the Ba Surrha would soon hear about them, and steps would be taken to see that conservatism won the victory over commercialism.

All the morning we followed the trail along the wide reaches of the Wadi Hadhramaut in the direction of el Hedgerain. Abdu was telling me a story of a goat who climbed into a tree and stayed there in high contentment for two months. Coming to where the wadi broadened, for a period we led our donkeys forward upon a high-perched viaduct. The rain storm had not touched this district, so that we followed the viaduct, on account of its smoother surface rather than to obtain safety from flood water.

At the point where the Wadi Hadhramaut widened into magnificence, el Hedgerain reared up—a cliff town, perched upon cliffs, three hundred feet and more above ground level. Tall date-palms promised shelter to the weary traveller, while above them, grey ramparts climbed up and up to a domed blue sky, patched in cloud, akin to cannon puffs, that lingered in the air above a medieval fortress in this land where movement was reluctant. Other sections of the town perched similarly at the various points of the compass along the wadi, each about two miles distant from the others, so that el Hedgerain is shaped in the form of a star-fish, left high and dry by the receding waters from what may once have been a wide and beautiful river.

We made our way towards the main clump of buildings. Pillows of cloud floated motionless in the sleepy sky. The bold ramparts of the wadi walls imprisoned the town with their superior height. Nothing moved in the landscape except ourselves, and from the fortress no one came out to meet us.

We had arrived at the hottest time of day, so I was thankful to avoid ceremonious greetings, and to be able to fling myself down and rest in el Hedgerain, a town reduced to torpor by too much sunbathing. Seeing I was preparing a meal, a deputation of the townspeople came forward, jovial enough when they drank and clinked my tea in their glasses; but I had a strong impression of a hidden antagonism —the first mass hostility I had encountered in the Hadhramaut, and it made me wonder.

Abdu began to look scared, and bit at his fingers, and I had to tell him, in English, to pull himself together. Arabs despise no one more than a coward, and a brave face put on unpleasant events will go further than anything else to carry the day. I liked much better the attitude of the ascaris, who, true to their masters, treated el Hedgerain with lofty contempt, keeping, however, a firm hand on their rifles. Apart from a nod here, and a smile there, I kept myself aloof, unbending as little as possible, and refusing ungracious invitations.

"You will be staying the night?" they asked, "so that you will sleep in the palace of the governor."

I looked up at the towering building stretching into the sky like a castle in Spain, and tried to imagine how squalid the interior could be. I shook my head, saying that I preferred to sleep in the open, without the oppression of four walls.

The townsmen looked at each other with sidelong glances, giving the impression of people plotting to make me stay, but uncertain how to succeed. One of the deputation removed his outer robe, and sat on it, a hint that we might expect to be here a long time. They kept repeating insistently that I could have a terrace with a wonderful view; in this way I would avoid the wind and the wolves, not to mention the sandstorms that might be expected at this time of year.

But I firmly declined their suggestions, and said I was quite used to sleeping in the open, and preferred it.

"One is more free," I remarked with emphasis.

Out of the corner of my eye I could see a look of fear stealing over Abdu's face once again. The deputation shrugged their shoulders at my insistence, and presently they departed, fluttering their long gowns, making me think of a row of important church dignitaries in England.

Towards dusk it began to rain so hard that after all I had to obtain some shelter, and asked for the way to be shown to the governor's palace. The ascaris doubted the wisdom of this move, but they came along without fear, and they brought Abdu with them.

They declared that the slave governor would be offended with me because I had brought no letter of introduction from the Sultan, and though they hoped for the best, they did not know what might happen.

Freya Stark has described this slave governor in detail— a slim dark man with a pinched face and the eyes of an Indian.

He has built up a reputation for rudeness and he is treated rudely by the personages of el Hedgerain. His position is an extraordinary one, only possible for a ruler, tucked far away from the world in a Hadhramaut valley: he is a black man ruling brown, a slave holding sway over his masters, a chieftain whom the Sultan ignores, and whose existence is barely tolerated by the local inhabitants. Why he came, how he climbed to power, or why he stays— no one seemed to know.

But we were his guests—or was it prisoners? I liked to think the position might be dangerous, though I don't suppose it was anything of the kind. . . .

At this point there entered the scenes a Seyyid, loved by all, a man who had become poor since he had given away so many presents during his lifetime. Hearing of our treatment at the hands of the slave governor, who had wished at the best to entice us into his palace and then ignore us, this Seyyid had come to offer us the hospitality of his house. He was a gentle being, bent and sedate, and painfully concerned at my treatment by the official representatives of the Government, though he never so much as blamed the slave governor by one word. I accepted his food, but I refused the offer of staying in his house, saying that I was quite comfortable where I was, for it would have been even more discourteous for me to leave the slave governor's palace once I had got there, than for the slave governor not to receive me or give me food, which was actually the case.

I gave the old Seyyid a tin of Maasnah honey as a present before my departure. In return he showed me his passport, and I discovered that for many years he had traded in Java, as did quite a number of young Hadhrami men. When he had returned to his country he found his wealth unnecessary and so distributed it to those who needed it.

.   .   .   .   .

With the coming of a new day I found to my surprise that Sheik Sa'id, whom I had been fortunate enough to meet at Aden, had already sent his car to meet me, and was now waiting at the limit of its southward journey under the foot of the cliffs, seven miles down the wadi. The bearer of this news was the Munsab of el Meshed's son and heir, riding on his father's grey horse. He was an intelligent young man of perhaps five and twenty, well built, sitting his horse like a soldier, and impatient over the treatment I had received from the representative of the Kaiti Government.

Abdu, his composure recovered now that friends were so close, took a high-handed view of things, begging me to punish the governor in some way and put him in his place.

I said I would send for the slave governor and see what happened.

After several attempts to round him up, my ascaris finally brought him to me while I was having lunch. He sat down with an ill grace, while I tried in vain to shame him by recounting the help and kindnesses I had received on every stage of my journey. But he seemed unmoved, except for his face, which darkened as though with evil thoughts. I found him difficult in many ways, yet there was a bearing about him that suggested that if only he could change his attitude and inhibitions, whatever they were, he could easily become a leader of the people. He had power and strength within him and I could see how it was he had become governor; here was a beardless, black Saul needing badly the harpings of a young David to charm him to better moods. After fruitless conversation, I tested him in another way. I began dictating aloud to Abdu a dispatch, first to the Sultan's minister in Mukalla, then to the Aden authorities, and finally to the Ba Surrha, in each of which I mentioned the situation at el Hedgerain, though I never intended the letters to be sent. The governor shifted about on his couch of cushions uncomfortably; he clenched strong hands across one knee, but he made no move towards reconciliation or friendliness; he neither smiled not stormed, but sulked blackly, and then in the end, while I was dictating the last of the letters, he went out alone.

I must say I rather admired him for keeping to himself, without a word of explanation or recrimination, although his conduct stood out by contrast with other Arabian chieftains whom I had met. Everyone else seemed delighted at what had happened; the old Seyyid beamed his pleasure, even the local people present were glad, and Abdu felt I had cleared the air, perhaps, for the next passer-by. Turning to the young Prince of el Meshed I announced my readiness to start out for the car.

A Town in Wadi Du'an

Sultan Ali bin Saleh of Shibam—Abdu in Background

I was given the grey horse to ride, and as I looked back for the last time at the frowning citadel of el Hedgerain, medieval and menacing, I experienced a fellow feeling for Don Quixote setting out on his rickety steed. An hour and a half later I slid from the back of my mount and approached an American tourer of some remote period, happy in the protection of a large black hood. A cutting in the wadi bed formed by the rush of a recent rain storm, had barred the car's further progress.

Out of the interior there now stepped with all the ease and lethargy of your true Eastern gentleman, the representative of the Sultan of the inner Hadhramaut, a portly individual in a beautifully tailored white coat, with eighteen carat gold buttons, and sporting a blue fountain pen in a breast pocket. Except for the pen, which looked like a peep of blue sky appearing amid ample white clouds, everything about his attire was snow white, even his turban being colourless and of fine silk. Mixing solemnity and uncertainty together, this gorgeous figure greeted me officially on behalf of the Sultan, reading out an address in a voice no one could hear. The chauffeur, on the other hand, had little time to spare for formalities: the little man in khaki-coloured jacket and black Javanese fur fez smiled coldly at me, shook hands quickly, muttered a welcome, and at once jumped back into the car. We all took our places, the heir of el Meshed, Abdu, and myself sharing the back seat, with my more valuable papers and instruments sandwiched between our feet.

The caravan, my badu and the ascaris, were ordered to take on the donkeys to el Meshed, and find their way there before midnight. Salim, the ascari leader, anxious no doubt for a lift, decided he ought to be my personal body-guard and attendant: he crouched on the running-board, his rifle between his knees, one hand on the wind-screen, the other on the door to steady himself. On the other side of the car a mighty negro, the bodyguard of the Sultan, was doing exactly the same thing; the two made faces at

each other across the back of the car. The negro waved
Salim aside with the dignity of a king, but the ascari
ignored the gesture with the unconcern of an emperor,
and nobody else interfered. We were now rushing at
twenty miles an hour over the sandy floor of the wadi,
such speed appearing incredible and exhilarating. The
rains had come and gone—had they not gone the car could
never have left Shibam—the rills hollowing clefts in the
soft floor of the wadi, isolating hard rocks and ridges which
we bumped over as though playing a game of leapfrog.
After the speed of donkey-back travel, I felt like a person
who is having his first ride, thrilled by new sensations of
speed, rejoicing in the momentum of effortless movement,
but a little anxious about the result of it all.

In three hours we had bumped a three days' journey along
the wadi, and as the sun slipped behind the distant cliffs of
sandstone and granite, we saw our first glimpse of el Meshed,
the open town of pilgrimage.

The ruins of Ghebun tempted us to linger for a little near
the site of what must once have been one of the proud
incense cities of the ancient trade route. We walked for
half a mile, since even the Sultan's car could not climb
up the sides of boulders; the black soldier, rifle slung across
his back, deeply interested himself in assisting me to search
the debris for any signs of rubies or emeralds. Ghebun,
until quite recently, used to attract archeologists, their
rewards being often liberal, and including such things as
inscribed stones of value. But to-day Ghebun is a bald
ruin, its surface cleared of every possible precious thing and
all I found were fragments of pottery, sadly broken, but of
beautiful colour. Colonel Lake, I heard, had visited the
site: another of those fascinating mortuary mounds of
Southern Arabia awaiting the verdict of expert excavators.

.   .   .   .   .

The young Prince of el Meshed had gone ahead while I
was treasure hunting, so that he was able to welcome me

when I arrived at the town, its three mushroom-shaped
mosques ghostly and glimmering in the twilight.

The rooms of the palace were larger than most of the
others I had visited, the walls and pillars richly but crudely
coloured with a raw vermilion as though someone had been
trying to paint the town. The lack of whitewash in the
rooms looked at first sight peculiar, and in the dusk, lit
by an occasional pressure lamp, the walls but dimly visible,
one could imagine oneself living inside some monster, just
as Jonah had done.

I slept on a terrace, despite a shower-bath of rain in the
night, and the new morning, arising golden-footed, brought
with it my donkey caravan and the ascaris sent to escort
me by the Ba Surrha of Du'an. This was the end of their
journey, so that I handed them over letters saying how
faithfully and well they had served me. Their smiles did
not disappear, even though, to Abdu's evident horror, I
had forgotten about the highly-important question of back-
sheesh. But I wished to test their integrity, and it was
only after they had turned the corner that I called them
back and made them a present. They seized my hand until
I thought they would pull it off.

For the next lap of the journey, camels took the place of
donkeys; they seemed to bring bad luck to my baggage, for
it was to have many adventures before I saw it again.
Before leaving el Meshed in the car the young prince
presented me with a most unexpected gift—the first English
book to find its way to that tiny inland town. The book
was a thriller by Oppenheim, and I left behind in its place
to start the English library of those parts, a delightful book
by Eiluned Lewis, dealing with children, called *Dew on
the Grass*.

We arrived at Katan a little before noon, swirling through
the streets on the strength of a loud-voiced electric horn;
the metal work was hot enough to burn the envoy's hand
when he touched it by mistake. Our meal at Katan consisted of more varieties of biscuits than I had dreamed

existed in the world; to these were added a dozen tins of different fruits, dates, fondants, sugary sweets and glasses of tea with or without milk. We sat up to a table, but the Sultan's representative and Abdu ate the sticky mess of tinned fruit with their fingers, and I was the only one to use a spoon; when the meal was over the Arabs began to look really uncomfortable so that I suggested we would be more at ease sitting on the floor. Everyone was grateful, the change of position making conversation flow freely once again. In two hours' time another meal was announced—lunch, consisting of chicken soup, rice and bread. But I could do no more, and left the others to settle down to their siesta: soon afterwards we set out in the car to Shibam, where ruled the Sultan Ali bin Saleh.

About tea-time we saw cliffs jutting into the middle of the wadi, cliffs that either hid or resolved themselves into an astonishing sky-scraping city, a thousand palm trees marking the spot where five wadis met. I rubbed my eyes in wonderment at this vision of New York in Arabia, and before I had lost my astonishment, I found myself outside a most beautiful villa, one of the finest I have seen, belonging to Sheikhs Sa'id and Hussein, and used as a guest house for Aden officials on their annual visit.

CHAPTER TWELVE

WONDER CITY OF THE EAST

MOST OF THE village-towns of the wadis have been built either adjacent to, or a little way up the enclosing walls of rock, and thus blend into their background, whereas Shibam upthrusts in the middle of the Wadi Hadhramant, exciting the eye to wonder.

Five hundred houses, each of them a skyscraper, standing on a slight eminence, cluster together to form one massive block of buildings. Shibam in the near distance is an unearthly citadel that might have been built by Aladdin out of mirage and magic ; architecturally it belongs to the incredible imagination of the Arabian Nights, to the prodigality of an Haroun al Raschid, rather than to the sober daylight of the twentieth century. Shibam, a table-land of houses, is the Arab's answer to the age-old oppression of the Djol and its mountainous wilderness.

Five hundred skyscrapers, standing back to back, their heads whitewashed as though going grey with age, leaning inwards to increase their basic strength, combine at first glance into one tremendous family mansion containing about fifteen thousand inhabitants. In fact, the best description of the capital of the Inner Hadhramaut might be to call it the world's mightiest block of flats. If Grosvenor House, made somehow of mud and with loopholes for windows, stretched the length of Park Lane, it would give some idea of how Shibam arrests the eye in the distance: a walled city without walls, the houses themselves supplying the fortification, their sides sheer, their tiny windows spaced at uniform distances; not a city in the accepted sense of the word, for it is the great houses that form the wall, four square and impregnable to the hostility of rifle fire. The windows are high set and any tribe setting out to storm the city would find no foothold whereby to make an ascent, while defenders would have the advantage of being able to pour things down upon the heads of the attackers in the manner of the Middle Ages.

The authors have not made a circuit of the walled cities of the world, nor even a small percentage of their number, but it would seem certain that Shibam stands by itself, without rival or counterpart—a mediæval fortress that is modern, a city of mud and marvel constructed to defend itself by means of its own houses.

Castles, perhaps, approach closest to the architectural idea on which Shibam must have been first raised; yet no castle has ever been able to house many thousands of people in comparative comfort. The walls of towns can be scaled after the expenditure of sufficient perseverance, but the shells of skyscrapers, whether constructed of concrete or mud, are beyond the reach of ladders, and the forcing of a single window would never permit of an armed entry in sufficient force for purposes of attack; to undermine and blow a breach through one house, would simply mean another and another would have to be served in the same manner, once the narrow, connecting street had been barricaded.

The idea of a self-protecting skyscraper fortress, belongs to genius. Shibam is a tall story—until you have seen it. Until gunpowder burst upon the scenes of history, the Arab conception of Shibam must lay claim to a foremost place among settled communities and their defences against wilderness and those who wander in it. Few of the fortified towns of Europe old and scarred in warfare, can have been either so formidable, or so up-standing.

The entrance to this unduplicated city is by way of a sloping cobbled roadway which leads to massive wooden doors, only opened during the hours of daylight. Though the archway—the only chink in the town's mud armour, is an open courtyard of quadrangular shape, generally filled by rows of camels gravely chewing time away. On the right is Government House and the petrol garage belonging to the R.A.F.; the town stretches forward and to the left.

It has caught up into itself much of the vitality of the trading territory that once supplied the opulence and riches to Araby, and local tradition insists that the skyscraping town was built by the old inhabitants of Shabwa, moving here on account of changing conditions.

Shibam to-day has an unequalled trading position in the inner Hadhramaut, for it is situated at the meeting place of two main, and three subsidiary wadis, a focal point of trade routes. It stands on a slight eminence, but in those early Bible days when the wadi was a wide river, it could not have existed, and Shabwa must have been the wonder city of the neighbourhood.

Nowadays the whole vitality of the region has become concentrated in Shibam, city of caravans, heart and brain of a large area of wilderness, stimulating and supplying the arteries of trading enterprise. Tortuous streets, turbaned merchants, a Sultan, and hosts of traders contribute to the leisurely activities of a city in which most traffickers work on a commission basis. There must be a great deal of this sort of business going on at this mart and clearing centre for commerce.

Shibam mixes town and village life, the main shops specialising over local goods, while those in the side streets are general stores in existence for people living in outlying districts at the tops of skyscrapers. Chickens run about everywhere, contesting odoriferous alleyways with the pedestrian, but children are mostly banished outside the town to spend their days playing sand castles in the wadi bed—an excellent idea, especially suitable to a town that stretches upwards rather than sideways.

The inhabitants belong to the increasingly popular army of those who wear shirts instead of coats; they have white shirts with turned-up collars, these shirts being tucked into a kind of skirt, falling below the knees. Tall, white figures, focusing and attracting the sunshine in contrast to the darker, dirtier houses, throng sandy-coloured streets with the stiff walk of horsemen, their faces tufted by beard and moustache, daggers in their belts.

Freya Stark makes mention of the beautiful blue cloaks worn by the women, as though the sky, cut out into pieces to suit the eternal plaint of Romeo, were walking upon earth. But I saw no signs of these; the nearest I could find were faded blue one-piece garments, bleached a lighter colour than is customary, by washing and sweat.

But if colour had fled from the streets, odours of all kinds added to the excitement of populous alleyways. An Eastern town has to be visited in the hot weather to gain any idea of the scope and possibility of smells let loose to outrage the nose: sickly sweet smells that close the eyes, sour smells, odours of decaying onions, unmentionable smells, and butting through the others with a malignant strength the nauseating tang of goat. A sight that is unpleasant can be avoided by shutting the eyes or looking in another direction, but man has not learnt how to close his nostrils at need. The Arabs have compromised over an ever-present problem by developing a kind of immunity derived from long association. No doubt nature has stepped in to assist them, and their noses no longer register what has become commonplace; possibly this has something to do with the fact that Arabs as a rule are not good judges of character, since it is a dictum of mystics that the sense of smell plays a leading, if unconscious part, in the detection of personality.

The sanitary arrangements of Shibam have not emerged from usages of the Middle Ages: drainage falling from the houses, runs in open sewers down the centre of the side streets; only in the main streets or the square of the camels, could I breathe through my nose in any comfort. If the town had not been built on a sloping incline, prolonged drought might make it unsupportable even for Arabs.

Abdu and I went on several shopping expeditions. Ali, the barber, harangued Ali, the confectioner, and in the surrounding booths the sound of bargaining filled the air. The second Ali had a face the texture of leather with two eyes hot and angry like coals in a brazier. When I went to his rival across the street, he ran across and attacked him, connecting all his female ancestors with she-dogs and swine; he pulled out a knife to settle the matter of who had the best goods for sale, slashing furiously at the rival confectioner. I had never met shopkeepers before who battled for customers with knives and were more jealous of privileges than children. For a moment I thought Ali of the glowing eyes would plunge his knife into me, shedding blood to cover the insult of my having left him for another. Abdu had to explain that I was a Nazrani, and that it was our custom to buy, if possible, from two people at once. I pointed out, too, that the flies were quite impartial about their appreciation of the goods of both merchants.

Walking in these streets where progress has not yet entered, I noticed none of the things familiar in cities of the West: no telephone or telegraph wires overhead, no motor cars, no post office, no police stations or police force—just permanent habitations for the needs of men and women, walking and talking during the daytime, resting during the heat of midday, and sleeping in the cooler sanctuary of night.

Apart from Palestine, there are only a few telephone lines in existence in Arabia, for the beduins cut them if they leave the shelter of the towns. King Ibn Saud, himself, the modern Haroun al Raschid, introduced the telephone between Jiddah and Mecca, only after difficulty, and no monarch is more open-minded or easily accessible, and none knows better the possibilities and limitations of his people. Strong opposition to the telephone gathered strength among the sheikhs and religious leaders, clinging to the past with a kind of faithfulness. They regarded an invention which could talk through the walls of houses and cross distances faster than the wind, as clearly the work of the Devil. Ibn Saud listened to them patiently and then sent them away, saying he would think the matter over.

A few days later he summoned the opposition to Mecca, having had time to make a plan of campaign. "You may be right," he told them, "when you assert the telephone is the work of the Evil One. But I wish to make certain whether this is so. What would you say, suppose the words the telephone speaks to you are the words of the Quran, the holy book?"

"In that case we could say nothing against it," the deputation replied.

Ibn Saud, who had ordered a call to be put through at a certain time, now requested the leader to take up the telephone and listen. The old man's face registered horror, unbelief, and then agreeable surprise. The voice belonged to Sheikh Abdullah of Jiddah, but the words were the words of the holy book.

Mecca was satisfied, and the telephone made its official entry into Saudi-Arabia. . . .

.   .   .   .   .

After walking about in Shibam I was always glad to get back to the outlying villa, where I lodged in peace and comfort.

Sheikh Sa'id was the first to come and shake me by the hand, for this was his home he placed at the disposal of guests, and Sheikh Sa'id's hospitality is well known among people in Aden. A man not tall, plump without being fat, one or two gold teeth, slanting eyelids over dark brown eyes and eloquent hands welcoming me in the doorway— this was my first view of my host. Sultan 'Ali bin Saleh would be coming at four o'clock, he said, perhaps we could then have tea all of us together; in the meantime I was to consider myself the master of this house and my slightest wish would be obeyed by his servants who would be about the grounds. Having satisfied himself that I was content and desirous of resting after my motor journey, he smilingly bowed his leave and I was left with Abdu.

We did a little unpacking and then I suggested that the Arab should take some rest. We passed into our separate quarters until the warning came that the Sultan was about to drive up in his touring car.

Sultan 'Ali, very tall, very thin, Arab gentleman, with eyes not unlike a camel's, which are large, soft, gentle and sincere—these eyes were expressive of His Highness' entire personality and intentions—had the most eloquent hands I ever saw amongst educated Arabs.

He sat with me on a brocaded sofa. We talked through an interpreter after exchanging a few greetings in his native tongue. Abdu, who was a little put out because he had been woken from what was no doubt a very restful sleep, stood awkwardly first on one foot and then the other, while he gazed steadfastly at the carpet. Sheikh Sa'id had settled himself upon one of the plush chairs that folded up and beamed at me in unmistakable friendliness.

We talked of many things; of my stay in Mukalla; the journey across the mountains to Du'an; the trouble I had had in el Hedgerain; of his own palace where I had eaten that day some tinned fruit and biscuits, and lastly of my longing to be the first Christian to reach Shabwa. Very little was said about previous travellers at this first meeting, but it was quite obvious to me that they had left impressions on the people which would benefit their successors.

We drank tea in pseudo-European fashion, the Sultan politely drinking the first glass of milky liquid and then refusing because he had done his duty. Tea held no soothing charms for him, but he had a weakness for Mocha coffee.

He shook hands in his gentle manner and went out quietly, leaving behind him a sense of peace and well-being. He would come and see me again, he said, and in the meantime he would not rest until he had obtained the services of guides to take me to Shabwa. He could not be certain whether his calls would meet with success, but he would make every effort to try and organise a caravan for me which would attempt for the first time to take a European to the holy city.

When we met again, soon after a strong and resonant voice, floating out to the villa from the summit of the town, had called faithful Moslems to prayer, I questioned Sultan 'Ali bin Saleh about the Queen of Sheba.

"Do thoughts of this Queen of the South ever enter your mind?" I asked, "or the minds of those in authority?"

"She interests all the learned in these parts," he answered in his musical, slow-worded voice; "she is not forgotten here."

"Are there any records or writings in your towns that have outlined the past?"

The Sultan shook his head. "You must go to the Yemen, to the capital, Sana. I have heard the Imam possesses libraries and many manuscripts. His letters he sprinkles with red sand to show his descent from the very far past."

Sultan 'Ali always wore a red fez on top of his thick black hair: he was Indian to look at more than Arab. He brought his little son to see me, a boy with the melting eyes of the gazelle, who looked at me without shyness or awkwardness and then seated himself on a cushion, folding feet and hands.

"I should favour books about this territory," the Sultan said. "If you are thinking of writing a book and will see that it is translated into the language of my country, I will guarantee 1,500 copies are sold among my people, and of these I will take two myself."

Abdu, who had been making his own inquiries, informed me privately that the ruler of Shibam had rebelled against the old Sultan (now dead) of Mukalla and had been deposed and banished. The present Sultan had pardoned him, and he had come back to live in peace and quietness, dividing his days between his town house and his palace at Katan.

I gathered he had only two wives, one to welcome him at each of his homes.

Women married to the richer citizens have an easy though endlessly enervating existence, since slaves carry out the entire household duties, leaving them free to look after the children and spend long leisure-hours at tea-parties. Gramophones play fatiguing repetitions of music, without beginning or end, and after midday, during the heat of the siesta, tom-toms, often beaten by women, thump away insistently at monotony. Discords breaking out from time to time from behind the little, lofted apertures of harem apartments, could be put down by the charitably-minded to the gramophones, and by the cynics to a superfluity of wives. Abdu told me that some Moslem scribe whose name he had forgotten, had once written down a description of women, as follows: "From ten to twenty, a repose to the eye; from twenty to thirty, fair and full of flesh; from thirty to forty a mother of boys and girls; from forty to fifty an old woman of deceit; fifty to sixty slay her with a knife."

Somewhere or other, either read or told, I got possession of a ridiculous story explaining how it was that flat roofs had come to bless the Arab. I think it was one of those travellers' tales that move about and test the sense of humour. . . .

In the days before flat roofs had descended upon the houses of the faithful, a certain town existed famed for the beauty and charm of its women, so much so that it called down upon itself the unwelcome attentions of the chieftain of that country. From time to time his followers would arrive and shout: "Wives! Wives! for the King," leading away the fairest and rarest.

The terrified town dared not resist its destiny, for there were no woods or thickets close at hand in which to hide the women; nor were there cellars to the houses. But one day a holy man, a wanderer, recommended the men to flatten all their roofs, and send their wives to live at the top of the houses, out of sight. When the chieftain's followers arrived the next month and cried: "Wives! Wives! for the King," the townspeople replied that none were left, and this in truth, on closer inspection of the houses, appeared to be the case.

After the supply had failed a second time, the chieftain, whom Allah had afflicted with a slight deafness, saddled his best camel and came to investigate for himself. When they saw him entering their town in person, the women started weeping and wailing, filling the air with their cries: so much so that the chieftain said to his men: "This place is clearly bewitched. These unnatural roofs are haunted with cats many in number, and it is no wonder to me that the girls of the town grow plain, since it is little sleep they can get." Whereupon he went his way, and that city was left in peace.

Which, of course, does its best to explain why roofs are flat and cats are so unpopular with Eastern harems.

.　　.　　.　　.　　.

Sultan 'Ali bin Saleh was a highly educated man, ready to talk on many subjects, and we had one or two interesting discussions on Arabic life and letters. At the villa belonging to Sheikh Said I had many restful hours of reading, helpful in gaining a little fuller insight into the inner workings of the life of Islam.

One began better to understand how it is that Moslems are the rigid conservative element among the population of the earth's surface, setting their face against sudden changes, trusting to revelation rather than revolution, believing in unhurried hereditary process instead of progress. Islam has become a disorganised political society founded on an undeviating body of religious doctrine.

The devout Moslem is taught to cultivate an attitude of confidence in the divine government of the world and a ready acceptance of whatever fate is apportioned to him. He must accept with patience and resignation the course of human events, as being the result of the operation of divine wisdom, even though the workings of it may be to him obscure. This lesson is constantly reiterated in the works of the later theologians, particularly in the writings of the mystics, and is set forth in the Quran in the well-known story of Moses, when he asked permission of one of the servants of God (whose name is not mentioned in the sacred text) to accompany him on his travels. Common opinion has identified this unknown personage with the mysterious being, Khidr, who is reverenced throughout the whole Mohammedan world as a deliverer in all occasions of peril. In the Quran he is only described as one to whom God vouchsafed mercy, and to whom had been communicated knowledge.

He is represented as being at first unwilling to allow Moses to travel with him on the ground that Moses would be guilty of impatience with him, as he could not be expected to show patience in matters that he did not fully understand. However, they set out together and embarked upon a ship, in which the servant of God proceeded to stave a hole. Moses protested, saying: "Hast thou staved it in so as to drown the crew? a strange thing, indeed, it is that thou hast done!" The other answered: "Did I not tell thee that thou wouldst not be able to have patience with me?" They went on farther until they came upon a boy whom the mysterious stranger put to death. Moses exclaimed in horror: "Hast thou slain one who is free from the guilt of blood? Surely thou hast done an evil thing!" Again comes the protest: "Did I not tell thee that thou wouldst not have patience with me?" Moses begs to be excused, and agrees that if he again asks such questions, he shall no longer be allowed to remain in his company. They come next to a city, the inhabitants of which refuse their request for food and will not receive them as guests. The travellers find a wall, which is on the point of falling, and the companion of Moses proceeds to put it into a state of good repair; whereupon Moses again criticises his action, saying: "If you had wished you might surely have received a reward for this." The servant of God can bear this interference no longer, but exclaims: "Now it is time for thee and me to part; but I will first tell thee the meaning of those matters in regard to which thou couldst not have patience with me. The ship belonged to some poor men who toiled upon the sea, and I wished to damage it, because coming after them was a king who took every sound ship by force. As to the boy, his parents were true believers, and we feared lest he should cause them distress through his perversity and unbelief when he grew up, wherefore we desired that God should give them in his place a more virtuous and affectionate child. As to the wall, beneath it was hidden a treasure belonging to two orphans, the children of a righteous man, and I built it up so that the treasure should remain concealed until the orphans were fully grown, and not of my own will did I do this, but by God's direction. Such is the interpretation of that which thou couldst not endure with patience."

Another story of Moses—told by one of the Mohammedan poets, Jalad ud-Din Rumi—tells of how he came across a shepherd who was praying aloud to God in language which seemed to the Prophet to be shameful and blasphemous. He was saying: "Oh, God, where art Thou, that I may become Thy servant and sew Thy shoes and wash Thy head and bring milk to Thee, at bedtime, Oh, Thou, to whom all my little goats be a sacrifice." Moses rebukes the shepherd and bids him shut his mouth and stop such raving and such blasphemy. The shepherd rends his garments and, sighing, goes into the desert filled with shame and repentance. Then God rebukes the Prophet, saying: "Thou hast parted My servant from Me. I look not at the tongue and the speech, but at the inward spirit and feeling. I gaze into the heart of the worshipper and regard not the mode of expression."

The rapid success of the victorious armies of the first two generations of the Faithful under Omar and Othman, and the command in the Quran to wage war against the unbelievers, bequeathed to later generations the aggressive ambition of making Islam a dominant power in the world.

So long as there was unity of government in the Moslem community, whether the capital was Medina, Damascus, or Baghdad, such an ambition could be cherished; but Spain made itself independent of the central power as early as 756, and the break up of the rest of the empire proceeded rapidly after the death of the Caliph Haroun in 809; and the last Caliph of Baghdad, Musta'sim, in 1258 perished miserably at the hands of Tamerlane in the city where his ancestors had ruled for nearly five centuries. By this date the political theory of Islam as elaborated by the Moslem legists and theologians had caused the institution of the Caliphate to be regarded as the core of the organization of the community, for the Caliph was held to be the source of all authority, and all officers of the law ultimately derived their appointment from him. So the fiction was maintained that the Caliph was the head of the whole Moslem community throughout the world, even after the holder of this ancient office had ceased to be able to exercise any effective authority. The Caliphate recovered a small measure of its former glory when the title was taken over by the Ottoman Sultan, and in the days of the decline of Turkish power, Sultan Abdul Hamid II (1876-1909) endeavoured to add to his prestige by a revival of the old theory of the Caliphate. He claimed that all Moslems scattered through the world, whatever might be the Government to which they owed political obedience, should recognise him as their leader. But it was Abdul Hamid who ultimately brought about the ruin of the institution whose past glories he had endeavoured to restore, for his despotic rule created in the minds of his subjects feelings of antagonism and distrust towards a political theory which could be made the instrument of such tyranny, and the abolition of the Caliphate by the Turkish Republic, in 1924, was the logical consequence of the deposition of Abdul Hamid in 1909.

The sacred law of Islam claims to be all-embracing, and concerns itself with every department of the life of the believer —religious, political, social, domestic, and private. It even lays down rules for the proper use of toothpicks, and prescribes limits for the activity of the painter and the musician.

If the sacred law was inoperative, it was said the fault lay in the evil state of the times, and all would be set right after the coming of the Mahdi (the rightly guided one), who would be sent to subject the world to Islam.

Every devout Moslem considers himself to be a member of an almost ideal society, which is bound ultimately to overcome hostile forces and make the "law of God" prevail. The memory of the glories of the Caliphate in the past is a stimulus to such a hope; meanwhile, all believers are brethren, and this brotherhood of faith succeeds in breaking down barriers of race and country, and finds outward expression in some characteristic form of dress or appearance—such as the clipping of the front of the moustache, the avoidance of certain articles of diet, and in regulations regarding the methods of eating, greeting and praying.

.　　.　　.　　.　　.

The ingrained dignity and good taste of the true followers of the Prophet are largely the outcome of their religious code.

[1]The right hand is reserved for all the honourable tasks, including shaking hands, the left hand for less nice duties of living. Yawning is considered ill-bred, though sneezing is praised. The nose must be blown where no one hears the noise or can take offence; spitting, if necessary, must be done towards the left, since a guardian spirit is thought to walk on an Arab's right. No pious Moslem either hurries or loiters unduly since both are regarded as unbecoming to the dignity of manhood. It is written in the thirty-first sura of the Quran:

"Distort not thy face at men; nor walk loftily on the earth; for God loveth no arrogant vainglorious one. . . . But let thy pace be middling; and lower thy voice; for the least pleasing of voices is surely the voice of asses."

Much of the end of the Prophet's life was spent in answer-

---

[1] *The Desert Gateway* by S. H. Leeder.

ing the questions of his followers, eager to know the right
and the wrong ways of behaviour.

One of the first questions an Arab believes he will be
asked on his day of judgment, is in what manner he accumulated wealth on earth and if so, how he spent it. Usury is
firmly forbidden to Moslems; Arabs who make a fortune
and die rich men are still looked upon by the pious with
contempt or indifference. Mohammed himself died in debt,
some of his belongings being held in pawn by a Jew. He
formulated the guiding principle that the poor will attain
the middle heavens hundreds of years before the rich.

In this rather splendid code laid down as principles of
deportment or conduct, one item has conspicuously caught
the opposition of critics—I refer to the Moslem treatment of
women. Why should they be condemned to veil and harem,
and on what grounds could polygamy be authorised, if
not encouraged?

The Prophet, in company with other Arabs of his day,
definitely held the view that woman was a step lower than
man in the ladder of creation; in an original epigram he
announced that woman was a bent rib and could not be
straightened. Having abolished the system of exposing
girl babies, he possibly considered that the surplus women
would be best provided for under the harem system; certain
it is that he meant no unkindness or belittlement, for no
man owed more than he to Khadijeh, the widow, his first
wife, and to young Ayesha, and a strong case can be argued
in favour of the veil both as a protection against dust and
also a respected symbol of protection against insult or outrage
by men. It is interesting to remember that the Prophet
guaranteed the rights of martyrdom to all Moslem women who
died in childbirth, a status accorded them by no other race
or creed.

. . . . .

The tribesmen of the Hadhramaut and its inner capital
are not, however, particularly religious, and long-established
custom moves them more than zealous faith. Shibam does

little in the way of public prayer in a region that was civilised before the days of religion.

Looking through the gateway to the town, it is the market square which takes the morning rather than mosque or minaret; as many as a hundred and fifty camels sometimes stand awaiting the call of the caravan. They journey into the wilderness or thread their way down the cultivated wadis, connecting links of the landscape, occasionally carrying on their backs a little of the aromatic gums which once made the people of the valleys and their incense trade pre-eminent throughout Araby. The old, fragrant highway has gone, but the camels still tread the unforgotten paths of the past.

The only modern transport touch is provided by three motor cars which are secretly run on British petrol. The R.A.F. garage and petrol store have been broken open and pay toll towards the upkeep of the twentieth century amid these withered places.

Shibam is surrounded by the green of palm groves and the refreshment of many wells, and in this respect resembles Damascus, emerald of the northern deserts. The Prophet, viewing Damascus and its orchards from afar refused to enter lest he should no longer desire to seek Paradise; he never came south, but the history of the Hadramaut belongs to the period of Moses and not Mohammed.

In the market square play-acting takes place each day in the cool of the evening. The actors raise their hands, declaim, gather into groups and sometimes pirouette in a kind of climax. I sat on the balcony of Government House by the side of the Sultan, but I could not fix my attention on the actors for he was busy talking.

There is a regular rhythm of life and vitality animating most Moslem towns, and Shibam is no exception. The people follow the daily time table of the sun, the forceful energy of their lives and everything they do, and they knew nothing of the insistent chime of the clock.

Starting at sunrise, gaining full momentum by seven o'clock, the human current of the town's activities dies low during the siesta hours of midday, flares up again into a peak of sudden recrudescence at sunset, and finally fades into the quietness of approaching night that brings darkness, not lighting-up time.

At sunset when the caravans assemble, and later when the sky is cloaked with dusk, Shibam, like Baghdad or Damascus, becomes for a little while a city of mystery and even enchantment. After the hot and dusty day, everything awakens into a sudden vitality. There are shadowy streets and sinister doorways and strange street cries; the smell of wood-smoke becomes an incense linking the mind back to the fragrance of past things.

"Y'Allah! Hurry up!" cries the vendor of beds before closing down his shop. "This way for the big family man."

"W'allah!" comes back the reply. "Keep them for thy many mothers-in-law."

Shops are soon shuttered and deserted, and a thousand hubble-bubbles awake into activity, winking at each other when their owners apply the blazing charcoal with a pair of tongs. Somewhere, someone strikes up a discord or two on a little stringed instrument which is called an oud. At first it sounds as if the Sultan is kicking his slaves downstairs, but when the time is accompanied by a mournful, monotonous chant, joined to those queer, inhuman quarter tones that only Arabs can produce, the music begins to become timeless: it is present, past and future, the dirge of the desert, the song of the naked skies, the ancestral call of the caravan.

Elsewhere at street corners you can see animated crowds indulging in another art, the art of talking, which on the East is allied to story telling. Wisdom has alighted in three things says the proverb—the brain of the Frank, the hand of the Chinese, and the tongue of the Arab.

But presently the moon appears and the haunting songs cease; the tales are all told for that night. As if acting on some hidden signal, everyone starts to disperse and return home to bed.

Only the watchman is left standing motionless beneath the stars of the Arabian night, waiting for to-morrow.

K

CHAPTER THIRTEEN

I TALK TO PHILBY AND LEAVE FOR THE GOAL OF MY AMBITION

SITTING IN THE evening on the terrace of Sheikh Sa'ids comfortable country house, I could watch sunset changing Shibam from a grey frown into a fairy-tale. In appearance the house resembled a small villa, the walls tapering towards the blue of the sky, the corners rounded and the whole effect extremely original; it was the first time that I had seen a house of this design built in mud, but going on to Sewun some time afterwards, I noticed the type was growing in popularity among houses ordered by the richer merchants.

The villa was a refreshing landmark in that bleached and scorched valley, because the outer walls were not only patterned at the tops and along their faces but were relieved by the use of pastel-shaded colours. To enter, one walked up a slope and through a strongly built doorway let into the defence wall, crossed the courtyard and mounted perhaps half a score of inviting steps. The kitchen was immediately on the right, primitive as Arab kitchens go, but the charcoal fire was sufficient for ordinary needs of cooking. The stairs were at the left, and straight ahead was a narrow T-shaped room, large and airy, used as a dining-room; on the south side of this room, at each corner, were two grilled doors, leading out into an open, high-walled court-yard containing an unexpected swimming bath twelve feet square and four feet six inches in depth. The water, raised from a well inside the grounds, replenished this bath every third day, and here I spent many delightful hours splashing in the luxury of super-abundant water during the ten days I spent in the August swelter of Shibam.

Upstairs, a large room, anxious to please, provided a display of luxurious and characteristic furniture: plush coverings of green and purple stared at red ornaments and two long ornate mirrors standing in the middle of each of the narrow walls; the longer sides of the room were broken up by windows, shuttered and glassless, but playing their part in the decorative contest. A terrace shaped into a wing was a far far better place than anything I had known since Mukalla, for it took the eye to peaceful gardens of feathery green, motionless in the heat, but musical with the voices of tiny waterways dribbling from the mouths of wells.

On the 16th August Sheikh Sa'id came rushing to me full of the news that St. John Philby, King Ibn Saud's adviser, was on his way by car and had already left Katan for Shibam. The Englishman had come from Mecca— the first time a car had accomplished the journey. In his excitable way Sheikh Sa'id shouted out that Philby had come down in four or five days with two cars, twenty camels and fifteen or twenty men; but in actual fact, as I learnt afterwards, the long journey from Mecca had taken three months and the personnel and number of camels varied considerably from the first erratic report.

Rumours began to fly about that the Englishman had been to Shabwa and had explored the secret city, but rumours gather weight quickly in countries lacking telephones or telegraph, and in due course St. John Philby, who put up at Government House, Shibam, came round to see me.

He was first sent out to Arabia in 1917 by the British Government because he had the distinction of being an Arabic scholar. Since then he has adopted the Moslem faith, made a pilgrimage to Mecca and been chosen as confidential adviser by the King of Saudi Arabia. He smokes an English pipe, but otherwise prefers Arab customs and

eats his food as close to the ground as possible. He is an
ardent motorist, and had travelled by motor car (excepting
of course the Channel crossing) from London to this far
away, sunburnt city of Shibam.

We had once met at a lecture given by the Royal Central
Asian Society in London. I had then written to him, telling
him of my projected trip to Southern Arabia in search of
the lost cities of the Queen of Sheba, and asking him for
advice.

This was three years ago, and somehow or other as he
walked on to the terrace, I had an absurd feeling that our
Arabian meeting was going to be stiff and crippling—a
sort of "Dr. Livingstone-I-presume" encounter.

A bearded, stately-moving figure, robed in the long
flowing robes of the north, sauntered on to the terrace.
He might have been an Arab sheikh as he came forward in
his slow, deliberate way and shook hands. If he had first
commended me to the safe keeping of Allah I should not
have been surprised.

Fortunately Philby is one of the most natural men living.
We were soon talking and smoking away in friendly freedom
with Shibam looking on loftily from the distance.

Yes, he had been to Shabwa—had only just left it, in
fact. He had spent five days there, his every public movement carefully watched by the inhabitants except when at
midday it had become too hot for them to stay outside.

He was disappointed by what he saw. Too much of the
town lay hidden beneath sand mounds or crumbled into the
disruption of a prehistoric past. Little could be seen or
found there, and the buried site left to decay too long, had
become a case for trained excavators rather than explorers.

He found no ruins of the sixty temples recorded by Pliny
in the days when the town was the flourishing capital of the
Himyarites. Writing later in *The Times*, he doubted whether
sixty temples could ever have been contained within the
compass of its walls. The discrepancy between ancient
tradition and record and present day remains, he thought

could possibly be reconciled by the notion that many of the buildings of the old town may have been built out of rock salt, unlasting and crumbling into nothing.

I told him that in the far inland Sahara, near Lake Chad, I had once come upon a village built entirely from the rock salt of local mines. One had also to consider the upward-growing tendencies of Hadhramaut cities, their girth limited and slimmed by the river wadis. Arabia of the south had thought of skyscrapers long before America had been separated from China on official maps, and a good-sized town can be contained in a small compass if the population does not object to perching in the air.

Philby agreed with Craufurd that Mareb may have been the more important city and the centre of the Sheba dominion. He came to think afterwards that the old name of Sabota was not so much Shabwa alone, as the whole district lying between the junction of the Jauf and Mareb areas and the Hadhramaut. Such a district may well have had sixty temples to Astarte and the rival gods.

In any case, he told me, I could do little good now by getting to Shabwa. He had been there before me and found the city too far gone in age for ordinary exploring purposes.

Before he left, I took him to see the swimming pool, asking him if a dip would refresh him after his long journeys. He declined: "I never immerse myself in water," he said: "it brings on the fever."

He wished to continue his motor drive down Arabia as far as the Red Sea, but I pointed out to him that he could never conquer the difficulties of the Djol in his car, and would have to reckon on a few days walking or donkey-back travel. When he understood this, he decided, since his journey had already occupied three months, that the extra lap was not worth while, and that he would return to Jiddah, visiting some of the wadi towns on the way. In his opinion I had no chance at all of attaining success, although I heard later, when I met him again most surprisingly and

unexpectedly, that he took my part in opposition to the
Sheikhs of Shibam who were offering odds against me.

.   .   .   .   .

After he had gone, reaction set in, and for the first time in
Arabia I felt thoroughly depressed and dispirited. I could
not concentrate my attention on anything; nothing seemed
of the same importance now that the secret city had at last
been unveiled—and by someone else. For months I had
been aiming my energies at a certain dimly-defined but
none the less substantial goal; now, though I had nearly
arrived, the end of the journey seemed no longer to exist.

Shibam could offer nothing in the way of diversion or
palliative for my mood, so I had to be content with watching
a spectacular sunset that for once looked lonely and tinged
with regrets. I wondered whether this lingering farewell of
something bright and beautiful was not the saddest thing I'd
seen. First gold was thrown into the sky, and then blood.
The prodigal display of dying colour riveted my attention in
spite of myself. As I watched, the fortress houses of Shibam
darkening into shadow, looked like an immense caravan
halted for the night—once purposeful like myself, but now
static and stranded in immobility. Colour and certainty
had gone from the day and the soft bloom of dusk was an
enemy stealing up unawares.

That night I went to bed without doing much in the way
of sleeping. . . .

Robert Louis Stevenson has written with the inner
conviction of genius that it is better to travel than arrive.
His statement remains unchallenged by the man who
spends deliberate time changing a place that is close for
one that is distant—but one small exception exists. This
exception to the rule of arrival loomed large in my mind
that night. It may be better to travel than arrive, but it is
best of all to reach the unknown FIRST, before it has been
circumscribed or materialised by others, and while it still
remains a secret.

It is a curious fact how the desire to be first, to autograph, as it were, a small piece of the future, possesses men's minds and prompts their movement; and I was no exception, lying on a rug on the terrace at Shibam. The difference between first and second has caused men to risk death in the clouds above the Atlantic, to jump to their death from aeroplanes, to spend long hours seeking for success. The difference between first, second and third has controlled the destinies of racing since man first contended against man, and those unplaced are forgotten in the struggle for supremacy.

My hope had been to carry through Craufurd's work by finding Sheba's cities of Mareb and Shabwa and putting them on the map again. Romance lay buried there, and Bible history incense-laden from the past. Mareb had been forbidden to me and now Shabwa had been reached.

I regret to say that night I wrote in my diary: Sick as hell. Shabwa looks almost shabby at the moment. Even in Arabia, mass effort and organisation seems to pay better than single-handed adventure. The days of the soloist are numbered.

.   .   .   .   .

The clear sunshine of the morning, falling across my face, helped to dissipate the cloud burdening my mind. I thought to myself that I was honestly glad it was Philby who had reached Shabwa first, rather than the representative of some other nation. At any rate the prize had been won for British exploration, and by the successor to Lawrence, an Englishman who had made Arabia his home.

I was glad to see him when he turned up again two days later after having made a trip up the wadi. The same dignified, commanding figure addressed me in the same unhurried voice.

"I've discovered I was not the first to get to Shabwa," he said. "I've just heard."

"Heard? Heard what?"

"I was beaten by several months."

"I looked at him in astonishment.

"Hans Helfritz, the German. His third attempt. He has written about it. The book is just out."

"Well, I'm damned!" I exclaimed, and that was all I could say for several moments of real emotion.

Hans Helfritz is a well-known if hitherto unlucky traveller, a young journalist, who is also, I believe, a doctor of music. Helfritz has made three journeys in the Hadhramaut; at the first attempt he had aimed to reach Shabwa, but his beduin guides, fearful for their lives, carefully avoided the district, and he made for Mareb, hoping for a sensational scoop. But the Yemen town was jealously guarded, and at Harib he was captured and flung into prison at the orders of the Imam; the Aden authorities ultimately procured his release from Sana, and he was sent down to the sea coast, under guard, to embark on a boat. On his third journey, Helfritz reached Sewun about the same time that Freya Stark lay dangerously ill at Shibam, the city of her dreams thus put beyond her reach, but surrendering to the perseverance and enthusiasm of the German who became the first European to succeed.

.   .   .   .   .

Setting out from Shibam as I had done, he planned forcing an entry at night; he discerned a ruined watch tower, sudden low walls looming, and a small mosque, decorated with rams' horns at the four corners. Helfritz and his guide sheltered in the little outlying rest house, hiding themselves until dawn, when ten friendly bedu, leading some camel transport, joined them. More and more bedu thronged the guest house until the German was discovered. In the confusion he managed to slip out and investigate the ruins, armed with a camera and a loaded revolver. He found the town to have been built between three low hills, which are now mortuary mounds of half-hidden granite blocks; on top of sand and stone, the bedu had built themselves primitive huts out of limestone, supported by tablets and stones of the past. Sheltering behind a ruined tower on the second hill, he was attacked by screaming women who rushed at him, throwing stones, the children with them behaving by contrast in a friendly manner; hurrying on, he reached the third hill, discovering, lying in a hollow between the hills, a princely building which he took to be the old palace of the kings. But by this time the women had called up their men folk, and bullets had began to take the place of stones, so that he hastened to his guide and the trotting camels, pursued by the farewell of rifles. . . .

Philby, coming down from the north, drove out of a sandstorm on the evening of August 8th, groping his way in thick darkness that suddenly rolled away in blanket fashion to reveal the presence of Shabwa—the dome commented on by Helfritz, and the mud-coloured village on its ridge. The arrival of two motor cars out of the storm drew out the entire male population, about 300 men, while the women screamed and crowded on the adjacent roof tops.

The inhabitants, awed into welcome by this sudden visitation, and show of force, formed a long line, each tribesman in turn touching Philby's hand and kissing the air when passing. Four goats were produced for dinner.

Careful measurements and inspection enabled him to reconstruct obliterated remembrance of a walled city, beautifully situated on an island ridge of rocky hills in the midmost part of Wadi Arma. The old Sabota had three gates, but the main entrance faced the north, or cool side. Remains and tumbled debris he mentally reconstructed into an important main street, guard houses and a few dominating houses; the high note of the town was evidently a large building standing confronting the skyline, three quarters of the way up the slope; this structure (round which a paved path still runs for some fifty feet), thought by Helfritz to be a palace, Philby put down as being a temple to Astarte.

Poverty, superstition and fear rule Shabwa to-day. Some Arabs speaking to me later on the subject cast down their eyes and looked uncomfortable. They seemed a little ashamed of this blot on their cleaner desert horizon, of this black sheep of the family bringing disgrace and disrepute to neighbours.

Many an Arab of these parts kills or robs his enemies at frequent intervals; sometimes he turns highwayman and swoops on caravans, but he would not dream of breaking the ordinary laws of hospitality or shooting the stranger within his gates.

Shabwa crouches in the sands—sphinx-like, even to those who live next to her. She can be compared to an old wisdom tooth, left too long unexcavated and unprobed and now poisoning her surroundings.

Salt has been the connecting link with Sabaean, Himyaritic and Arab kingdoms; two salt caravans leave the district each year, one going to Shibam and the other to the Du'an valley. Besides eating salt the Arabs rub their babies in salt to promote hardihood and save washing. Many beduin women believe it is unlucky to wash their children for the first year.

The second salt caravan, proceeds to the Du'an valley direct, across the mountains, following a switchback pathway that trades the best terms it can with desolation. This is the way by which the brothers Ba Surrha wished me to approach. The journey of the traders would probably occupy four days, since commercial caravans in Arabia usually go hard at their task, taking their leisure when the journey has been completed and not in the half-way stages; to get from Du'an to Shabwa by this little known route would have probably taken me a week. I can say little more about this line of approach, without having tried it, but the journey would be across the grain of local geography, up and down mountain chains and not along them.

I sat out in the terrace when Philby had gone and had a good think. It seemed strange to me how this forgotten

Turning the Corner in Shibam

The Road to Shabwa—Salim and Saleh Plot

city should have held out for several thousand years, veiled and withdrawn from the eye of Western curiosity and research, to be discovered in a moment of expansiveness twice within a year. Such occurrences in the narratives of exploration are none the less dramatic because they have happened before. I had left England, thinking I alone had set a course for Shabwa, and now here I was being told the threshold had been crossed already twice. Helfritz and Philby had both got there.

.   .   .   .   .

The day after Philby's motor car had disappeared in a cloud of dust, Sultan Ali ben Saleh arrived to discuss my plans for the future, expanding into an affectionate interest in me. He brought with him his little son, smiling gravely to himself, and a cooling Arab drink, highly scented, reminding me of hair wash sold in expensive and exclusive London shops.

"You will still travel to Shabwa?" he demanded in his soothing voice that somehow made me feel luck might be awaiting me. "I have two guides who will start with you immediately."

I answered that I was not going to give up all my plans, now that I was so close. If he had been successful in finding me two guides, I would try to reach the incense capital myself.

"A man who loves a woman is not satisfied if it is someone else who has seen her," the Sultan exclaimed, and his little son nodded his head vigorously, as much as to say that he was a true man of the world and knew all about it.

Sultan Ali had come to the conclusion that my best chance of success would be to continue as I had started, dressed in Arab clothes, since Europeans were not wanted and Christians were not tolerated in the lawless district I was about to enter. But with a wisdom some would call cunning, he pointed out that the position had changed since Mr. Philby (called in the North, Sheikh Abdullah and in the Hadhramaut, Sheikh Abdullah Ibn Saud) had passed through the country, visiting Shabwa, and that this change might be turned to my advantage. He suggested it would be safest for me to dress in the clothes of an Arab from the North, then the inhabitants might think I belonged to the party they had already seen; in this way my lapses from prevailing custom and conduct would not excite curiosity into danger. I would be well advised to feign dumbness, but I might be expected to be able either to read or write.

I went downstairs to see how far Abdu had progressed with my simple evening meal. I found my servant near the bottom of the steps squatting on his heels in front of a huge bowl of rice and meat; he did not look up when I hailed him but went on eating, stuffing his mouth with his fingers. I called to him in rather a surprised tone, "Are you not going to get me a meal?" He did not answer, but went on gobbling, until I told him there was no reason for him to eat my meal in addition to his own; then he came out with a torrent of abuse in Arabic, little of which I could understand. He spoke also in his broken English and told me that he was going to leave my employment on the morrow because I expected him to work without opportunity for pleasures or profits for himself. He picked up a kettle and took threatening aim at me, but he was so trembling with rage that he could not release it. His past ill-humours and moodiness had now boiled up to a climax.

I left him alone, putting down his actions to fear of Shabwa and the gnawing emptiness left behind by absence of Carte—his favourite drug. All night and most of next day he sulked like a schoolboy and would no nothing for me.

I began to think my traveller's luck had completely deserted me, I knew I would probably not reach Shabwa without Abdu.

He began to make busy preparations for return to the coast, and I suffered the discomfort of feeling I was too young and beardless to hold the obedience of a tough old Arab sailor who had turned mutinous, but, unaccountably, when the two guides turned up and I departed with them into No Man's land, Abdu Noman marched by my side.

I passed no remark or comment on the situation, nor did he. We walked along occupied in a wide but sympathetic contemplation of the back view of three camels plodding in front of us up the sandy floor of the Wadi Hadhramaut.

CHAPTER FOURTEEN

DESERTION

I HAD NOT shaved since the day I left Aden; if my beard was a little straggly, I at least had a firm moustache, and with my skin blackened in the sun, I felt that if I did not wash for the next few days I might pass as a typical Nejdi Arab. The wearing of flowing robes gives a man a curious enveloping dignity, and a long head-cloth, combined with cool, empty sleeves and a voluminous white garment, turned me into a son of the desert.

I was not impressed with my two beduins, for they were wild and unkempt, dirty and short of temper; but the Sultan had arranged with a rich merchant that a deposit should be laid against my safe return, thirty silver dollars being handed over as a form of security.

Abdu was uncomfortable. He had not the guide's avarice—they had already demanded the whole of the money before departure—he had not my ambition to realise, nor had he faith in his own powers of combating the journey that lay ahead. But he came. Our stores had been prepared the evening before, consisting mainly of meat taken from a shark's hump, and dried, a dish much to the liking of local beduin. We had loaded the camels as lightly as possible so as to make good speed, and we hurried for three hours before making camp at Dal-Rak, a place where a bush called Meswak grows, useful for allaying thirst if the twigs are chewed.

We slipped quietly out of Shibam without being noticed by the inhabitants; I was no longer an Ingleezi or Nazrani, but another one of those strangely garbed Arabs to be seen any day in the streets of Mecca.

I told Abdu that since I was a sheikh, I had better have a name. He suggested Yussein, but I told him that if I chose a name continually used in the North, it might help to strengthen my disguise, and so I became Sheikh Feisal and I suggested he could be a Seyyid from his own country, the Yemen. This pleased Abdu well enough, and he confided our new status to Salim and Saleh, the guides.

As we rode along Abdu recounted how across the wadi on the northern cliffs, high above the valley, was a building which had a gate and a lock of gold: one of the many fabulous stories of places and people that are to be found scattered up and down the southern extremity of the Arabian peninsular. The building was haunted, said Abdu, by the Djinns. It was only three hours' journey away, but anyone who touched that lock of precious metal fell dead as if electrocuted. I asked Abdu if he believed the story. He was not sure, he said, since people sometimes exaggerated, but stranger things had happened in Arabia. Apparently Colonel Boscowen heard of it, and set out to visit the building, yet for some reason he never got there and it may be that his guides, fearful of what might result, led him away from the spot. He brought back with him from the near neighbourhood, a large stone, worn with ancient writing, probably Himyaritic, that is now in the garden of the guest house.

With the exception of prowling, half-savage dogs which attempted to steal our food supplies, night was peaceful, and dawn staining the sky found our camels lumbering down the centre of the wadi towards the west. We were travelling fast. Henan was our first objective, and I fully expected that Philby, with his cars and his escort, would have passed us before we reached that border town.

By midday we had come to Katan, and there the guides purchased food for our camels, while we put our backs against a palm trunk, deriving what shelter we could from the blazing sun. We rested, and after lunch would have dozed but were awakened by the sound of a motor. This, I thought, must be Philby, but instead it was the Sultan, who had stayed the previous night in Shibam and had then come on to Katan to see me off.

During the afternoon, a car raced by in a smudge of dust, a miniature sandstorm blown from the racing wheels. Half an hour later when the cloud of its passing had mingled with the sand dunes, came a merry singing of beduins, strange to those parts, and perhaps twenty gaily bedecked camels of the fast racing breed, trotted past, their movements keeping time with the lilt of the singing. This was the debonair, devil-may-care retinue—Saudi soldiers—that had come down as an escort for Sheikh Abdullah Ibn Saud. They did not see us, and my beduin's remarks were wasted upon hot air.

We followed the soldiers, and in a little more than half an hour we entered a fresh region, a delight to the eye: sand dunes, piled not too high, clothed by clustering bushes, some brighter than emeralds in colour and others the tone of uniforms in the Royal Air Force, both a pleasant relief to the powder sand stretching for five miles between the wadi cliffs.

Once, no doubt, the valley had been nourished by a river, but in this twentieth century the sea was sand and the ships were camels. The sky was gentler than I had seen before and I saw my first Arabian butterfly.

We found our way through these dunes, and as the day stooped westward we walked upon more level ground into the splash of sunset; we drank at a whitewashed fountain and passed beyond the old fortress of Henan, perched high on a little mountain like St. Michael's in Cornwall. Our advent created a stir, for we were the second party of travellers to come that day. As we swung round the house of the head man of the village, I saw to my astonishment, the Ford car which, earlier in the afternoon, had gone past so hurriedly, and which announced the presence of Philby.

Our caravan unloaded, we stretched out our blankets at a distance of about three hundred yards from the mosque.

Henan is not a walled city, but here the headman, who is rich, pays money to the beduin leaders of those parts. By this means, though they may be of different tribes and normally fractious, he retains many of them as a personal bodyguard. Henan remains safe and apart, untroubled by the distresses that go on around, having bought its freedom and paid for peace.

After sitting down to a plate of baked beans, Philby came over to me. He had eaten, he said, but would be glad if I would visit him when I had finished my meal, for he was giving a radio entertainment to the villagers and the head-man that evening. He was surprised we had made such good progress. He himself was expecting the arrival of his second car, but until it came, he would remain where he was.

.   .   .   .   .

At about eight o'clock, I sauntered through the dark, moonless night in the direction of the paraffin flares grouped near the Ford, around which crouched a slowly-increasing circle of the people of Henan. When I first appeared, many of the people pointed and shouted "Nazrani" at me, but the arrival of Philby, known to them as a Moslem, brought a hush.

I sat with him on a rich carpet. We rested our backs against the running board of the Ford. In front and partly surrounding me, lay the radio set, the batteries, and several cases and tins in which Philby collected and kept his specimens of flora and fauna and the insect life of the desert. Moths and insects of many kinds were attracted to the glare of the pressure lamps, and whenever he saw one that was unusual or new to him, he popped it into his little lethal bottle. This form of collecting went on while conversation was in progress. Faintly, as he turned the knobs of the radio, came the sound of weird eastern music. This was the broadcast from Cairo we were waiting

L

to hear, followed by the news from Cairo, broadcast in three languages—Jewish, Arabic and English. The broadcast was not a success, for atmospherics and the noise of distant storms obliterated most of the sound. I was told that the desert, which one might expect to be so good for receiving, is among the worst places for wireless.

But if the beduins and tribesmen and the richer people of Henan were disappointed, Philby himself was satisfied. He was able to check his chronometers with the time signal.

The insistent noise of the broadcast sounded like artillery being fired. My host waved his arms, said a word or two and dispersed the gathering. I noticed how much difficulty he found in conversing with the Hadhrami.

In the south, they use for the most part, the language of signs; words are left out and their place is taken by the movement of the hands or arms. Philby, practising his "handies," sometimes confused the beduins, and made them laugh. Then he would exclaim fiercely: "Why do you not learn to talk properly? How can you expect me to understand, when you wave your arms about in a meaningless manner?"

Good humour, often contributes to Philby's success in Arabia. He keeps his men together by a happy knack of creating a laugh at critical moments, and also by being strong enough to turn a discordant member of his retinue out of camp, having first made him appear small.

With his usual thoroughness, he had come down through the northern tribal territories on his journey to Shabwa, picking up here and there the head man or sheikh of the tribe; thus ensuring the safety of his party and the goodwill of the owners of the territory through which he passed. He believed safety lay in numbers. He had collected about twelve tribal sheikhs.

When I was on the point of leaving, Philby's beduins brought him a large wooden bowl, three-quarters full of warm camel's milk. Every night, he said, he drank a quart of camel's milk, and suggested that when the occasion offered, I should do the same, for it was both pleasant and health-bringing, varying not greatly from thick cow's milk.

The night was cool after a roasting day and it was interesting to me to hear Philby remark that he had not found his summer journey hot until he reached Shabwa and Shibam.

. . . . .

I had breakfast at dawn, and with my two guides and the three lightly-loaded camels, started out at a good pace towards the west, travelling along the right side of the Wadi Hadhramaut, that wide highway of camels for thousands of years. So straight was the valley that at the hour of sunset, for many days, the sun could be seen vanishing before our eyes into the sea of sand.

I began asking the two guides, Salim and Saleh, about details of Shabwa. They seemed suspicious of my questions, but I learnt three tribes—the Sa'da, Azken and Radha —shared Shabwa between them without a common leader, and this partly accounted for their lawlessness.

I began to feel certain as we progressed that Shabwa would be more south-west than on the maps. At midday we passed the village of Rubaiyz and a little beyond we made camp near some wells, where we encountered goats attended by beduin women, offering me a chance of testing the success of my disguise.

I told Abdu that I should talk very little and that he must be prepared for anything that I might do. I walked out into the desert and took some photographs, and after a quarter of an hour, I came back to a tent which had been pitched with the aid of two weary bushes. Already the beduin women, fear overcome by curiosity, were squatting in the shade of the canvas, and when food was prepared they came close enough to touch my clothes, while their unwashed fingers jabbed at a pile of rice and fish. They eyed me from behind their veils, in a manner not so much suspicious as curious, and I think they were sure in their minds that I must be one of their kind.

It has been said, and truly said, that Arab women, particularly those who live the wild life of the nomad, are quick to discern deception in a traveller. They are peculiarly antagonistic to anyone not of their own race and religion, and here was I, a considerable distance from civilization, sharing my food with these half wild and savage women of the wilderness. I was more alarmed of them than any men, and I talked but little since I was a sheikh and obeying the rules of hospitality as set down by the Prophet Mohammed. Nothing more was expected of me, though they may have wondered if they saw me make a note in my diary and take a photograph with my Ensign Midget—a camera which I could conveniently conceal in the palm of my hand. They clustered round me like vultures with their flapping black clothes and queer head wrappings, and presently when I tired of their curiosity, I reclined full length on my back and went off to sleep.

At two o'clock we broke camp and prepared to move.

It became evident as we progressed towards Shabwa that both Salim and Saleh were independent, reckless types caring only for their own stomachs, and I became convinced that if I had not left part of their wages behind in Shibam as security, they might easily have gone off and left me to find my own way.

Neither Abdu nor I could do anything with them. Whenever I asked the name of a mountain or similar landmark, they demanded money in return. I told them plainly that if they insisted on collecting cash in this way, nothing would be left to give them by the time the end of the journey was reached, since they would have already had it.

This threat worked for a time, though when seeking information about certain wells, I soon discovered that they had either lied to me or had been ignorant and refused to acknowledge the fact. Since we kept to the north side of the valley, I asked my guides, who had just killed a snake in the trail, whether or not Shabwa lay straight ahead, for the maps had shown it farther to the south. They insisted that not only was Shabwa straight ahead, but that it would be found on the side of the wadi we were skirting—the same side.

Since I could get so little topography out of my guides and I wished to check up exact positions, I began to rely more and more on my camera for visual records; to halt the caravan, whenever a picture had to be taken, would have been tiring for the camels and annoying to the guides, so I walked for the greater part of our day's trekking, being free in this way to stop whenever I wished.

.   .   .   .   .

About three in the afternoon, I stayed behind to take photographs of a ridge of hills we had just crossed. I had with me a dozen dates in a handkerchief; but no money. I took several pictures before starting to catch up my caravan. Rather to my astonishment not a living thing was in sight, but I did not worry, merely hurrying my pace to follow the marks of our three camels. They were plain to be seen; two guides had been riding, and Abdu's footprints in the sand showed that he was wearing sandals, leaving imprints clearly distinguishable from those of the camels' pads.

I plodded on for about half an hour, expecting any minute to see in the distance amongst the shrubs and sand dunes, the bobbing forms of the hooked-necked camels and their riders. All at once I noticed that Abdu's sandalled footprints were no longer to be seen; I thought he must have mounted the third camel, but I could not quite understand what had been happening or why I had not caught up with the caravan by this time.

A little later I began to be worried, since the tracks of the camels were behaving oddly. They zigzagged, broke up, and seemed to show my guides were hurrying away from me, as if determined, that I should not catch up with them or risk their lives in Shabwa. Had they taken what they considered to be the best opportunity to give me the slip? A stretch of hard gravel made detection difficult, but I scanned the ground, hoping to see a turned-up stone here and there. My caravan, I had now become convinced, was trying to desert me.

I had to face the facts. Without guides I was lost, but since the friendly cliffs were close at hand and since I had been told the way to Shabwa lay straight ahead, I went forward in that direction. Perhaps my entry into the ruined capital would be alone.

I scanned the cross trail of a passing caravan of at least twenty camels, leaving it behind as I kept the westward direction. My mind was busy. I thought of Shabwa and its importance as a salt-bearing district; I thought of Philby waiting for his second motor car at Henan; I thought also with envy of Salim's prowess in reading the trail. Many times he had pointed out the track of a camel or a number of camels, in a matter-of-fact way saying how this was so-and-so's camel and tired, or this was the camel that so-and-so sold and which had been resting in a certain valley but a short time ago; or on another occasion he would say, here is a party that has passed—they are bad men and have been hurrying; later he would come across pursuing trails, reading the day's old story of the chase by marks in the sand. In explanation of his ability he said he looked at the pressure of the pads in the sand and gauged the distance of the animal's stride, these telling him everything he needed.

After looking about for some time, I came across a fairly well worn trail close under the cliffs of the wadi. It seemed to be a little way off from the route we had been following since leaving Henan, but it was a trail, and since it led westward towards Shabwa, I felt it would be wise to keep to it. By the time the sun had sunk into the bed of sand on the horizon, I began to be thirsty and when darkness fell I could no longer be certain of the trail. But the looming cliffs on my right held me steady upon a westward course.

Here and there the cliff face broke away into a miniature valley that I would be tempted to follow, and only the soft brilliance of Venus, a lantern in the heavens, kept me going forward. I think at that time I still hoped I might be wrong about the desertion of my caravan and that they might be practising some trick or that they would now come back and look for me.

With the coming of night, it occurred to me that they would light a fire and its blaze would attract my attention; but after an hour, when nothing had happened, doubts came into my head, and I cast anxious glances up and down the valley, and on every side, peering into the darkness.

I was alone in an abandoned part of No Man's Land, and knew I was up against it. My only provisions were a few dates, and the desert wells of Arabia even when existent, are often impossible to find without local knowledge of their whereabouts. Wanderings are only pleasant when within reach of water.

.   .   .   .   .

I remember sitting down to consider the situation; then I went on again. Once I mounted a rock and called out with all the power of my lungs, but only my own voice was thrown back at me in mockery. The night wore on and I divided the hours between halting and moving on again, since I was too anxious to sit still for more than a few minutes. At every new point of vantage I scanned the wadi bed by the light of the stars. I struck a few precious matches.

Recalling the actions of Salim and Saleh the previous day, I came to the conclusion that my guides had not left me out of anger or carelessness, but because a plan of desertion had been formed in advance. I remembered how the two of them had gesticulated on several occasions, employing a violence that Abdu had thought suspicious.

Why Abdu himself should have gone off with the guides, leaving me in the lurch, I could not fathom, and his defection after our weeks together was upsetting.

Wandering on and on I found myself getting faint and dizzy. I knew I must rest and try to sleep, but it seemed to me to be the final confession of weakness.

I was beginning to feel desperate—when I heard distant voices which I could not credit. Was I dreaming?

. . . I thought it might be a trick of nerves, but when the voices became louder I knew I was no longer outcast.

Camels and their riders loomed up suddenly.

We exchanged the Moslem greeting.

"Salaam aleikum."

"Aleikum es-salaam."

The newcomers eyed me with curiosity, for my garb was unusual and I was alone. I asked if they had seen my party, and I described Abdu, who I said, was a Seyyid from the Yemen escorting my beduins and three camels. They must have thought it strange that an Arab should mislay his caravan, and I told them the first story that came into my head, by way of explanation, adding that my name was Sheikh Feisal. This announcement was greeted with shouts of hilarious laughter, and one after another, they repeated "Feisal, Feisal" in my ear. "Why are you not armed?" they asked, and hoping for the best I answered that my rifle and other weapons were on my camels, which I was expecting to meet.

I asked for some water, and they allowed me to drink from the goat skins slung across the camels. They were impatient to move on, and when I asked whether Shabwa lay straight ahead, the leader laughed and was joined by the others. "Shabwa," he said, "is on the other side of the valley. You have been going in the wrong direction."

"I am recently from Henan."

"This is where we are going," the old tribesman replied.

"Then may I join you until my beduins are found?"

This was agreed upon, and we set out at a fast pace.

They told me that they had come from Radet es-Sa'ar, a village so poor that it carried on no intercourse with its distant neighbours, but on this one day in the year, the old man, his sons, and their women folk, were taking firewood on the backs of their camels to sell in Henan.

I had certainly been fortunate, for this trail was rarely used and the wells, scattered at great distances, are hard to find.

I was surprised at the pace the caravan moved. Occasionally the young men would take a rest, squatting uncomfortably on the bundles of wood, perched high on the backs of the camels, but the women folk and the old leader never paused, and maintained their pace until we came near to a well where a blazing camp fire filled me with momentary hope that my guides had been found. The crackling flames lighted up the faces of two women, one old, her skin like a parchment, the other young and obviously a slave. They were grinding coffee beans, and soon they would be making bread, and we should have a meal, for this was to be a camp; a short one, to give us a brief rest before dawn.

The moon had climbed high into the sky clothing everything in a spectral, almost phosphorescent light.

All sorts of questions were put to me.

I shared out my twelve dates, which were accepted with delight. Other women arrived, tousled shepherdesses, who, having corralled their goats, squatted with us and bandied words one with another; the younger members of this family party were lusty people, full of the fun of life and fitting badly with my mood of melancholy. We chewed chunks of doughy, unleavened bread, which we dipped into a wooden bowl of milk; and I lay down upon a dirty rug with an empty feeling in the region of my stomach. I put my head on my elbow and took a last look at the sky. For once it was not comforting. But in a minute or two I had fallen into an exhausted sleep, to be awakened an hour later by the noise and bustle of hurrying men, loading sacks of firewood on the backs of the camels who were bellowing hideously into the night.

Gradually I was able to master the situation in my mind, and it occurred to me there was an outside chance that if I camped with the shepherdesses and their goats I might in some way regain contact with my beduin guides; on second thoughts, however, I came to the conclusion that the possibility of meeting them anywhere near this unknown spot was so slender as to be not worth considering. No other party of Arabs might be passing for a long time. I risked being marooned in the wilderness, unable to go anywhere or do anything for weeks.

After anxious thought, I decided in favour of going, not staying, and this was what the old chief had expected.

We took our farewells of the women still crouching round the dying embers of the fire and our caravan picked its way eastwards toward the dawn and Henan.

.   .   .   .   .

My pressing need was still for water. Not until now had I realised, personally, the part water plays in the life and history of the Hadhramaut. The story of Arabia is built not upon the sand, but upon water—the dayspring of the desert and the controlling force of plenty.

I thought of Mareb with its great dam that had kept out the dead fingers of the desert for historic centuries. I thought of the wells which had lined the single track of commerce up which the Sabaean riches had once passed. I thought of Sheba and the artificial thirst that Solomon had once created in her by the use of incense and spices.

Whether Shabwa possessed a great dam modelled on the one at Mareb is not clear, though it is certain as daylight that an extensive irrigation scheme existed for the wadi, the last remnants of which are used by the bedu to-day. There were cunning sluices and controlled watercourses linking up with the great river that is now no more than billows of sand blown by the wind.

Shabwa in its young, green days, must have stood up
—an island of prosperity amid abundance, linking the trade
of the Wadi Hadhramaut with that of Mareb, Main and
Nejran, leading back to dim remembrance of Old Testament
times, when Sheba was Queen, ruling the prosperity of
Southern Arabia in fact and in legend.

CHAPTER FIFTEEN

SHEBA AND SOLOMON

IT IS POSSIBLE that Sheba and her Queen, the Queen of the South and of the morning, the most romantic feminine figure of the East, may never emerge fully from the sands of antiquity. The footprints are there by which to track the story of Sheba and Saaba, the perfume of the past still lingers over the incense countries, but the twentieth century may never succeed to its own satisfaction in tracing these imprints home or digging out exact facts and stone figures to satisfy Record offices and museums.

Yemen and Hadhramaut are not Egypt; no crowds will gather round the newly-discovered sarcophagi of royal resting places or gape in wonder at funeral regalia, though the Queen of the South and her Sabaean contemporaries are thousands of years younger than the Pharaohs, laid to rest in the Valley of the Kings; no photographs exist or are ever likely to exist of Balkis, Queen of Sheba. Yet a fully equipped expedition exploring carefully the Sheba district from Mareb to Shibam, from the mountains where flourished the tree of frankincense, to the wadis where passed the caravans, and mighty skyscrapers arose out of sun-baked mud, may well come upon last links that will settle the Sheba riddle beyond doubt. Inscriptions and remains are there for the finding. Arnaud, Halévy, Glaser and one or two others have made a beginning, but much might still be learnt of the Kingdom of Saaba, gold-producing, incense-growing, purveyor of African ivory—one of the most fascinating and least known of the Bible empires. The country is not easy, the tribesmen are secretive, hostile, and sometimes fanatical, the sand has covered up the past: for these reasons, and because early inscriptions are undated, unquestioned and exact detection of Sheba and her times may fade into the years rather than grow clearer. The Sabaeans are dead, their memories but dust and ashes, but Sheba herself does not fade from the imagination of the East. In Southern Arabia the learned know her name and revere her memory much as we think of King Alfred or King Arthur. In Abyssinia she is the day star in the darkness of the past.

Solomon, wise man of the civilised world, the established ruler of position and property, mated with Sheba, the barbaric princess, the lady of moon-lit caravans, and their union, the meeting of fact and fancy, proved irresistible to the imagination of Arabia and Abyssinia. Much is known about Solomon, his ways of life, his houses and his chief cities; by contrast, the veil of mystery that has surrounded through the centuries the queen from foreign parts added to Sheba the appeal of the eternal feminine. In the age of gold and incense, man, wise and majestic had married woman loving and lovely and both were royal in their own right, and the royal circlet of romance was thus completed. For the first and last time the sun and the moon had met and mated together.

What she has lost on the ground of certainty, Sheba has gained in more heavenly realms, holding unchallenged her position of almost divine right by virtue of her inclusion in the three holy books of the nations—The Bible, the Quran, and the Kebra Negast of Abyssinia, the Book of the Glory of Kings.

Hidden away in the morgues of Sana, capital of the Yemen, Commander Craufurd, for long adviser to the Imam, has found ancient manuscripts written on age-old parchment, telling of a caravan headed by a beautiful Queen journeying to see Solomon. Arab writing and records are mostly apocryphal, few books have been published or printed in Arabia, and to this day newspapers,

when existent, come from Cairo, but Craufurd's pains-
taking search has recreated echoes of far off Saaba glories
and has made the latest contribution to the portrait of
Sheba, the inscrutable.

Balkis, cited in the Sana records as daughter of Shar
Habil, was born at Mareb, capital city of the Sabaean
empire. Her mother was Ekeye Azeb, a princess of
Abyssinia. She spent many years of her childhood in
Abyssinia, returning to Mareb just before the death of
her father. By the laws of her country, the heir had to
be elected by the people, and was compelled to pass a
test of nine requirements, the most important being physical
fitness and orthodox religion. Balkis, according to the
Sana story, was the first woman candidate for the Sabaean
throne, and she was lame. She was, however, the most
exotic and glamorous woman ever seen, surpassing with
her beauty anything that had gone before, so she was
elected without difficulty.

She was slender as a gazelle in the hills, fair skinned, her
features were chiselled and she had almond eyes. Her
voice was the lilting soprano of a highland woman, for
Mareb, the royal city, was built among the mountains
nearly 7,000 feet above the sea.

The city was probably of no great size; the palace,
according to Craufurd, was constructed with foundations
of gold, silver and copper on the step-pyramid basis. The
royal dwelling place overlooked Lake Moeris, an artificial
lake formed by damming up a valley, and known to legend.
The famous dam of Mareb, a wonder of the Arab world,
converted the hills into watersheds, conducting water to
the neighbouring region, silver or silver-lead being used for
cementing the conduit pillars into place. Centuries, flowing across that ancient landscape, saw the disruption of
the dams and the drying up of soil into sand, some say
because the Himyaritic civilisation led away prosperity
from the hinterland of the caravan routes down to the sea,
and others because the inroads of water rats, in addition

to neglect, caused the lock gates to burst, and the water supply to fail in a parched land.

Some of these cities of the Old Testament were garden cities, surrounded by the green haze of orchards, water running musically through the centre of the town and fountains splashing in the shaded gardens of the rich. Sunshine gilded the houses, drying up refuse and decay; pillared temples glistened at the end of streets broader than those to be found in Eastern towns to-day; bearded men and their womenfolk, primary colours brightening their clothes, walked to the place of caravans or to shadowed temple ceremonies, dust settling upon them as they went, unhurried by the hoot of motor horns or the roar of mechanical traffic, man's modern slave which is fast becoming his master.

In such surroundings as these Balkis, the Queen, lived and moved in the unfettered freedom of women, seventeen hundred years before Mohammed invented veils and the harem system.

She can best be read about in a book by Sir William Budge published by the Oxford University Press, called the Queen of Sheba and her only son Menyelak.

.   .   .   .   .

The story of Sheba and Solomon starts with Tamrin, master of caravans, and business manager to the Queen of the South. This Tamrin who could command five hundred camels and seventy ships, and traded in the grand manner, came within Solomon's orbit when the King of Israel had circularised merchants with a list of materials necessary for building the House of God. Red gold, "and black wood that could not be eaten of worms, and sapphires," were needed from Arabia, and Tamrin was the man to supply these requirements.

Tamrin was so struck by the wisdom and royalty of Solomon that, on his return to the South, he could talk of little else. He told Sheba of all that he had seen, the

wonder and the graciousness of the great king who had
nothing false about him, and nothing wanting, and who
received information from others and imparted it two-fold.

Each morning—the freshest hours of the day and
the polite time for paying visits in Arabia—Tamrin
would sit down and tell Sheba of Solomon. And woman-
like she wondered, and pondered, and wept a little.
And she found it in her heart to envy Tamrin who had
travelled northwards.

The journey was long and difficult, not lightly to be
undertaken, if she was to find knowledge and majesty
personified sitting on a throne. More and more questions,
she asked Tamrin, until finally she decided that she
must hear for herself the words of Solomon.

"I am smitten with the love of wisdom," she announced
to her counsellors in explanation of her departure, "and
I am constrained with the cords of understanding, and
my heart seeketh to find understanding." Put this way,
there was no answer that could stop her from starting.

And so she set out to cross the length of Arabia.

The Queen made innumerable preparations for her
journey, and the Kebra Negast tells how "seven hundred
and ninety-seven camels were loaded, and she set out on
her journey and followed her road without pause, and
her heart had confidence in God."

She must also have possessed pride and confidence in
her caravan. Nearly a thousand camels, a long line of
expectation, a chain of commerce and corded circumstance, donkeys without number, horses and chariots,
not to mention an array of courtiers and attend-
ants, between them probably helped to form the largest
caravan seen at any time in Arabia. When Sheba went
northwards to visit the King who had taken possession of
her thoughts, she brought with her the most expensive
gift ever given to a man by a woman. The wealth and
value of the caravan Sheba took to Solomon has been
computed at twenty-five million pounds in modern cur-

rency. Most of the precious gifts known to the millennium before Christianity must have found their way into Palestine: incense, spikenard and aromatic gums, all the perfumes of Southern Arabia, tortoiseshell from Malacca, gold from Ophir, bales of ivory, apes strapped side by side with peacocks from the East. Because a young woman was in love with manly wisdom, Asia and Africa walked arm in arm in this unimagined display, and costs became unaccountable.

The Queen was still a girl in her first allurement. She had staked everything on her decision, as women have done since the beginning. Somewhere afar off, an echo blowing with the wind across the distant hills, she saw life waiting for her, sharpened into significance, promising the answer that united mind and heart and has been sought by men and women down the ages. And because, like most women, she was disquieted, she determined to start out with all the support that pomp and circumstance could give her.

There is a description of Sheba's caravan and its endless procession, recapturing perhaps glimpses of what the eyes of the Israelites saw when the advance guard had passed by on their way to Solomon at Gaza.

" . . . Behind them, were the porter slaves of Balkis, from this side the mountains of the moon, where the sources of Nile are. They were black; their loins were girt with leopard skins and their bodies were rubbed in white and vermilion, half and half.

"The child Balkis was an atomy, lost in a great silver chair. Only her eyes were seen under her veils, burning yet not consumed.

"Behind her were horses prancing in their chariots, and all the army under a storm of flags."

All mention is omitted of the route taken by the caravan, but it is an easy matter to visualise camel and donkey straggling from the tops of the tablelands up the back of Arabia along the immemorial trading route between

M

north and south. Leaving the Jauf area, it would have
plodded past Nejran and Taraba, then slightly East of
Medina up what is now the Hejaz, across the Red
desert to Maan, Petra, and so to Palestine, a journey of
some thousand miles—when taken at a camel's pace, a
journey not so far removed from the "ends of the earth,"
by which it has been described.

A Queen, her treasury, her heart, her court, were on
the move, and it is easy to imagine how the journey passed
into legend. The walled cities opened their gates in wonder;
the watchman on the tower, rubbed his eyes and cried
out in astonishment; humble shepherds on the hills must
have thought Astarte herself had left the evening star to
visit them. The desert spread its carpet for the imprints of
her passing, and the stars at night in number as the sands,
roused from their loneliness, looked down with brighter
interest. The curlew called the royal tidings along the
furrowed forehead of the Djol, and beduins left their fires
to watch the royal caravan go by.

.   .   .   .   .

Solomon, possessed of advance news of Sheba's coming,
made ready for her arrival. He ordered propitiary perfumes to be burnt: "styrax, Indian aud, oliban, male
incense and moon coriander, white myrtle and rose-
odoured ledanon." No doubt—man of the world though
he was—he found himself to be in a pleasant state of expectation and excitement. The wives that he knew became
as nothing in his sight when this Queen among women
approached.

A good deal of nonsense has been written about Sheba
possessing a goat's foot. Abyssinian legends describe her
as being magically healed of her infirmity when she reached
Solomon, fortunately before he had seen her. Possibly she
was lame; but the Arabian stories are probably closer to
the truth when they say that all Sabaeans were credited
with goats' feet, their towns being in the mountains.

Solomon, however, according to the Arabs, wished to make certain, so he devised a deception which gives an instance of his dramatic, if in this case, rather expensive, wisdom.

He caused a courtyard to be constructed of crystal, very brilliant and dazzling in the full sunshine, and at one end his throne was set up awaiting the embassy from the south.

And Sheba, dismounting from a silver chair with the sun full in her eyes, stepped upon the courtyard that seemed to her at first to be liquid water, so bright were the reflecting gleams from the sun. In her sudden bewilderment, the young girl acted on instinct; she lifted the seven dresses that covered her, and Solomon looking down from his throne saw that her feet were similar in shape and size to those of any maiden.

His doubts set at rest, he proceeded to pay his royal visitor honour. He sent her the best of everything and each day he arrayed her in new dresses. They visited each other, becoming daily better acquainted, the moon reflecting the rays of the royal sun.

Balkis, the beautiful, expanding at Solomon's feet, could observe every detail of this King of Kings—his wisdom, the subtlety of his voice, the extraordinary poise and composure surrounding him. She compared him to a pearl in the sea, a pomegranate in the garden, the morning star among stars; but Solomon, the wise, apparently never flattered her, keeping his own council.

Among the attributes presented to him by Arab romancers, was the understanding of the speech of birds as well as beasts, so that Balkis must have been given a liberal education during the six months she stayed with Solomon, watching the construction of the Temple, talking with the King, and being instructed in wisdom.

One day they met a labourer carrying a weight upon his head. The King bade him stand, while he made discourse, as the Prophet Mohammed did hundreds of years later, on the subject of compassion.

"I might have been the stonemason and he the King. What is there to choose between us except a difference of places? What would come to the world without compassion one for another? Blessed is the man who knoweth wisdom, that is to say compassion and the fear of God."

Struck by this example of Solomon being able to place himself in another person's shoes, Sheba was emboldened to tell him about her religious difficulties.

"Whom is it right for me to worship?" she asked the King. "We worship the sun according as our fathers have taught us to do, because we say that the sun is the King of the gods. And there are others among our subjects who worship other things. Some worship stones and some carved figures, and some worship images of gold and silver. And we worship the sun, for he cooketh our food, and moreover he illumineth the darkness and removeth fear; we call him 'our king,' and we call him 'our Creator,' and we worship him as a god; for no man hath told us that besides him there is another god."

Solomon, a master of words, answered her in this fashion:

[1] "Verily it is right that men should worship God, Who created the universe, the heavens and the Earth, the sea and the dry land, the sun and the moon, the stars and the brilliant bodies of the heavens, the trees and the stones, the beasts and the feathered fowl, the wild beasts and the crocodiles, the fish and whales, the hippopotamuses and the water lizards, the lightnings and the crashes of thunder, the clouds, and the thunders, and the good and the evil. It is meet that Him alone we should worship, in fear and trembling, with joy and with gladness. For He is the Lord of the Universe, the Creator of angels and men. And it is He Who killeth and maketh to live, it is He Who inflicteth punishment and showeth compassion, Who raiseth and Who bringeth down. No one can chide Him,

[1] *The Queen of Sheba, and her son Menyelek*, (Oxford University Press) page 28.

for He is the Lord of the Universe, and there is no one who can say unto Him, 'what hast Thou done?'"

Sheba promised that she would not worship the sun, but would worship the Creator of the Sun. She told Solomon that she could not stay indefinitely, but must be getting back to her own people and country.

When he realised she was determined on departure, the King, apparently, was more than sorry. In the resounding words of the Kebra Negast, he said to his own heart, "A woman of such splendid beauty hath come to me from the ends of the earth! What do I know?"

Perhaps a little tired of profundities, he decided that what he did know was that he desired to mate with the beauty of the Queen of the South. He asked Sheba to become either his mistress or his wife: the distinction is not clear as noonday when it is considered that Solomon had four hundred wives and six hundred concubines complicating his domestic affairs.

Sheba very properly refused to have any dealings with his private life, and prepared to start on her return journey. A Queen of Sheba could neither take the position of mistress nor share the throne with four hundred others.

It was then that Solomon, caught between the snare of dishonour and the shock of being refused, thought out another of those simple artifices which the centuries have not forgotten. Where a lesser man might have tried to change the decision by intoxicating the senses of the Queen, the King of Israel thought out a plan depending solely on water for its success, water that has been a key word in Arabia, elaborated by the need of thirsty centuries.

The accepted story of the stratagem by which Solomon overcame the scruples of the Queen of Sheba, abbreviated almost to vanishing point, is an example of how much can be said in a few words.

She went to Solomon the King, and he said to her, "whence comest thou?" And she answered and said, "I am from the country of Ethiopia," and he showed her the ten Commandments of the Kingdom. And he gave her strong meat and drink. And Solomon slept. And there was water he had set out there in his wisdom, and as he woke up from his sleep, the Queen was pouring out some of that water into her bowl so that she might drink. And Solomon seized her hand and said to her, "Was there not an oath between us? I swore not to approach thy vessel, and thou didst swear not to approach mine." And she said to him, "Let me alone. After I have drunk thou canst fulfil thy desire."[1]

A much longer and perhaps clearer account approximates to the Arab version, and has been translated by Sir Wallis Budge:

[1] . . . Solomon . . . invited her to come and dwell with him for a season so that he might complete her instruction in wisdom. The queen accepted his invitation and removed to his house, and a place was specially prepared for her from which she could watch the great banquet which he had arranged to hold in her honour: she could see everything and not be seen. The chamber in which she sat was decorated with precious stones, costly carpets covered the floor, purple hangings covered the walls, and the air was redolent with the perfumes of oil of myrrh and cassia, which were sprinkled about, and with the scent of aromatic powders which were being burnt in vessels placed in the room. In this fragment chamber she was served with a sumptuous meal, and she ate freely of the highly-seasoned dishes which were set before her, and drank her fill of spiced wine. Solomon intended that both the peppery meat and the spiced wine with its sub-acid flavour should both increase her appetite and make her thirsty, and they had this effect. When the royal banquet was ended Solomon came to the queen, and said to her, "Take thou thine ease for love's sake until day-break." And she replied, "Swear to me by thy God, the God of Israel, that thou wilt not take me by force. For if I, a maiden, be seduced, I should travel on my journey (back) in sorrow, and affliction, and tribulation." Solomon said, "I swear unto thee that I will not take thee by force, but thou must swear unto me that thou wilt not take by force anything that is in my house." And the queen laughed and said unto him, "Why, being a wise man, dost thou speak as a fool? Thinkest thou that I shall steal anything, or carry off out of the house of the king, anything that the king hath not given me? Do not imagine

[1] *A History of Ethiopia*, vol. 1, pages 197–199 and 203. By Sir E. A. Wallis Budge.

that I have come hither through love of riches. Moreover, my own kingdom is as wealthy as thine, and there is nothing that I wish for that I lack. Assuredly I have come only in quest of thy wisdom." And Solomon said to her. "As thou wouldest make me swear, swear thou also to me, for swearing is meet for both (of us), so that neither of us may be unjustly treated. And if thou wilt not make me swear I will not make thee swear." And the queen said unto him, "Swear to me that thou wilt not take me by force, and I on my part will swear not to take thy possessions"; and he swore to her and made her swear.

Then the servants prepared a bed for Solomon on one side of that chamber, and a bed for the queen on the other. And Solomon told a man servant to wash the stand that held the water pots, and to set in it a vessel full of water whilst the queen was watching, and having done this to close the doors of the chamber and go to bed. This order was given to the man-servant presumably in the Hebrew tongue, which the queen did not understand, and when it was carried out the young man went to bed. And the king went up to his bed and the queen to hers. The chamber was lighted by "shining pearls" which were set in the roof, and by their light, which was as bright as that of the sun, moon, and stars, Solomon watched the queen, who had dropped off into a light slumber. Presently Makeda woke up and found that her lips and mouth and throat were dry, and that owing to the peppery food and wine of which she had partaken, her throat was parched, and she was exceedingly thirsty. Though she smacked her lips together and moved her tongue about, no moisture came to her mouth, and she determined to get up and drink water from the vessel which she had seen the young man place filled on the stand. For a time she lay watching Solomon carefully, and having made up her mind that he was asleep, she rose up silently and, making no sound with her feet, crossed the chamber to the door, and going to the water-stand, took the vessel in her hand to drink from it. Now Solomon had not been asleep, and when he saw the queen go to the water pot, he leaped up, and seized the hand with which she was lifting the vessel to her lips and stopped her from drinking. And he said to her, "Why hast thou broken thy oath that thou wouldest not take by force anything that is in my house?" And being afraid she replied, "Is the oath broken by only drinking water?" And the King said, "Is there anything that thou hast seen under the heavens that is of more value than water?" And the queen said, "I have sinned against myself and thou art released from (thy) oath; but let me drink water for the sake of my thirst." And Solomon said, "Am I truly released from the oath which thou didst make me swear?"

And the queen replied, "Be released from thy oath, only let
me drink water." And he permitted her to drink water, and
after she had drunk water, they slept together.

.   .   .   .   .

Sheba's visit was now drawing to a close. Solomon
himself could hold her back no longer and freely gave
her leave to depart. A King of Judah, a Jew, had
mated with an Arab Princess; on their walks through the
city, alone in the palace, in public meeting and talking
the stars out of the sky in the privacy of night, they must
have done much for the problems of Arabia, reconciling
many things, but leaving one great problem still unsettled
—a discord that divides Arabia into conflict to-day, and
is as old as its hills: the fadeless controversy between Arab
and Jew, between the sons of Shem, quarrelling, as families
do, over their birthright, lying between the middle and
the southern seas.

Before she departed Solomon once more loaded Sheba
with gifts. He gave her six thousand wagons and camels
laden with desirable things; he presented her also with a
vessel for the sea, and a vessel for traversing the air, which
is the first mention made of an aeroplane. Solomon, we
are told, made the aerial vessel by means of the wisdom
of God.

Both he, and the beautiful Queen of the South, became
fabulous figures, the frontispiece in the story of Araby.
They were a highly unusual pair, never duplicated before
or since, and if they were not quite capable of everything,
posterity has tried its best to make them so.

As a poet, who is now dead, has said of them:

> " She was Queen of Sabea
> And he was Asia's Lord,
> But both of them talked to butterflies
> When they took their walks abroad."

CHAPTER SIXTEEN

THE FIRST MENELIK—AND THE LAST

THE REST OF the story of Balkis, Queen of Sheba, has not reached its final chapter until to-day, when Haile Selassie has lost the throne of Judah and left Abyssinia to be ruled by Rome.

Sheba, the girl Queen in love with manly wisdom, is still surrounded with a haze of tradition and tale, but the name of her first-born, Menelik, has trodden the roads of history. It is generally accepted that the Solomonic line of Kings ruled in an unbroken line over Ethiopia until the red-haired Judith, flaming into evil ascendancy, founded the Zague dynasty at Aksum. Shoa became the sanctuary for the dispossessed seed of Solomon until the royal line was restored, like a precious painting, about the time of the first Edward in England.

According to the oldest Ethiopian literature, God placed a pearl in the body of Adam to be handed on through a series of holy descendants until it entered the body of Hannah and the Virgin Mary. This pearl, being a sign of divine intention, passed through David and Solomon and came to Menelik's brother, so that Sheba's seed, when crowned in Ethiopia, became known as the line of King of Kings through virtue of their royal parentage.

Balkis must have pondered over many things when her caravan filed away on the return journey to the south, down the old incense road that perfumed the obsequies of Bible history.

She had seen and loved the wisdom of the greatest king of his day; she had stayed six months with Solomon, Lord

of birds and genii and men; she had become a woman of
wider horizons and deeper understanding, her spirit ful-
filled and refreshed after the test of the long and wearisome
journey across a dried-up wilderness in search of wonder.
The sprawling shapes of the hills, parched as she had been
for need of water, the skeleton trees touched by spring so
seldom, the corrugated cardboard road, the clamour of
the caravan, the influence and the infinity of the
night, the shining loveliness of the moon, now lonely no
longer, must all have appeared different, their focus of
visibility changed, to the Queen returning to her greener
realm of pomegranates, melons four hands thick, and
abundant water flowing upon the heights of the hills.

Whether she told her princes and courtiers, at this stage,
of the destiny she carried in her womb, is not related, but
it is probably that the boy Menelik was born, or at any
rate, reared across the Red Sea, among her own people of
Ethiopia rather than in Mareb or Shabwa.

Craufurd's researches have convinced him that Sheba's
mother was an Abyssinian princess belonging to the
southern half of the old Saaba Kingdom, and it seems
natural enough that the Queen's choice turned in this
direction where her son's environment was concerned.
Possibly the nobles of the real Sheba district had other
ideas for the marriage of their beautiful Princess, and
resented the Jewish influence that had been brought to
bear on their dynasty.

Whether Balkis stayed always among the palaces and
orchards of the Yemen, or whether she spent much
of her reign with Menelik in what is now the Tigre
province, is not clear, but the fact emerges that Menelik
is more African than Arabian in upbringing and outlook.
He belongs to Abyssinia rather than Arabia, though his
mother reigned in the cultivated garden that is still a
fertile corner of the Yemen highlands.

The Queen had started on her long journey to the
North a young girl, she returned nearly a year later, a

woman. Her pilgrimage had flowered in a way that is usually only found in fairy tales, and now it was to bear fruit in a son. Except for the thought of the four hundred wives in the background, nothing could be more romantic or completed than the legendary amalgamation between Sheba and Solomon. She found fulfilment, she looked into the bearded face of wisdom, she took back with her no regrets, no disappointment or disillusion, no possibility of inhibition or change at any future date. The inner treasures she had won were unalterably hers. Her romance was now beyond the reach of failure, decay or frustration. How many women can say as much? How many discover a happiness that neither flies nor fades?

Sitting above the waters of Lake Moeris, watching her people singing as they cut the bark of the incense trees and controlled the sluices of prosperity, she could say to herself, "I charge you, O ye daughters of Jerusalem, by the roes and by the hinds of the field, that ye stir not up my love. . . ."

And again:

"Who is he who cometh out of the wilderness like pillars of smoke, perfumed with myrrh and frankincense, with all powders of the merchant?"

Sheba, in her honey-coloured beauty, perhaps more than any golden words of Solomon, was herself the Song of Songs.

So she reigned and passed into the frame of legends, abdicating before she grew old. Her son, Menelik, heightened into manhood, came to her to demand the birthright of all sons—a sight of their father. Balkis had her answer ready; she had held it secretly on her finger all these years. Presenting Menelik with Solomon's special ring, she sent him forth to obtain his father's guidance and blessing.

·   ·   ·   ·   ·

Tamrin, master of caravans, now grown grey in the service of Saaba, was recalled for purposes of escort. When

the two of them reached Gaza, the Israelites who saw
Menelik were so struck by his "awesome" appearance and
likeness to Solomon that they sent representations, spies
on horseback, to Jerusalem in order to see if the King
was really there or had suddenly grown younger.

They made obeisance to the King, and delivered
themselves as follows: "Hail, may the royal father live!
Our country is disturbed because there hath come into
it a merchant who resembleth thee in form and appearance, without variation. He resembleth thee in noble
carriage and in splendid form, and in stature and in
goodly appearance: he lacketh nothing in respect of these,
and is in no way different from thyself. His eyes are glad-
some, like unto those of a man who has drunk wine, his
legs are graceful and slender, and the tower of his neck
is like unto the tower of David, thy father."

Solomon and his son met joyfully. The caravan master
gave the assembled audience interesting details of his
country; he declared that the climate was better than
Judea, without burning heat or fire, that men did not
die of the sun, and that the tops of the mountains ran
with water; he concluded courteously by saying that his
country lacked one thing—namely, wisdom, and for this
reason they had made the journey. . . .

After Menelik had been publicly recognised as a de-
scendant of the royal house of Judah and certain time had
elapsed, he announced his intention of returning to his
mother and to the mountains he loved. The old King
did his utmost to dissuade him, promising him many things,
but ultimately he saw fit to harness his son's determination
for their mutual advantage.

Solomon possessed a colonisation complex. He desired
his children to inherit the earth in the best interests of
expansion. He also wished his seed to be as the sands in
number. It was for this reason (the chroniclers relate)
that he mated with a thousand wives; but providence
evidently did not approve his ideas of family emigration,

for he was blessed with no more than three sons. Judah and the Jews have never become formidable in numbers; no more than fifteen million Jews are scattered throughout the world at the present time.

Menelik told his father of his wish to take away with him one thing in addition to a blessing: the Ark of the Covenant.

At first Solomon was aghast, but when he became a little more used to the idea he said to his son: "If it be the will of God, the Governor of the Universe, that thou shalt take away the tabernacle with thee, it will be an easy thing for thee to do. But do not, I pray thee, let me know about it."

He had bade the nobles prepare to send away their eldest sons with Menelik to found a new Jewish kingdom in Abyssinia, the southern half of the Saaba kingdom. The young Israelites resented this forceful treatment; particularly disliking the idea of a more savage country without a religion, they decided their only possibility of happiness would be to steal the Ark of the Covenant and take it into exile with them.

This removal corresponded roughly to a modern emigrant of importance taking by force with him to New Zealand, say, the Crown jewels together with the State carriage and one of the King's sons.

Azarius, son of Zadok, the priest, thought out a plan; death, if it came to the conspirators, would be in a holy cause. Money was collected by Azarius to further the plot, and a carpenter was commissioned to construct a framework of wood, exactly similar in size and shape to the Ark of the Covenant. Menelik, ignorant of the stratagem, was persuaded to obtain Solomon's permission to offer sacrifices, and the king, generous in a big way, presented the young men with 100 bulls, 100 oxen and 10,000 sheep. The following night, the conspirators substituted the framework of wood for the real Ark, carefully replacing a covering exactly to match the one they had taken, composed of the finest golden wiring.

Azarius and his followers waited surprisingly a week, then the Ark was placed in a wagon. Surrounded by stores and dirty clothes, and together with Menelik, the whole band fled southwards at fierce speed, passing eventually through Egypt. It is said, the cat-headed and dog-faced idols fell to the ground in fragments when the Ark of the Covenant passed.

Pursuers were sent out by Solomon and the nobles of Judah, who followed the tracks of the flight without catching up with it. Passers-by, when questioned, replied: "We have seen a great King and his numerous soldiers, and the Ark of the Covenant was with them. And they were travelling along like the clouds when they are driven before the attack of mighty winds for a very long distance. . . ."

.   .   .   .   .

Back again in safety within his own country, Menelik was received with acclamation; Jubilee trumpets sounded, the Ark of the Covenant was placed on Mount Debra Makeda, which evidently provided the Ethiopian name for the Queen of Sheba. Zion had come to rest in Ethiopia; for the first and perhaps the last time, Africa was equipped and endowed by majesty.

Before joyous multitudes, according to the ancient tradition, the Queen inaugurated the new Solomonic Kingdom. She gave her son 17,700 chosen horses, Arab and African steeds, besides the throne of the kingdom, and she made a farewell speech to the multitudes which has not been forgotten.

"[1] I went down like the great iron anchor whereby men anchor ships for the night on the high seas, and I received a lamp which lighteth me, and I came up by the ropes of the boat of understanding . . . I went to sleep in the depths of the sea . . . and it seemed to me there was a star in my womb, and I laid hold of it and made it strong in the splendour of the sun; I laid hold of it and will never let it go. . . . I went into the blaze

[1] The Queen of Sheba and her only son Menyelek. (Page 154.)

of the flame of the sun, and it lighted me with splendour, and I saved myself by confidence in the footprints of wisdom, and not myself only but all the people of my country, and not those only but those who travel in their ways, the nations that are round about. . . . ."

Age has done well by the beautiful Balkis, Queen of Sheba and mother of peoples. Aksum has been a holy city largely on her account; the Ark of the Covenant is said to lie buried somewhere beneath the city. Where history starts and legend ends it is still difficult to decipher, though it may be taken for certain that a Jewish invasion or influx into Abyssinia did take place in connection with the Queen of Sheba, and the Saaba kingdom became important enough for Rome to enter the field of events. In recent years the wheel of fate has spun round to old numbers again, so that once more Arab, Jews and Romans have been in conflict for ownership and supremacy.

The trumpets of Abyssinia, celebrating Sheba and Solomon, will never be heard again, the trump they sounded has lasted nearly 3,000 years, blowing unchallenged from the heights of Africa, this side the mountains of the moon, across to Araby; but now their thunder has been stolen, their sovereignty superseded, by Mussolini and the modern bugles of Rome.

.   .   .   .   .

Mussolini took away the Lion of Judah to ornament Rome; Titus removed the seven-branched candlestick from the Temple when he stormed Jerusalem.

It is curious to note how often, and at what important moments, Arabs, Jews, and Abyssinians have intersected each other's history.

An Abyssinian soldier is said to have helped St. Paul to make his escape from the city wall at Damascus.

The Abyssinian Negus befriended the first Moslems who fled from Mecca and obtained safety in his kingdom. Mecca for a time was even afraid of an Abyssinian invasion to help the Prophet they had cast out.

The Jews of Medina gave their assistance and welcome to Mohammed when he escaped from Mecca, and it was when he lost their support that he took to the sword.

At the time of the late Abyssinian war, the Arabs, in order to do what they could for the Negus, refused wherever possible to supply animal transport to the Italians.

It is also curious how the temple area, and the Temple in Jerusalem has never been rebuilt by the Jews since the coming of Christianity and Jewish disruption, so that their chief link and sequence with the days of their ascendancy remains severed—the days of King Solomon and the Sabaeans, whose fame, at one time circled civilisation.

CHAPTER SEVENTEEN

THE INCENSE-CARRIERS AND THE WADI HADHRAMAUT

THE SABAEAN EMPIRE, whose destinies the Queen of Sheba once shared, has provided one of those mysteries of history which remains partially veiled, and the Sabaeans rank with the Kmers of Angkor as a race whose coming to, and going from the stage of civilisation has never been explained. Thousands of years ago, when Britain was still an Ultima Thule and Imperial Rome had not yet arisen, the land of Saaba was renowned throughout the civilised world; its name was circulated as a household word for wealth and luxury, and it had the practical monopoly of the incense trade—that old and bearded trafficking between Asia and the classical countries. The Sabaean Empire developed a legendary and fabulous splendour, glowing with the force and inner fire of the rubies that are still found from time to time in Southern Arabia. The riddle of Saaba, which has puzzled scholars and explorers alike, has been kept up into modern times, since entry to the heart of the old kingdom is still extremely hazardous, quite apart from the fact that the boundaries of the empire have never been mapped. This gap in the records of history and geography is pleasantly stimulating, for it is good to know that a few apertures remain along the increasing encyclopaedic wall of hard facts. Bricks, scholarly mortar, and stone inscriptions have been contributed from time to time to the Saaba breach, but there is still room for the passage of doubt and controversy in the circuit of a people whose trading enterprises are thought to have stretched tropically far south to Zimbabwe in Rhodesia.

Saaba is the ancient name for the peoples of Yemen. The name is first mentioned in the tenth chapter of Genesis where Sheba and Hazarmareth (Hadhramaut) are called Sons of Joktan, descending closely from Shem and Noah. Confusion has arisen owing to the fact that Sheba is marked with Dedan on the early Bible maps on the Persian Gulf, and the south-west corner of Arabia is labelled Joktan. On the other hand, the Sabaeans had many colonies and dependencies, including Abyssinia, and in various records the names Sheba and Saaba are interchangeable.

The Sabaeans were known to have been great traders, from the days of Solomon to those of Cyrus, and they purveyed for the most part incense, precious stones, ivory, ebony and gold,—all the things which the average person would be likely to include in the presentation of a barbaric caravan.

Ezekiel, when prophesying the destruction of Tyre, a city whose artizans helped Solomon to build the Temple, calls attention to the trading business of his day:

> Arabia and all the princes of Kedah, they occupied with thee in lambs and rams and goats; in these were they thy merchants.
>
> The merchants of Sheba and Raamah, they were thy merchants, they occupied in thy fairs with chief of all spices and with all precious stones and gold.
>
> Haran and Canueh, and Eden, the merchants of Sheba, Asshur and Chilmad were thy merchants.
>
> These were thy merchants in all sorts of things, in blue clothes and broidered work, and in chests of rich apparel, bound with cords, and made of cedar, among thy merchandise.
>
> The ships of Tarshish did sing of thee in thy market: and then wast replenished and made very glorious in the midst of the seas.

The first authentic inspection of the Saaba kingdom from outside was supplied by the military expedition of Aelius Gallus, sent out by Augustus Cæsar in 30 B.C. This was the first official contact between Old Testament days and classical times, and was described by the Greeks.

The cupidity of Rome derived little satisfaction from the expedition owing to the manœuvres of the middle men of the incense commerce—the Nabataeans. These Arabs of the north did not show the Romans the caravan route; instead, they recommended them to a port abutting a waterless hinterland, so that on arrival in the south the soldiers were too weak and reduced in numbers for action.

A hundred years or so later an anonymous writer wrote the Periplus from which voyage narrative, together with the comments of Gallus, Pliny's account of the Yemen is largely taken. The contemporary Sabaeans and Homerites are described, and their trading relations with Rome, at that time probably the largest city in the world.

Strabo, the Greek commentator, of the third century, tells of four great nations who flourished in the south: the Mineans, capital Ma'in, the seaport at Carna; the Sabaeans with their capital at Mariaba or Mareb; the Catabanes, living close to the straits of Bab-el-Mandeb, and in the east the Chatromotitae (Hadhramis), their capital resting at Sabota.

It is particularly noteworthy that the Mineans were a Hadhramant people, advancing into the Jauf area from the east. They formed, it is thought, an island of rivalry within the wide-flung ocean of the Sabaean dominions, though some scholars consider that they were an earlier civilisation. At any rate they had separate kings and they were buyers and purveyors of the frankincense of Sabota and the Shabwa district.

For a brief spell only the veil was lifted from the mysterious Sabaean traders and agriculturists, by mention from two or three classical writers; then the incense land was curtained off once again from outside view, and, after the coming of Mohammed and the Moslem conquerors, slipped into its old seclusion guarded from trespass by hostile and war-like tribesmen.

For many hundreds of years people in Europe knew little more of the land of Sheba than what they read in the early writings of the Bible. From the days of the Queen of Sheba to those of Napoleon this unusual gap in Western knowledge continued to remain more or less unbridged, the actual ground totally unsurveyed. Even when the first explorer arrived, the jest of isolation was not finished, for the first deported inscriptions, consisting of porphyry blocks, could not be deciphered. No one could be found capable of reading them. The language was so old that it had become lost; the people who wrote and carved those inscriptions had been born too close to Noah and Abraham.

Tablets and inscriptions copied by Arnaud at Mareb found an interpreter in Ossiander. But it was not until Joseph Halevy entered the Jauf area, covering ground untrodden by Europeans since the days of Gallus, the Roman commander, and bringing back with him 800 inscriptions, that some of the past was recaptured and antiquarians and archæologists exchanged facts for fancy, stringing definite stones on to the jewelled story of Saaba and Sheba.

The oldest Sabaean coins in existence show an owl standing on an amphora, clearly copied from the early Greek mintage. The alphabet, if it can be called such, consists of twenty-nine consonants and lacks vowels, but it resembles Ethiopic, and is traceable to the influence of Phœnician mariners. Even in the Arabia of the Old Testament many of the amenities of life were owed to sailors and the sea. Solomon was not able to construct his Temple without the assistance of the architects from Tyre, and the Sabaeans could not have scratched their simple records on stones if the Phœnicians had not given them a start.

A Caravan Moves along the Ancient Incense Highway

The New Generation Looks on from the Wadi Hadhramaut

Hamdani, one of the few Arab chroniclers whose observations are taken to be authentic, saw the famous dam at Mareb a thousand years ago—only Arnaud, among Westerners, has seen it since those echoing days when the Near East was ringing with the crusades and Cross and Crescent struggled for mastery.

The gradual dessication of the country, changes in the trade routes, and the slackening of local effort, rather than the interruptions of conquerors, brought about the death of an empire which held the arid fields of Southern Arabia fruitful and powerful for more than twice the duration of the Roman Empire.

The broad outline of the last period of the Sabaean Kings has been found in the Axum inscriptions in Abyssinia. The Sabaean Himyaritic period starts about the time of the Gallus expedition, and has left its footprints in the Hadramaut valleys. In the sixth century, the armed forces of Abyssinia, supposedly Christian, over-ran Himyar and his princes, until checked for a time by the Jewish dictator, Dhu Nurwas, who persecuted Christians and tortured them. With the arrival of militant Moslems upon the scenes in the next century, there was the spectacle of three of the four great religions of the world at grips in armed encounters.

Siwah is supposed to be the first Sabaean capital in those pre-historic and pre-record days when the Sabaeans had priest kings bowing the knee to Shams and Astarte. But little is known about the city or its site. It is like the peoples of 'Ad, whom the Arabians believe vanished into thin air, destroyed by a destroying hot wind which blew ceaselessly and with terror for a week, passing up the noses of the tribesmen and turning living bodies into dead men.

.   .   .   .   .

Most important of the ancient highways belonging to the people of the south was the Wadi Hadhramaut, linking the incense country with the northern route from Mareb

and Nejran. Running east and west, four hundred miles
of history as well as geography, the broad track of the
Wadi was the shorter side in the right-angled route of the
spice commerce, travelling into classical temples and
sweetening classical corpses. It was also part of the over-
land commercial highway between India and Egypt,
tapping the very heart of the incense-growing districts,
than which none were better or more honoured among
cultivators, and whose sweet savour launched a thousand
caravans.

Ophir, in the firm belief of Craufurd, lay once upon a
time at its sea-washed mouth. If the river that once ran
down the wide reaches of the Wadi was no river of gold,
no Pactolus, the port at the eastern exit must often have
overflowed with golden cargoes. Some of the treasures
of Solomon's mines in all probability found their way into
this harbour of fame and fable.

At the other end extended the sand desert round Nejran
which has encroached upon and engulfed the western exit
of the great Wadi through the years, transforming Shabwa
from a popular city to a village of mud hovels. Motoring
down this way, Philby came across what he took to be traces
of old tributary streams, contributing to this main artery
of ancient thoroughfares.

·   ·   ·   ·   ·

There are three master roads of history whose mere
mention stirs an illumination in the mind; incandescent
names, they burn in the imagination with a glow that
cannot be extinguished or denied. Not only the great ones
and the free ones of this earth have reacted to their spell,
but almost all men who can read. Everyone who has seen
a ship sail over the skyline into blue seas, or strung camels
setting out along the gigantic desert road, must have
tingled to the sound of the golden road to the Indies,
the silken road to Samarkand, and the incense road of
Arabia.

Oldest of them all, bound up in a dim way with religion and origins, life, and especially with death, is the ancient incense highway of Araby.

Which experience would have been most satisfying in these annals of adventurous travel, undertaken by nations rather than individuals: to have sailed into New Worlds with Drake and Magellan? to have set out with the speed of Mongol horsemen on the silk road across the roof of the world to the great Khan enthroned in China? to have traversed the inscrutable desert in the company of caravans and their corded bales of incense?

Unfortunately each of us has only one life to live, and cannot choose whether he would be born into the reign of a Queen of Sheba, a Kublai Khan, or a Queen Elizabeth. Nor can he be in two places at once, though this apartness is fast being reduced by the transit of the modern aeroplane, able to control the span of continents, if not the centuries. Travel, in its more mystical aspect, is essentially a striving to come to terms with the unities of time and place, progressing at rare moments, almost of reincarnation, back through the centuries.

The three historic roads of organised wayfaring not only caused races to be captured by a wind of movement, but also gave those races the commercial gains necessary for massed impetus. The riches of Peru and the Indies caused the emergence of Western Europe, the wealth of the silk road gave to the Tartars Asiatic supremacy, the long-hoarded gains of the incense trade, collected through the centuries, enabled the Moslem Caliphs to afford to set out to conquer the world.

Pliny gives a glimpse of what the incense trade meant to antiquity when he mentions that Rome sent a sum, equivalent to a million sterling, to the Near East in payment for cosmetics, incense, scents and silk. "Too much," he complains, perhaps somewhat unjustly, "are the ladies costing us these days."

Traversing the sandy infinities of the Wadi Hadhramaut, beneath a summer sky so blue that it looks as if it could never know the shadow of a cloud, progressing by means of camel caravans, does not seem so far removed from Sheba and her days as the tally of years suggests. A Bible is better than a guide book in these places.

Instead of going west for its principal markets, the diminished incense trade has turned east, back upon itself. Trade to-day is with Aden, Dharfur, Muscat and Bombay. Frankincense and myrrh are still produced in quantity in the Gara mountain district towards the extreme eastern limit of the Hadhramaut. El-Hafa, the principal port, exports a thousand cwts. annually to Bombay to scent the gloom of Indian temples.

History and Geography have walked side by side up and down the Wadi Hadhramaut, and at times Religion has joined them. The trade, until the sea routes were opened, meant life to Southern Arabia, and it ministered principally to the needs of worship and death.

The Wadi Hadhramaut to-day is firm sand, sometimes yellow and sometimes of a pinkish hue, empty, bare, sun-struck, it stretches from the No Man's Land west of Henan, away to the borders of the sea. It is desolate and lost, yet bounded by the comforting limits of tremendous cliffs that throw almost solid shadows; it is utterly lonely yet peopled at intervals by surprising cities; it is without doubt one of the most remarkable and paradoxical places on the map of geography.

The only landmarks are the drinking places, white-daubed and domed, looking in the distance like the tombs of saints. They are maintained and filled by the slaves of the nearest town, the work of replenishment being a sort of ritual on the part of the city corporation or some wealthy Seyyid.

I scratched up the sand on one occasion and found it to be of no great depth. The river in the dim past must have flowed over a granite and limestone bed. Under temporary conditions, after rainstorms, the river returns magically for a week or two, but the rainfall is not consistent enough to maintain fluid conditions, and the watercourses play hide and seek in the sand.

The only district where scrub flourishes is round Henan but camels are not allowed to eat the two-foot green shrubs, standing high and dry on little mounds anchored by their roots in the shifting sand. Between Shibam and Katan, I noted that the Arabs have built rough reservoirs in the Wadi bed, but so severe had been the recent storms that all were broken down and few had succeeded in catching rainwater. Round Shibam there must be at least 200 wells, and the Wadi is cheerful with water-courses and the feathery green of palm trees. Some of the date palms live to a great age, and when they become unfruitful the Arabs cut off their heads. This drastic operation renews the vitality and fertility, but, being a last resort, cannot be performed successfully a second time.

I thought it curious that the Arabs did not grow orange groves, and I was told Jews are addicted to the culture of orange trees, but that the Arabs prefer their many kinds of date palms which thrive without attention, provided their roots obtain the blessing of water at fixed periods.

Between Shibam and Terim, palm trees dot the sands in groves and even woods and are the wealth of the district.

The townsmen are free inhabitants, as distinguished from the Seyyid aristocracy, the feudal tribesmen and the beduins.

The lawless beduins interest themselves from time to time by sniping from the table lands at those who pass by in the valleys. Some of the wealthy landowners have dug trenches so as to walk about unscathed in their property, and they sometimes use a portable tin breastwork, transported or worked by slaves, that intervenes between their bodies and the dangers of the hills.

Except in the sun-baked towns, men live dangerously in the Wadi Hadhramaut, and the caravans journey east and west, going about their business under the protection of antique muskets that keep outlaws to the uncertain distance of rifle fire. The main intercourse now takes place between Shibam and Terim, and southward down such wadis as Du'an, towards the sea coast. But the vitality of the district has been dying for several hundred years, and many of the young men emigrate to Java and Singapore. The product called gum arabic, used for making sweets and on the flaps of envelopes, now comes to the merchants of Europe almost entirely from the Sudan, being tapped from the acacia trees, which are bled at the times of rising sap, principally in December and January. Thousands of tons of gum arabic, pure in quality and soluble in water, are exported annually.

Freya Stark, during a brief visit, traced out many of the old incense routes in her book, *The Southern Gates of Arabia*. Yet so far as I know, no white man has ever traversed the length of the Wadi Hadhramaut from the Jauf area west of Shabwa to the sea.

Leaving the mountains and the desolate Djol, and travelling in the Wadi, one finds oneself stepping out into the desert and the incommunicable peace of the desert. After the stony, inhospitable heights, firm sand underfoot comes as a blessed relief. At El Meshid the Wadi is seven miles across—wide as an arm of the sea, reaching out towards the horizon with the longing of all really flat places of the earth. The camel caravans are a progression of dots, a sort of desert decimal system, the palm groves are the upright contrast to continuous lateral lines, the cliff walls, when in proximity, frame the long perspectives in phantasy. Time and distance fade into insignificance in that unending sunshine and are lost to view. Yesterday is the same as to-morrow, the rocks are scorched or glared into unreality, and moving forward, man becomes in himself the beginning and the end of movement—a dot in the control of some far-off destiny.

A sense of illusion hangs over the wadi walls and communicates itself to this desert journey that is yet enclosed.

These cliffs are so high that they form ramparts limiting width but not length; they continue with the insistence of some accompanying fate, and their height and their grandeur dwarf everything, whether living or dead, within the limits of the Wadi below. Looking up at the huge ascending faces of these cliffs, four, five and six times the height of St. Paul's Cathedral, date palms become toy trees out of Noah's Ark, and the houses in the towns no bigger than dolls' houses.

A Wadi town close against a cliff wall reminds the eye of card houses built to amuse, and of no particular permanence. Even some of the skyscraper buildings run up by the inhabitants to confront overwhelming surroundings do not appear in any way outstanding. Contrast distorts and belittles. No one notices a sandfly when it stands alongside an elephant. New York could be placed alongside these giant cliffs without attracting attention, and its tallest and most sky-pointing buildings would not look particularly high.

Nature looks down on man and his mansions, and ever the wadi stretches wide arms east and west, the old incense road, often golden at sunrise and sunset, a river of water once and now a river of sand.

Most of the towns, El Meshid, Katan, Sewun, are built on the south of the wadi where shade lasts longer. The caravan tracks are mostly in this area. On the unused, northern side I found many traces of very ancient habitations whose ruins still perched upon the sides of the cliffs and whose history probably went back to Himyaritic and Sabaean times. They mostly lie between Henan and Shabwa. . . .

It was this northern side of the Wadi Hadhramaut that I came down on my melancholy return journey from Shabwa.

CHAPTER EIGHTEEN

HENAN AFFAIRS AND THE RETURN TO SHIBAM

THE CARAVAN OF the wood-carriers made slow progress in
No Man's Land.

The trail along the wadi was difficult to follow and often
the old leader had to converse with the younger members
of his family, and they would scout in various directions
before the caravan could proceed. These stops and sudden
changes of route were tiring and I came to the point when
I felt ready to drop.

The moon had dipped and faded into the hills, but the
stars shone brighter with its passing, and a ridge of hills
which seemed vaguely familiar to me rose nearer and
nearer as we stumbled through the sand and between the
tufted bushes. The young bedu began to sing, their voices
fitting well with the melancholy of the night.

Little was said to me, and my thoughts concentrated on
the fate of Abdu, my instruments, cameras, and more particularly my bags of silver. I hoped strongly we might
reach some half-way village before Henan, enabling me
to come to grips with circumstances and perhaps make a
fresh start; as it was, every step was taking me farther away
from Shabwa.

We came to the ghostly ridge of hills when dawn had
tinted the sky; it was the gap through which I had passed
the previous day on my outward journey. Soon the sun
shone fiercely and I asked for a lift. When the old weather-
beaten leader of the caravan, father of the family, refused
to burden his camels any more, I summoned my pride
and determined not to petition him again. We came to

the well shared by the beduin women and their goats,
but to my surprise there was no one about, and no possibility of any help in that quarter. I had been told that
we should get a drink here, but the caravan did not stop,
and we jogged or walked away from that water although
I knew that the beduin goat-skins were empty and I saw
no chance of a drink before reaching Henan.

I was beginning to find my masquerade irksome. I had
begun not only to think I was an Arab but actually to feel
like one, so insinuating is the influence of environment on
a human being, hundreds of miles away from civilization.
But now that I was returning in these unpleasant conditions,
I began to wish myself clothed like a European once more,
representing a definite nationality, rather than a fish out
of water, longing for liquid more than anything else.
I had set out to find Shabwa as a thief in the night; my
attempt had been in the form of a dash, and though when
I had left Henan I had met with a small ambush, because
I had not paid the demands of a sheikh of the territory,
the danger had not amounted to much, and had not in
any way affected my chances of reaching Shabwa. It was
not the rigours of the desert, nor the barriers of the local
inhabitants that had prevented my arrival, but rather
the cunning of my two beduin guides whom I had taken
on trust, chosen for me by the Sultan.

When the sun rose in power, the spirits of the Arabs
rose with it, and I became subjected to many jibes and
hearty laughs. Occasionally the old caravan leader became impatient with his followers, since I think he was
afraid in his heart lest, if they carried their efforts too far,
he would not receive the money I had promised him for
taking me back.

An amusing incident arose that I think was invented
in the mind of the old leader to test out my bona fides,
although he must have been certain enough by this time
that I was no follower of the Prophet. He turned towards
the north, and kneeling in the desert prayed as all Arabs

have been bidden to do, in the direction of Mecca. He signalled to me to join him, but I refused; so did his followers, and I am afraid he made a sad mess of family prayers out there in the wadi, clearly showing he had forgotten the Moslem precision of prayer, and turning the ridicule of the others from me on to his own head. It was a most laughable sight to see the old man bobbing up and down in the desert looking back every now and then to see if he was doing his bowings right, and it was with great difficulty that I kept a straight face. He reminded me of something sprawled and meaningless and of the earth rather than the sky; I had seen a zoo bear behaving in the same way, dividing his time between two feet and four.

We came upon some large birds which obligingly remained on the ground instead of flapping into the air. The bedu began to stalk them, crawling along and taking advantage of every possible piece of cover in the cleverest fashion, but they spoilt the effect when they came to level their old matchlocks, either their aim or their rifles leaving the birds where they were before.

My thirst was now overpowering.

We did another two hours of blazing trail before reaching the cool sanctuary of Henan. I had just sufficient strength left to go to a house and beg for water without showing the Arabs how finished I felt.

I was thankful the journey had come to an end, for it was evident enough to me that my safety had depended upon the avariciousness of the caravan leader exceeding the enmity of his followers, and I did not know which was the stronger.

·   ·   ·   ·   ·

I now found myself back at the house of the head sheikh of the village, a quiet man who had made a fortune in Java, and had returned when still young to his home town, his riches lifting him up to be leader of the community. His word or his money was law, and a command from him was sufficient to provide me with attention and hospitality. I stayed in his house and explained my position to him while he listened with the courteous attention of the educated Arab; he was a real friend in need, for he at once offered to loan me money to pay the beduins, and he arranged for some soldiers to search the desert in order to bring back the two guides who had abandoned me.

It was three days before they were brought back. They were found in the neighbourhood of Shabwa, though they had carefully avoided the place itself. I was within a few hours' march of the ruined town, if I had known the correct direction to take. The sheikh told me, to my surprise, that St. John Philby and the Sultan, who had arrived at Henan the previous afternoon, had returned to Shibam, word having come that the Englishman's second car had broken a back axle. It was curious that both of us should have had trouble, Philby with modern mechanical transport, and I with transport that had stood the test of time since the days of the Bible.

While waiting for news of my caravan, I spent much time with Balak bin Zaid Bedek, a merchant of Fuwa, who had come to Henan. He held the position of inspector of schools, and he introduced me to the local schoolmaster, who took me over his building, showing me how young Arab children are taught.

The Prophet is still the Headmaster of Islam. Arab children start their education by being taught the many names for Allah, and the Quran is their lesson book. Saints supply numberless convenient holidays and the boys spend no more than three hours a day in the schoolroom. Their memory obtains the best training, for they learn many pages of the Quran by heart. Boys practise pranks as they do the whole world over ; the brightest boy in the Henan school was half-Japanese spending term-time with his retired father and his holidays with his mother in the East Indies.

The whole village of Henan turned out to see the entry of Abdu and the two guides, escorted by the soldiers. They walked in jauntily, the ascaris swaggering a little, sticking out their chests and beating their hands on the butts of their rifles. I think that Salim and Saleh were in doubt as to whether they were being brought back in triumph or disgrace, but I saw their faces fall when they saw me. I had nothing to do with them, and I did not talk to Abdu until we were all returning to Shibam, the two guides under arrest.

Abdu was full of explanations and excuses. He seemed to be genuine in his remorse, and said he had had a bad time. When he had first missed me, he had called the attention of the two cousins to my continued absence, but they had merely shrugged their shoulders and said no doubt I should catch them up. Abdu had asked how I was to be expected to overtake them when I was not even in sight and they were going faster than they had done before; by way of answer they changed their course, moving over to the south side of the valley. When he remonstrated with them, they said that they had to cross the valley since Shabwa was on that side. Abdu did not know what to do; he could not make them stop and he did not dare to stay behind himself; so he had gone on, trusting to the providence of Allah to guide my footsteps after them. He had hoped I would find the way all right, for he knew I was used to desert travel, but when night came on he had become doubly anxious, not only for my safety but for his own. He had searched out a long pole and strung a lantern on the end, holding it high above his head for most of the night. I told Abdu that I had been careless in allowing the guides to have a chance of giving me the slip, but that he had been cowardly in not staying behind to tell me when the guides had changed direction.

While at Henan, and on the way back to Shibam, I had plenty of time to think over my position and future plans.

Checking my stores, I found that half my instruments were damaged beyond repair and that I had barely enough money left to take me back to the coast. My recently found enthusiasm for becoming the third white man to reach Shabwa had begun to evaporate. Philby had described it as disappointing, and I did not seem to have enough money to organise a fresh attempt to get there. If the old incense capital had been veiled and unvisited, I should not have been content to turn my back, but in the circumstances, thoughts of fresh undertakings and new country to cross began to occupy my thoughts. The Yemen was most unfortunately barred to me, otherwise I might have ventured further into the Sheba country round Mareb and Jauf. The Empty Quarter stretched invitingly to north and east, but a man going there without careful preparation and forethought, would only succeed in wandering into wide emptiness, deserted of every form of interest, and reaching at the end to nothing.

The old allurement of the unexpected and the unknown began to lay hands on me again. The old and insidious deceit of getting somewhere *first*, of discovering wild secrets of nature which others had never come upon before, took firm root in my mind.

I had been told that an unexplored route lay across the mountains to Shihr, that wild and unvisited tribes had their habitation in those mountains, and that only the presence of the abundant rains which had fallen recently made this wild tract of country at all possible even for camels. I began to wonder what I should find if I went that way—and wonder is the champagne the traveller drinks to refresh himself in the wilderness.

.   .   .   .   .

Immediately upon arrival in Shibam, Salim and Saleh were flung into prison. The trial was to take place in a day or two when the Sultan returned from his palace at Katan.

o

The Sultan had left to enquire about a man who had been murdered for his rifle. Twelve months previously a beduin had stolen a rifle; this year at the fête held in Katan, the same beduin recognised his rifle in the hands of another man and accused him of being the thief. The beduin had been shot, and his murderer had managed to make his escape in the confusion. Thirty police had been sent after him, but the narrator of the story explained to me with a smile that it was certain the thirty police, or even a hundred police, would never bring their man back once he had escaped into his own country.

The Sultan's accredited agent took charge of the trial in his master's absence. He was slow, inconsiderate and overpowering, taking the line that I was giving him a great deal of trouble over a very small matter. The trial was fixed for one afternoon. I sent down Abdu to hear the result.

The decision made me laugh more than I had done for a long time. My guides, accused of running away with my property, had invented the Gilbertian defence of saying that it was I who had run away from them. I had not wanted to go to Shabwa so of course I had stayed behind.

Even the Arab jurists, eager to avoid disputes or a fuss with outlying tribes during a time of festival, must have had their doubts. They asked the two beduins to produce witnesses to prove their statement, and the beduins answered that they would fetch them, if set free for the purpose. Salim and Saleh were solemnly released, never to return. Abdu told me they were unlikely to venture near Shibam again until the Sultan had forgotten the whole episode.

"What would the Sultan do if he knew?" I asked Abdu.

"He would have them beaten, or perhaps they would be hung up by their heels to change the position of their thoughts."

But Sultan Ali bin Saleh remained in Katan, presiding

over the Feast of the Camels, which lasted for five days
and nights and attracted merchants from various points
in the Hadhramaut and Yemen. The last day of the
festivities had arrived, so I was too late to take part. I
saw no reason to approach the Sultan again unless I wished
to make a fresh attack on Shabwa, so I turned my attention
to the mountains.

I began to organise a caravan to take me to the coast,
determined to cover ground which had never been traversed
before. I made up my mind to forget Salim and Saleh
and to consider new and unexplored projects.

We obtained five camels and two men; one, a half-
breed, who had bought himself out of slavery, bore the
name of Komiss. He was one of the ugliest, best-tempered
men I have ever met. Later, at Sewun, we were joined by
one other recruit, an Arab from the lower grade. We
were told we were lucky to have procured camels, since
most baggage animals had been commandeered to help
merchants into Katan for the festivities.

CHAPTER NINETEEN

AN UNKNOWN DESERT EDEN

THINKING IT OVER quietly, it is queer how people go off to visit desolate places happily and with satisfaction.

The answer is not easy to find, but it is connected with the very essence of travel and it is often a matter of going back rather than forward into the unknown. Man gets back to nature, to the good earth, and to himself. The test of personality is not how a man appears to others, but how he gets on with himself. Some love themselves, a few hate, many under the stress of a too-crowded communal life develop a terror of being alone; but out in the wilds, reserves and reticences discarded, the traveller finds out about himself, and his footsteps lead into paths of peace.

There is something universal and enduring about the soil of Southern Arabia, something that is elemental, seemingly at any rate, beyond the reach of more than temporary distraction or unrest.

Passing through this ancient countryside, too old any longer to bear fruit, or make a pretence of vigour, one catches a sense of creation, deep-rooted and abiding, stretching back before the days of learning or even knowledge, to the first soil of wisdom. The land remains as it was in the beginning. The earth droops to an ancient acceptance. . . . man is just himself.

For four hours we jogged easily along the valley bottom eastward, sometimes on the south side, sometimes on the north side. Our camels were not heavily loaded, but because the day was hot and perhaps because our beduins inclined to laziness, we went on at an unhurried pace.

Abdu entertained me along the route with stories of massacres and single murders done by rival tribes and robbers. He showed me a spot where stains certainly showed on the ground, prompting him to invent the murder of three men who had left the village after taking their master's flock to sell at the market. "This is the *Kabile* country," said Abdu. "These towns hold no allegiance to the Sultan, humouring only themselves; and often the villages are besieged." One or two of these villages were connected by long passages, theoretically ideal, but useless in practice, for they could be used only while the tribes concerned were on peaceable terms. So far as I could gather the original idea of these tunnels was to enable the tribes to carry on an exchange of goods without risk of being exposed to the enemy in the open ground above.

Sometimes we swerved near a village and passed through palm plantations and fields growing vegetables, the green of which refreshed the dead, dry area around it.

In four hours we came to Sewun and made camp in the entrance of the mosque. Here, Komiss' friend joined our little caravan and we settled down together in the cool of the canvas, after unloading the thirsty camels.

We had camped unaccosted in Sewun, as though in a suburb, and it surprised me that this suburb should be to all intents and purposes undefended. The white-washed walls of the mosque were pitted here and there with bullet holes and a few yards away, standing alone like an island, was a tall fortress with no windows below twelve feet from the ground and then only slits large enough for someone to fire through. The door was solid as an elephant and looked as though it would stand many onslaughts before giving way.

In happy contrast to this scowling fortress were the children: girls ranging from the ages of six to fourteen, the eldest being of marriageable age, gaily bedecked and with dresses short at the front and trailing to the ankle behind, their arms overburdened with silver bangles,

heavy broad anklets above their tiny feet, and their thick
black hair hanging down to where curled silver necklaces
encircled slender brown necks.

I had almost forgotten that children could be pretty.
With them were young boys, from three to seven, for the
most part stark naked, friendly but shy creatures. The
girls had their faces painted the yellow of ochre, which is
supposed to keep their skin pale, a sign of beauty. One of
the girls carried a parasol, a little affair of silk and wood
which remained open in greeting to the sun.

They were not only intensely curious but entirely devoid
of modesty. They stared at me, relieved themselves, and
pointed their fingers at me. The bolder ones approached
nearer and touched my clothes, crying out in surprise at
the buttons. For a time Abdu, with the aid of Komiss,
tried to keep them off, but he eventually left them alone
and went off to prepare a meal.

In my audience were old and young alike, and the old
ones were like children in their talk, and the young,
for their part, because of their seriousness and lack of
frivolity, were like grown up men; only the girls giggled
and behaved as small girls often do.

We had pitched our tent, using the entrance of the
mosque for a wall; no one seemed to comment on this and
it did not hinder the muezzin, from the minaret above our
heads, calling the villagers to prayer in a strong clear voice.
There were two entrances to the mosque and since I was
resting in one of them, a man who wished to enter that way
was forced to step over my body, but he took it all as a
matter of course. I filled in my diary, took readings from
my aneroids and thermometers and then snatched a restful
hour's sleep before departure.

With our camels once again forging ahead, we swung past
the gateway of the walled city of Sewun at a left-angled
bend, we followed the wall along on the northern side
and noted its varying thickness; within a few yards
we came to a grill, iron-barred, set in a wall where it

met the ground. No one could squeeze their way through, but these grills allowed the exit of water during rainstorms.

It appeared to me that Sewun would be a difficult place to conquer, particularly as it is a self-supporting city, producing within its walls, cultivation and enough produce to keep the people alive in the event of siege; Sewun is one of the two most up-to-date towns in the inland Hadhramaut; the other being Terim, further east.

Two hours' marching brought us clear of the environs, and then we came to a valley more than usually dead, the track close against the south cliff, and beyond the cliff the mountains showing rugged and formidable. They wore a grave beauty impossible to capture on canvas or paper. A soft radiance from the sky lit up projecting crags, whose outlines were lost in the shadows of mauve and purple, blue and amethyst. The valley had been rounded, and for a while seemed to lean a little to the north, only to straighten out again at the first opportunity; its width had tapered slightly and I began to wonder whether I should ever see it coming to a point. Many times I had travelled up smaller wadis to their source where they projected from the foreheads of the mountains.

When we came near the village of Ishharr, our caravan turned due south into the Wadi Adim and we travelled along it for about three miles in the delight of pleasant discovery.

.   .   .   .   .

This was the local Garden of Eden, luxurious in a coat of many hues and with ripe fruit flashing colour here and there like a woman's frock in summer.

A greater surprise lay in store when we turned the bend and saw a wide stream flowing before us. We made camp beneath a flowering thorn tree that made a canopy above our heads. Stripping in the sunshine, I dived into the river, but could not reach the bottom.

This could lay claims to being the most delightful spot in the Hadhramaut, but the beauty is intermittent, for the local people told me the recent rains had brought it into being. The camels walked in and drank their fill, the goats and sheep of the villagers also, and the human members of our party last of all waded into the oily green river that enchanted us.

We had had an exciting morning before reaching Ishharr. One of our camels, a strong brute, ran amuck for perhaps fifty yards until finally his load came off with a bump and a bounce. We had difficulty in catching him, for he moved on directly we came near. Fortunately, this baggage did not belong to me, but was the personal belongings of our beduins.

Two camels had joined us when we turned off from the mighty Wadi Hadhramaut, carrying goods destined for Java. The last night in the Wadi Hadhramaut, we camped near a fort set amid a desolate area in the centre of the valley. The nearest village was five miles away, and as we passed it we were told that two men were murdered that morning and robbed of their money, and that the villagers, hearing the shooting, had rushed out and discovered the results of the ambush nearby a well and had given chase to the assassins. The murderers had run to the fort under whose walls we camped and there they asked for food and water, and not until they had gone on again did the Sultan's soldiers discover that they had unwittingly aided the wrong side. It is a strange story, but not an unusual one in the Hadhramaut.

We had slept for four hours, and been woken by the moon, which guided our steps into the coolness of night. The breeze had been southerly, making travelling pleasant. As the dawn broke, other caravans woke to life, and we hailed them cheerfully in passing.

.   .   .   .   .

We had now come to a place where I could easily have rested for many days. The luxuriant growth of trees, bushes and vegetables, the contentment of the animals, the fish in the river, made up a pleasing picture.

I had little thought that I should be diving and swimming in midsummer in the southern Arabian wilderness.

The current was fairly fast and the rocky bottom uneven and broken sometimes by sharp crags, but there were many deep places, and here I found that my legs were often attacked by a large species of fish, unless I kept swimming. The villagers declared the fish caught in these waters were not edible, and I wondered what manner of fish they could be. The water itself was too thick to see anything of them. In the shallower portions of the river, fish about the size of a small carp flashed their quicksilver in and out amongst the channels of the rocks; there were hundreds of them.

We had camped a little before noon, and an hour later the faint rumble of thunder came to our ears. The country was rugged here, broken but not steep, and the formidable cliffs of the Wadi Hadhramaut had melted away to mere banks of rubble. Many times I noticed black birds the size of crows, sailing above us, making a curious sort of chirping, and sometimes landing on the humps of our camels. They were evidently seeking food, and they seemed to find satisfaction in the wool of the beasts, while their owners contentedly chewed the bushes.

Abdu had a talk with me. He complained he did not like the Hadhramaut. He considered it to be a land of suspicion and murder; a lawless land. He said, also, that even where there is peace, the existence of the men and women was often of the lowest order and not the equal of his Yemen standard.

Before we left, an old man from the village came to me and eyed me curiously, trying to decide my nationality by my dress of blue shorts, blue silk shirt and Arab turban and sandals. I was a puzzle to him. Many of these villagers have never seen a white man, and possibly some of them did not know such people existed, but my skin had turned brown and in places was almost black.

It was three o'clock when we started off, and as soon as there was sand I attempted to walk with bare feet, but gave it up very shortly, as the ground was as hot as embers. I had never before experienced such heat on the ground, and when I thrust my thermometer into the soil the mercury rushed up to the limit, and I hastily plucked it out of the sand before it burst.

Our steps seemed now to be steadily mounting, and the country was wild and vast, no longer hedged by forbidding cliffs. It was not until after the arrival of the next morning that we came to a part of the valley that could be considered a gorge. As we crossed the backs of the mountains, slipping amongst the stones, our camels panting heavily, Abdu pointed out by the wayside a hedgehog, black as coal and just as dead-looking. I was rather surprised that such creatures existed in Arabia, and Abdu said they were extremely rare.

We went down a gorge opening into a plain dotted by big bushes. Clouds tempered the heat of the sun, and a playful breeze fanned our faces and cooled our legs as we went forward into a land older than Noah.

CHAPTER TWENTY

RACING THE RAINS, WE MEET THE FLOOD

IT WAS THE fifth of September and behind us in the north-west sat in the sky a beautiful rainbow, strong and brilliant, with a second one describing a fainter arc.

Two large birds, not unlike the kestrel, having white wings, black-tipped like mourning stationery, came to greet us at our midday camp.

Rain had made the ground softer, so we were able to discover the tracks of a gazelle. This led to wild excitement amongst the beduins.

The caravan began to follow a wobbling trail, a curious fact, since apparently there was no earthly reason why it should not forge straight ahead like a Roman road. We came to a cutting made by human hands in the mountains, and here there was an abundance of quartz in layers glistening in the sun. The colour of the rock apart from this, was a brick red. We found ourselves in a deep valley and here our voices played around us hoarsely when we spoke. Only four of our camels were loaded, the fifth, a young one, was not harnessed to the others, and allowed to wander as he wished. He must have been a source of envy to the rest, because he could contentedly eat from the bushes along our route; but the others maintained their pace without chance of straying from the narrow track.

When loading or unloading the camels, Komiss would start a sing-song after the manner of sea shanties, which the others joined whenever there was a chorus; and this rhythm undoubtedly helped the preparation of the camels.

Komiss and his companion were a welcome contrast to my last two guides. They found life a cheerful and willing business. I had no trouble at all from them. On occasions they would pick up brushwood along the way, so that we could enjoy a fire if we were wet when we made camp.

Sometimes distant storms flashed weirdly in the hills. After rain, the earth in the valley smelt of incense.

One day, sheltering beneath some rocks half way down a pass descending two thousand feet into a valley, Komiss talked about the future and its possible dangers. He explained that the beduins fear the rain in these parts. To get across the mountains a caravan has often to descend into the valleys. Sometimes these valleys, constructed with cleft walls, rocky and perpendicular, leave exits only at their ends. It is possible to descend into a valley with the camels, a wadi perhaps five or more miles long, and when in the middle, storms on the neighbouring hills may cause a million rivulets to cascade out of the mountain sides and fill the valley with a torrent of water. Therein lies the danger, he said. Komiss told us we must on no account go down into the valleys unless reasonably sure of quick retreat.

For the next few days we camped early in the morning and left again at one o'clock or earlier, for though the heat was then at its greatest, it was the hour when storms approached. We were forced to make our camp in the valleys, for only there was fodder to be found for the camels. We came in the course of time to a place called Arafar. Here there is a high mountain, on the top are remains of a small fortress-like building dating from the seventh century. It was built by one of the Prophet's disciples whom Mohammed had sent south to spread the gospel of the Moslem faith. When the disciple had come into a land of heathens, worshipping the moon and certain planets, as in the times of Sheba, he had made a roadway up the almost unscalable cliff and built his home. Whether he had chosen this eyrie to be as close as possible to the heavens, or to be safe from attack from below, imagination had to decide.

But Arafar was a most unusual kind of place, blessed with abundance.

Here in this village had come rich merchants to settle, and their industry had been imbibed by the people, who now possessed a rare spirit for work; here in Arafar the people had successfully conquered the arts of desert cultivation, and almost every kind of fruit and vegetable could be seen growing in the parched soil. Banana trees flaunted their boat-shaped leaves, there was a coffee plantation, dates, coconuts, potatoes and various other kinds of edibles. The head man was proud of his achievement, and when later I talked about him to the Sultan in Mukalla, the Sultan said he was glad to hear of such prosperity, and that he regretted more men did not live who knew what could be done to the country by the proper use of wells. It occurred to me to suggest to him that a number of enthusiasts might be trained and sent out to revive the decaying oasis. How English gardeners would enjoy carefully tending and nursing gardens from such barren beginnings, and getting something out of nothing!

Crossing the backs of the mountains and journeying down to Ishharr, every day, almost every hour of the day, the aspect of the country changed. Wide valleys would be flung suddenly aside for narrower gorges; cliffs of the wilderness would give place to the claims of sparsely growing bushes; and occasionally a flowering tree would pierce the monotony of dun-coloured sandstone; but it remained a country wild and untamed, linking man back to origins and first beginnings.

There were few settlers, and nomads roamed freely, seizing upon what they could find regardless of circumstances. The people of these parts were poor, even by beduin standards; ragged, often going foodless for periods, and with only the stand-by of skinny goats.

In many places we found traces of the storms of the past years. Once we descended a slope leading to a narrow valley whose walls consisted of red sandstone where we could

see, 250 feet above our heads, that the rocks had been shaped
by the swirl of waves when that gorge had been inundated
by a rush of water. Komiss brought to my observation one
morning the fact that three years ago in this very valley,
a storm had taken him unawares, and he had not been able
to get out quick enough. He had been faced with a wall of
water sixty feet high, tearing towards him. There was no
time to unload the baggage animals, and he had only
been able to save a few riding camels. While crossing this
region, he had frequently scrambled up the face of the cliff,
and been stranded for a week on its summit while the waters
subsided. He told me that when floods came it was usual
for the beduins to fire their rifles as a warning to other
travellers or villagers.

Strangely enough he told us his story only a short time
before we heard the rumble and crack of an approaching
storm. The wind turned into a gale, slashing the sand and
rain into our faces; it came at us horizontally; the camels
checked, but were driven on, and we all kept our heads down,
tying handkerchiefs over our faces as we faced the blast.
It was a strange experience to watch the other figures
pushing on against the tempest, for it looked as if we were
combating the sea world, rather than anything on land.

The sun had long since clouded over, and in the sand and
rainstorm even the half light had dwindled and all but
gone.

Komiss urged the other beduins to shout encouragement
to the camels, and we sang lusty Arab songs to hurry the
lumbering beasts. It was five o'clock and already night.
With the passing of the sandstorm, driven away by the
pouring down of rainwater from the skies, the lightning
flashed more continuously, and the thunder became
terrible.

The rain was lit up in sheets, and in the flashes I saw
Komiss urging on the camels. For two hours we went ahead,
contemptuous of our shivering bodies, anxious only to reach
higher ground. A shout from the leader announced he had

discovered a path that led upwards, for which he had been seeking. But in our ears came the sudden rush of water, a sound I had heard before coming from immense water-falls. I do not think we realised just how near we had been to disaster, but when we had climbed perhaps eighty feet, a wall of water about twenty yards below our level came surging along the channel and roared past, carrying boulders in its stream. . . .

It was a night without a moon, and only the now fitful flashes of lightning showed us how close we had been to the end of things.

The strain over, we all broke into song, our steps mounting us higher, until soon we were at a height of twelve hundred feet above the valley bottom. The river below was rising fast, and I wondered whether it had ever flooded the steppe we were now traversing. The rain continued and the wind was very cold; even the camels shivered, but we went on until we came to some dugouts, houses tunnelled away into the sandstone strata. These were the homes of a small party of shepherds and shepherdesses, their goats corralled safe from the floods. The moment we halted and climbed stiffly from our camels, the rain ceased. The wind dropped. The clouds broke across the sky and the moon peacefully and clearly lighted up our haven of refuge.

We were all anxious to unload the camels and get some movement into our bodies and warmth. We made a fire in one of the dugouts and our eyes smarted with the acrid smoke, since the only outlet was the door, but its cheerful blaze warmed our hearts, and we drank coffee and tea from little bowls of baked mud, the cups of those parts.

I asked Abdu the reason for the tunnelled dwellings, and he said it was because the people feared attacks from passing roving bands who travelled along the wadis. These little dugouts could not be discerned at a greater distance than a hundred yards, and they were situated on the less frequented side of the valley. A long way above the level of the bottom, they were reasonably safe from unwelcome attention.

Komiss was philosophical, but Abdu had grown wildly excited over our escape. He said that Allah had protected us, and he spent extra time over his prayers, no doubt thanking his Protector for special consideration.

After supper I wandered away with my torch to the edge of the steppe. The waters were still swirling and sucking in the wadi below. It was a rather awful sight. I could not repress a shiver. Earthquake, fire and flood, are all of them cataclysms, but now I thought flood was worse than fire and should go into second place, for it carries the weight of fear, without the warmth of excitement.

CHAPTER TWENTY-ONE

THE SAFETY OF THE SEA

I WENT TO sleep that night thinking that perhaps the journey to Shihr would take longer than originally planned. There was no more rain and the warmth of the morning sun was gratefully received by a steaming earth. At breakfast I asked Komiss about our prospects for the future. He said they were good. Provided we kept an open eye for the storms and avoided the narrow gorges where a caravan could easily be trapped, we ought to be safe enough.

The sun, making up for the coldness of the night, went to the other extreme and blistered our skins. Our journey had twisted alternately, since leaving Ishharr, starting due south and then swinging south-east or west, and back again, like the pointer of an erratic compass. My maps were no help to me. I had long since been baffled by our manœuvres. Only local knowledge appeared to be of any use in the task of path-finding.

It is a country where it would be easy to get lost, since there are few water-holes or wells. A country to be avoided except in the seasons of rain.

At our midday camp we heard the singing of distant beduins. Komiss was alert at once, and bade us hurry and pack. He took us round in a wide detour and we hid in a corner of the rocks.

The singing beduins came nearer and we caught the glint of the sun shining on their rifle barrels. They were a gay, debonair and free lot, and Komiss thought he read in their movements the intentions of a plundering band.

Soon after their passing we came out of the hiding and continued along the route, only to find after proceeding for perhaps a mile that the stragglers of the band were hustling along their lazy camels. There was nothing to do but go ahead and greet them in a nonchalant manner, and this we did. In number they nearly doubled us, but the sight of a European so astonished them that they did nothing but return our greetings and hurry on to inform the main body, casting backward glances every few yards.

Komiss confided that he thought there would be no trouble from the party, but that it might be wiser to break away from that wadi; while we were finding a new trail, he would cover our tracks and make new ones to mislead the possibility of pursuit.

While we were following this plan, more singing came to our ears and we hid again, wondering whether we had fallen in with another lawless band. We caught sight of the sun flashing again on metal, but this time it was petrol in cans strung across camels' bodies, four hundred in number, and seemingly a mighty concourse. The caravan carried petrol to the rich el Kaff's of Terim which some consider to be a more important town than Shibam or Sewun.

They passed us on the other side of the valley, nearly a mile from us, but we shouted to them and their voices came faintly back to our ears.

·　　·　　·　　·　　·

The country from now on grew more and more precipitous. Our camels lumbered up the sides of the steep mountains and shambled down, their loads constantly having to be readjusted. It seemed often as if their legs would not stand the strain of descent since they possessed no power to slow up, and only the constant care and control of the beduins kept the animals upon their feet.

This was a route used only at that time of year when there was water. Stench from the skeletons of camels constantly greeted us as we made our ascents and descents.

The animals had fallen off the narrow ledge, and tumbled below, either being killed outright by the accident or unloaded and left to perish. One afternoon while descending into one of these narrow valleys a camel slipped a little; he might have slid over the edge to destruction, if Komiss, who was riding, had not slipped from his perch and with rare presence of mind grabbed the camel's head, thus forcing the animal's legs back again to safety.

We reached a narrow valley, and thunder and lightning warned us of another storm. We went on faster, and the flash of lightning and the noise in the heavens crept nearer. The sky overhead was clear and untroubled, but Komiss, who was experienced in weather conditions, urged us to hurry since the storm had passed near enough to feed the streams leading into our gorge.

We were three hours racing along over shingle and rocks, and as the darkness came, enveloping the gorges, after a strong and insolent sunset, we hurried up the side of the cliff, winning more easily this time our second race against the rains.

Passing near a place where a camel had fallen, Komiss or one of the other beduins would stop to inspect the remains and would be able to tell us not only the age of the camel but the reason for its falling, whether accident or weakness, or too heavy a load; he, also, could give us the date when the mishap had occurred—as though trained like doctors in post-mortem proceedings.

It was on one of these occasions when Komiss stepped aside to inspect a large skeleton—which he said had lain there for three years, skin and flesh long since disappeared through the ravages of wolves and birds of prey—that the leading camel faltered and the second animal, strung by its nose rope to the leader, cannoned into it and would have slipped and gone below had not the rope held him.

There was little opportunity of relaxation on this last stretch, for alarms and excursions were frequent. Late at night sometimes, we would camp, since, when there was no moon, it was dangerous to attempt to traverse the rocky hills. But storms broke suddenly and we had to fetch in the camels, and hurry to safer ground.

The chief diversion in this unpopulated, hostile land, no longer cultivated into smiles by man, were the tracks of gazelle, and occasionally we caught a fleeting glimpse of elastic bodies bounding to safety. Komiss and the other beduins would take turns to stalk and shoot at gazelle, aiming in front of the flash of white underneath the tail, but their aim was bad and we had no meat until we reached the end of our journey.

Coming nearer to the coast, we spent a day crossing a wide plain; our steps taking us over little rivulets, and then the plain disappeared into the fastnesses of mountains which here rose to a little more then seven thousand feet. In the early morning the summits of these mountains would be hidden in low-lying clouds and at night our clothes would be soaked to the skin because of these mists.

There were more birds in the air and whenever we packed up and left a camp, crows would help us to clean up. It was in these mountains that one evening we came across a white-bearded badu who must have been at least seventy years of age, carrying a home-made spear. With him appeared his wife in rags, and a dog and donkey; walking exactly in their footsteps came a young man of perhaps twenty-eight years who was their son. They would have shocked vegetarians, for they had no property and Komiss told me that they lived entirely on meat, which the old man got each day with his spear. He was a remarkable figure, thin as a rake, but still alive and alert, and I wondered whether his prowess was sufficient to get food for the larder each day.

The last day before coming to the coast, we descended into the wadi that opened out to the shore of Southern Arabia. Behind us receded the tall mountains, their heads in the clouds, and then as we topped a little rise, we saw

The Leader of a Roving Band Demands Tribute Money

The Unmapped Mountains

for the first time for many months the silver flash of the sea. The sun broke through and made a new world of that wilderness, bringing cheer to us, and smiles of satisfaction to the friendly faces that now began to cross our path.

. . . . .

Shihr is a walled city, living on its industry of fishing, but outside, sprawled here and there, lie villages, dependent upon water from the mountains, and the donkey water-carriers trotted past us or met us along the path, busy about their business.

Shihr had a long wall of white surrounding the town, from which peeped houses of four and five storeys capped by four lofty minarets. This is a sea port second only in importance in Southern Arabia to Mukalla, where the coastal steamers call.

As we left the last outcrop of mountain to our left, Komiss pointed out a peak, distant by perhaps fifteen miles, and said that there was a hole, bottomless, haunted by the *djinns*, for many had tried to descend its depths, but had come back fearful of the future. Coughs and howls came up from here. Lights taken down had been mysteriously extinguished; even a modern electric torch failed to work in its depths. The Sultan had tried to order slaves to descend to the bottom and two men who were made to lower themselves, never came back. But I did not take the story of the haunted hole seriously, since many years had elapsed since the last attempt to discover its secret, and no doubt a legend was already growing up on the spot.

Outside Shihr are a lot of tumbledown dwellings made of wood-thatch and cloth. These are the miserable homes or hovels of the poorer beduins, where ill-fed children squatted and ran naked and unwanted. We passed by these suburbs and came to the gateway of the sea port, swinging into the narrow streets; on camel-back I could look right into the first floor windows. The construction of Shihr is reasonably good from an European standard, and we were led by an increasing escort to the house of the chief man, Shaikh Omar Saleh bin 'Ali, a short red-bearded, blue-eyed man, anxious to do all in his power to make me comfortable and happy. The Government guest house is a fine large building of white-washed mud, three storeys high and surrounded by a terrace. The usual plush couch, armchairs, and folding seats, were to be found in the reception room, and also a rich carpet itself carpeted in a thick layer of dust. Two slaves hastened forward to flick their dusters in order that we might sit down without too much concern for our clothes.

I took a seat at the head of the room, and Shaikh Omar took the other, and we both faced the entrance, through which poured ministers of the Government, merchants, and men of high standing.

My beduins asked for presents, and I distributed gifts to them. Komiss and his friend were the least mercenary of the guides I had employed, and I was sorry to see the last of them.

Shaikh Omar fidgeted with his beard and smiled approvingly and Komiss and the other Arabs shook hands, and said in parting that they hoped I would return again to Arabia and become their brother.

Then they went.

A letter was written by Shaikh Omar with the aid of his ornate, gold-embossed fountain pen which long since had given up regular work and had to be dipped into a bottle of ink. A message was sent to the Sultan in Mukalla to tell him of my arrival and to make arrangements for a car to take me along the road to the capital should there not be a steamer on its way.

The view from the windows looked eastward over the town and southward over the sea. Immediately in front, on the other side of the quadrangle loomed a fortress. I was told by an Indian doctor, who belonged to the court, and who stayed in the town as dispenser to the people without charge, that the fortress had been built as a defence against the rebellions in the times of the Kaiti and Kathiri struggles for supremacy.

We went over it, and amongst the ruins we found a courtyard with mosaic-patterned arches not unlike an Indian temple. We saw, also the entrance leading to a subterranean passage two miles long, and coming up eventually to ground level a long way from the town.

This was the secret of the Sultan, to be used only in times of emergency, but everyone seemed to know about it. We did not progress far down the tunnel because the smell inside was strong enough to drive us back in panic.

I was shown the dispensary, and then taken for a walk along the two miles front where the fishermen were coming in with their day's haul. A number of very large stingray fish were left on the beach, one of which had a span of seven feet. There was also a shark which had been brought in, but the rest were mostly unknown to me, varying in length from six inches to three feet.

Numbers of fish were thrown away for reasons which seemed to me obscure, but the Arab is neither a sailor nor a natural fisherman and leaves fish-eating to camels. There were thousands and thousands of crabs, none larger than five inches across, scurrying about the beach and disappearing into their holes as we approached and tried to pick them up.

.   .   .   .   .

On our return, we sat upon the little veranda of the dispensary and sipped coffee, talking of my journey, of Freya Stark and of others the doctor had known in the Hadhramaut. It was he who had perhaps saved Freya Stark's life in Shibam. Certainly he had been able to keep her alive until the coming of the Royal Air Force and Wing-Commander Haythorne-Thwaite. He had been resident in Sewun for a short period, and had come down to Shibam to attend to the English woman; he was interested in travel and told me news of an Egyptian party that had

landed at Hodeida and had gone up to Sana to interview
the Imam, in the hopes of being allowed to explore in the
region of Mareb, and though this party were Moslem, the
Imam had refused them permission.

They had come back and then travelled along the south
coast to Mukalla with the intention of going up country
and visiting some of the relics of past civilizations strewn
about in the mountains.

I asked if he found the practice of chemistry one that was
useful in this part of the world, but he said he was afraid the
Arabs did not take to medicines. If they did so at all,
he had to make them nasty otherwise patients considered
them to be useless. They were superstitious and steeped
in tradition and they disliked anything that suggested poison.
They were fearful for a child when unwell, but more
frightened of giving it anything medicinal.

Since the young Indian was in charge of passports as
well as health, he knew the movements of the two ships that
came alternatively to Shihr, and he told me the s.s. *Africa*,
the boat which had taken me from Aden to Mukalla was
expected hourly. We spent most of the next day walking up and down the sea shore. I thought of the walrus
and the carpenter. The fishermen insisted on shaking me by
the hand wherever I went; a little of this shaking of
hands with men whose palms stank of fish, went a long
way, and the Indian doctor sensing my distaste, bore me
away to talk politics in the house of a friend.

There was nothing much to do in Shihr and I waited
the coming of the Aden ship with an impatience shared by
Abdu.

CHAPTER TWENTY-TWO

REFLECTIONS ON SLAVES, THE SLAVE TRADE, AND ARABIAN POLITICS

A GREAT EXCITEMENT prevailed when the ship from Aden arrived at last and anchored in the bay, bringing in its hold a cargo of rice. Black slaves, their torsos shining and gleaming in the sun, worked at the unlading, chanting queer choruses.

The *Africa* looked a curious vessel as it bobbed up and down upon the crested rollers, with its ungainly funnel set well aft, and its extremely antiquated proportions. It gave the impression of being definitely home-made; in England it would long ago have been sent to be broken up, but in the eyes of the Arabs it was still a fine boat and a wonderful thing.

Abdu revived in an extraordinary way once he smelt Aden again, and rising from his sick bed with alacrity he assisted in packing up the pots and pans and general paraphernalia of travel. Directly I promised some of the stores that were left over, to Komiss, Abdu awoke to life, regained consciousness and asked me for the first refusal.

Shihr came down to the water's edge to see me off as I embarked in a little boat and was rowed out to the steamer. I shook hands all round. The Arab is always ready to shake hands, or at any rate to touch finger-tips, and does so ceremoniously on every possible occasion. It took a long time to say good-bye to Sheikh Omar and his friends, and I despaired of getting away, but suddenly my legs were seized from under me by two muscular negroes who, running swiftly through the green water, handed me over to two greasy natives standing in the boat. Abdu, in his semi-white clothing, suffered even worse than myself; finger marks were left across his tunic as though the carriers were criminals leaving their thumb-prints behind. A half-score of brawny arms pulled on the oars; we played leap-frog across the surf and then rowed easily towards the gangway of the *Africa*.

Once on board I went straight for the companion-way leading to the bridge to see if the chief engineer and the skipper would recognise me from the voyage out. I found them laid out flat taking a restful siesta under two green umbrellas. I sat down in an arm-chair and stretched out my legs luxuriously. Without waking the others I sank into a sort of coma; Arabia seemed to be far away, the desert to have receded into the land of half-dreams; I was back again in civilisation amongst the luxuries of clean food and soft beds.

The chief engineer was the first to awaken. He rubbed his eyes in sleep and then sprang up in amazement when he saw me reading the newspaper. He seemed astonished that I had returned safely and without visible signs of hard-ship. The murmur of our voices, droning in the hot after-noon, woke the skipper, who sat up with an oath.

We had a midday meal and were preparing to cast off when a shout from the shore announced a delay, and looking through my glasses I saw a twelve-oared boat racing towards the *Africa*.

There was something familiar about the seated figure in the stern, something I had seen before in the poise of the white-robed figure who was being hurried towards our boat. The focus of the glasses told me in a minute who it was making this last-minute arrival; it was Philby, taking most unexpectedly to the sea. My fates appeared to be bound up with this Englishman who had turned Arab.

I knew at Shibam that he had been forced to ride donkeys for a section of the journey down to the Coast at Shihr because his second Ford car had broken a back axle and there was no means of replacing it. The few cars that find their way into the Hadhramaut are transported over the Djol in parts and then assembled again. Philby had come down to Shihr and had then gone to Mukalla in order to wireless Aden for the spare part he required.

He clambered on board and greeted those on the bridge with his usual smile. "I heard you were just going," he told me, "and I was determined to meet once again before you left Arabian shores. I have been staying at Mukalla a few days while a back axle for my car was shipped out to me," he explained. He said that he was about to return to Shibam, then perhaps to Shabwa again, and afterwards over to the north. He asked me how my fortunes had progressed at Shabwa, and was bitterly disappointed to hear that I had not got there. He told me he had had a conversation over the radio with the authorities in Aden. They were very annoyed, apparently, that he should have come down with an armed band to force an entry into Shabwa, following this up by descending into the Hadhramaut and entering the Aden protectorate without having first obtained the permission of the authorities. He repeated to me some of the conversation, his grey-blue eyes twinkling merrily.

The *Africa* gave two hoots on her whistle, and the engines began to throb. "*Au revoir*," Philby shouted as he disappeared over the side into the rowing boat. "We will meet in London when I come over for the Coronation. Good Luck." With a final wave of his hand, he disappeared from my sight and out of this narrative.

As we swung clear of the reef and steamed westward, I turned over in my mind the sequence of my encounters with Philby, the last word of which I was not to hear until I reached Aden and talked to Captain Hamilton.

I then heard the other side of the story of Philby's expedition into the Hadhramaut.

Before Philby had arrived in Shibam, rumours filtering through the countryside had reached Aden that King Ibn Saud had sent down an armed force that had invaded

Hadhramaut territory. These rumours, together with the natural hostility of the local tribesmen, nearly brought about the death of the Arabian explorer, since, when he was at Shabwa, the beduins of the locality had encircled the ruined city, waiting for him to step into the ambush which they were preparing for him. Captain the Hon. R. A. B. Hamilton, the political officer who happened to be in the neighbourhood on a punitive expedition, held back the tribes with great difficulty, and prevented what might have proved a tragedy. He explained to the tribesmen that Philby was a friend, and when they would not listen, promised to get him away from their country if they would hold their hand and give him time.

He then sent Philby an urgent message saying he could hold up the tribesmen for five days, but no more. . . .

.   .   .   .   .

Back again at Mukalla, a boat put out from the shore, containing 'Ahmed bin Nasir, minister for Tribal Relations, who wished me to meet his lord and master, the Sultan.

It was pleasant to be whirled through the main street at Mukalla in a motor-car, this time without Abdu, for I had left him on the boat to indulge his moods out of harm's way. Once again I entered the drawing-room of the palace, and took my seat on the plush chair, while the ruler of the Hadhramaut was advised of my arrival.

Sultan Saleh bin Galib was a big man, standing over six feet, and heavily built. His young son, who accompanied him, had studied at an Egyptian University, and spoke English, but he was kept in the background of the conversation. We had a long talk about many things. We discussed politics, the doings of the Italians in Abyssinia, the politics of South Arabia and the slave traffic of those parts.

.   .   .   .   .

The slave trade is about thirteen hundred years old in Arabia, and is both universal and time-honoured.

Westerners generally gain the wrong idea of something, in itself objectionable, but which has grown up to be a part of the life of Arabia and the Arabians, and often some of the best part.

Western people shudder at the very word "slavery" because of the tales of physical cruelty, tales of plantation life in the Southern States of North America before Abolition —*Uncle Tom's Cabin* stories.

But in the case of the Arabian or Mohammedan slave, it is different. Many of the slaves are treated well by their masters. Many are contented. And therein lies the danger.

Only the more prosperous among the beduin or nomadic Arabs own a slave or slaves. A sufficiency of water and pasturage for his camels, coarse tobacco, black coffee, several young wives, plenty of rice, dates, and an occasional dish of camel or goat flesh would satisfy the most luxury-loving badu. It is the sedentary Arab of the town or village who is the main instrument for the present slavery conditions.

Slavery is congenial to the Arab character. The Arabs are a patriarchal people. A man's wives, children and servants are all very much under his sway and he pays no direct wages to his servants. He prefers them to come and ask him for a new garment, a weapon, a beast of burden, or a dole of money.

It is natural for a dependant who scents a chance of gratifying his self-interest more effectively elsewhere, to leave his good patriarch, go away and improve his prospects. This is very disconcerting to the benevolent patriarch, who, therefore, decides it is best to buy his servants outright rather than hire them.

Mecca itself, the holy city, meeting-place of the Mohammedan nations, pattern to devout Moslems all over the world, is the principal slave market of Arabia; but there are others. . . .

Passing down the streets towards the centre of a town during my wanderings, I frequently passed Abyssinians, negroes and half-castes, some badly and some well dressed, attending their masters or acting as a bodyguard. These were all bondmen. But nothing is ever seen of the hundreds of younger girl slaves who are kept close in the shuttered houses of the city.

Some of these towns have in their centre a slave market. The slave dealers arrange benches in front of their houses for the displaying of their merchandise.

Are they wretched? No! Many whom I saw in various towns were laughing and even joking.

The customers arrive, file slowly past, keenly surveying the slaves, discussing the while their needs with the dealers. On the invitation of a dealer, clients drift inside the houses, where they view the slave-girls.

A beautiful slave girl was offered to me for the equivalent of £5. When I signified to the seller that I was not interested, he became enthusiastic, for there is nothing except fighting that an Arab loves more than a bargain. The dealer settled down to it. Here was an Englishman with the Eastern love of haggling. Many cups of coffee, and perhaps a few hours' desultory talk—then a satisfactory sale. When finally he realised that I was not buying at any price he turned away, a disappointed man.

I happened to meet a man who had some kind of connection with slave dealing. A human bird of prey, he described to me the procedure of slave-running in the bad old days.

First of all a village is marked down where likely recruits are obtainable and boasting strong men and shapely girls. Then preparations are made secretly for a descent by night. Raiders with spears and rifles swoop down on the village, uttering fearsome yells, carrying fire and destruction before them.

From Abyssinia and the hills and fertile valleys of the Blue and White Nile streamed down the bulk of the black cargoes. Under Italian jurisdiction, this will probably no longer be possible, and if Mussolini carries out his bond, the slave raiders, with Arabia as their market, will have to look farther afield for their human merchandise. Liberia is their natural alternative source of supply. But even if Mussolini acts with equal determination in abolishing slavery in Abyssinia as when conquering their country, it will still be ten years before any real shortage of slaves is felt in Arabia.

The slave dealer painted a vivid picture in his description of a typical raid.

The darkness, the sudden yelling and noise have the stupefying effect of nightmare on the sleeping inhabitants. The village is set on fire and everybody put into a state of panic. Old people are thrust on one side, the sick and wounded are left behind, but the able-bodied are taken away to their unknown fate, fastened together in batches.

What do the unfortunate victims think of their plight? How far are the evils modified these modern days? Curiously enough, I was told that though the men are filled with despair, the women and girls often enjoy being forcibly abducted from their homes. Black girls sometimes regard the Arab slaver as a good friend, for he takes them away to see the world and seek romance, much as a ship sails away with the fancies of an English boy. If they are lucky and pretty enough, they may end in the town house of some rich mussalman, surrounded by luxury and ease.

The problem is one that can only be tackled from the place to which Moslem turns for its prayers—Mecca.

"Do you think it is right to carry on such a traffic, in these days?" I asked a high Arab official. "Is it not the will of Allah?" he replied. "The Moslem holy book says that a man may have slaves if he wishes it."

His words provided the answer to a problem that has been exercising the mind of the Arab world for many years.

Moreover, the creed of the Quran has it that it is a blessed act to free slaves. The Moslem's reaction to this is,

"How can I receive this blessing until I own slaves to liberate?"

Once having bought slaves the Moslem usually forgoes the spiritual blessing that goes with the freeing of his human possessions. The end of slavery in the East must wait until the Holy City sets the seal of its approval on abolition in every form, or until the import market is cut off.

There is usually a reason for everything; and there is said to be a very good reason for the Prophet's approval of releasing slaves, and giving them high powers.

It is recorded that at one period of Mohammed's martial career he was beset by a force that threatened to overwhelm him and his supporters. Came to the Prophet one day a slave man who claimed to have an original plan to save the citadel. "Build trenches," said the bondman. Now, to the people this was an unheard of thing, and the majority were against precedents of any sort. Mohammed looked doubtful: torn between curiosity as to the wisdom of the advice and a wish to experiment, and the hidebound council of his followers and friends at Medina. "Build trenches, Master of the Faithful," pleaded the slave.

Mohammed did; and the battle turned against the Prophet's aggressors. From thence did Mohammed recognise that in his slaves he might well find ones to lead and govern his people.

More than twelve hundred years after the Prophet's day, I found that slaves are still known to rise to high estate. There is the local governor of el Hedgerain—none other than Ubeid bin Salim, an African. The one-time governor of Shibam—Ferai Sa'id—now governing Seheil, too, is a bondman.

There is a peculiar tree in Arabia, the Zarr, with thick leaves poisonous to animals, and a flower like a sweet pea, whose wood is now used locally to make gunpowder.

But this fighting tree is not nearly so surprising as the modern slave traffic.

A little Arab sailing craft, a dhow, slipping across the water at night, sailing without lights, noses through rocky shallows into a quiet backwater. Its secret arrival provides moments of excitement and intensity. The cargo space of the dhow is not filled with ordinary merchandise, but with slaves, packed as tight as sardines in a tin; stowed abreast in rows, with their ankles chained to the bottom of the boat, they have no chance of escape.

These sailing vessels look innocent enough, but they may be part of the slave racket that has been going on in Arabia for hundreds of years.

A beautiful native girl of Mombasa, Kenya, came once to Southern Arabia in this fashion.

One moonlight night she ventured alone down to a well to draw water for her family, as she had done every night so long as she could remember. Suddenly five huge black figures rose from the deeper hues of the surround, and the song she was singing was smothered in the folds of a coarse sack. Five years later she was telling her story to a British Political Officer travelling through the country.

If a vigilant gunboat appears on the horizon when the slavers are at their illicit trade, tarpaulins and boxes are strewn on top of the human cargo. A few slaves may be suffocated; if any make a noise, they are promptly knocked on the head to intimidate the rest. No mercy is asked or given when running the black cargoes to Arabia.

Slave running and lawlessness have the advantage over civilised ways, for the dhows are fast, draw only a few feet of water, and can generally evade the law through knowing every inch of the district.

.   .   .   .   .

The political face of Arabia, unchanging for many years, has begun to alter slowly of late years and take on different expressions. The dominating features of the population for whom politics at all seem new, are, first the tribal, and then the patriarchal system. These can change only slowly

Q

through the centuries, being bound by age-old rigidity and custom, so that the changes, when they come, have to be from the outside and on top, rather than from below. What Ibn Saud thinks and plans is of far more importance than any social or progressive movements among the people themselves.

So far as anything is certain, Ibn Saud is working towards an Arab *bloc*, strong enough to be safe from foreign absorption and, at the same time, able to control its own destiny and make its voice heard. With intensely conservative and localised tribesman to be considered, he has a task requiring tremendous tact and diplomacy. Philby was asked on several occasions whether he thought the Arab King would annex the South. His answer was that King Ibn Saud already held the South in the hollow of his hand; his son had marched to Hodeida a year or two ago and had the capital at his mercy. But the northerners were content with a show of force, and afterwards concluded a favourable treaty, both with the Yemen and with Iraq.

King Ibn Saud's horizon, whether he wishes it or not, is bounded in some directions by the British and British interests and his friendliness and regard for the English is at present a definite part of his policy.

Arabia and the Arabs could not become an aggressively hostile power, unless a Holy War was declared, and even so, their rulers realise, after the Abyssinian surrender, that they could not take the field against the armed forces of a Great Power. Working on the old lines, and with the handicap of their unprogressive code of conducting affairs, they would certainly have no chance at all, and to change these ingrained traditions and ways of living, as Attaturk is doing in Turkey, would be impossible in a country still consisting of scattered, suspicious and semi-independent tribes. Modernism is unlikely to hurry the wheels of Arabian progress for a great period of time. Warfare, if it comes, is more certain to be localised between the Arabs and the Jews and the Arabs and foreign exploitation. There is talk of Arabia for the Arabians, largely called into being by the influx of a foreign class of Jew into Palestine. Yet the Jews and the Arabs are cousins, inextricably mixed by their history and geography, also the Arab is at the outset at a disadvantage, for he is no commercialist, distrusts capitalism, diffuses his property, owing to the laws of inheritance (primogeniture does not exist among the Arabs) and his power tends to become cut up. It is partly for these reasons that the Arabs feel that if they do not do something quickly in Palestine, it may be too late, though the undoubted future of the land lies in the amalgamation and friendly intercourse between these two kindred races, each contributing their own special qualities for the common good.

The Arabs would gain more now from the impetus of the Jews than from their exodus.

If the Moslems, however, are not likely to trouble the international horizon themselves, save only by a stiffening in national feeling and a more careful scrutiny of foreigners, they will, and are already, forging their way to a fresh and perhaps strengthened importance through other causes. The focal point of danger is shifting from Palestine in the North, long the battleground of rival interests and religions, to the lesser-known and hitherto remote corner, ignored by most—the South-west corner of the Arabian peninsula, now the very toe of importance.

The Yemen, the Aden protectorate and the Hadhramaut down to Shihr and Mukalla, are now becoming the controversial areas of Arabia, for they are linked with the new advances in Africa, with the Suez Canal and the highway to the East, and with the communications of various Empires. Arabia is not strong enough to cause trouble by itself, but allied to some greater power it might do much. Therein lies the doubt and uncertainty of the future. In alliance with the British, the Arabs swept the Turks out of the peninsular. Besides the Turks and the British, there is now another power that has appeared upon the scene—the old power of Rome, revived, to a certain extent, under Mussolini. As yet, local authorities do not know what the effects of Abyssinia going Italian will have on the territory across the Red Sea.

For the last ten years the Imam of Yemen has had a treaty with the Italians. As mentioned before, this treaty has just come up for renewal. When I first came to Aden the result was uncertain. Now it has been decided, and the decision is significant.

The Yemen has turned to Italy again, but only for a short time. The treaty has been renewed for a single year, which is an unusually short period. What does this mean?

The Imam is clearly giving himself time to see which way the wind will blow. In the long run he continues to flirt with Italy—but only for a short time. Is he to favour Britain or Italy, or is he to march hand-in-glove with Ibn Saud? The future is fluid for a few months, and during that time the seeds of future happenings will be sown. No doubt Italy would like to strengthen her sphere of influence in Arabia, and link it up to that of North Africa; with Abyssinia and Southern Arabia formally in his grasp, Mussolini might be able to turn the pincers on to Egypt next. He is working hard to impress the Arabs, especially on the radio. On the other hand, the Imam fears the possibility of an invasion of his country by Mussolini, under the pretext that was used in the recent Italian-Abyssinian War—the abolition of slavery and the slave trade. For this reason he cannot afford to cut the ground from under his feet by rejecting the hand of the British.

The politics of the Red Sea at the present moment are in a delicate condition The old land of Sheba has suddenly become important again, and fixed the attention of the outside world. Interested eyes are being cast upon the old kingdom of the trading caravans, as in the past.

Will there ever be another Balkis, Queen of the South and of the morning, sitting on the throne of Arabia?

The caravans of trade, embassy and diplomacy, are once more in motion, but nowadays they are going towards the land of Saaba rather than journeying away from it.

APPENDIX

SHEBA

The place name of Sheba has been used in this book to designate the Queen, more often than any other, since her real name must be regarded as still unknown, or at any rate unproved. There can be little doubt but that both Balkis and Makeda were given to her long after her death; one was attached to the Queen by later generations in Arabia, the other in Abyssinia. The earliest authentic mention of the name Sheba is in Genesis, where it is applied to one of the descendants of Shem.

SABA OR SAABA

The word Saba in its earliest form meant, "to make a trading journey. . . ." It was a collective word for merchants making the southern journey. It became the name of a district in south-west Arabia.

Sargon (715 B.C.) tells in his annals of the tribute of Shamsi Queen of Arabia and Itamara of the land of Saaba. Assyrian inscriptions of the time of Tiglath Pileser II make mention of Saaba, but even they are later in date than the period of the Queen of Sheba. They tend to show, however, that the Sabaeans, in all probability, originated from the north and east of Arabia, drifting southward towards the trade. The Mineans, on the contrary, were people of the south, the ancient Hadramis.

ETHIOPIAN CONNECTIONS

The Ethiopians had the word Saba from early times; with them it meant "men," and helps to designate the

Sabaean descent of the country. There is also a river
Mareb in Abyssinia. Mara, in Arabic, stands for woman.
The principal tribe of Semites to invade Abyssinia were
called Habesh, and they came from the Yemen. The
language of these Semites became known as Amharic;
the old Sabaean alphabet was cleverly turned into a
syllabary reading from left to right, and not the reverse
way as in the ancient inscriptions.

QUEEN OF SHEBA AND
COMMANDER CRAUFURD'S RESEARCHES

PLACE OF BURIAL

According to local information gleaned by Craufurd,
the Queen of Sheba is probably buried at Sirwal, approxi-
mately fifty miles north-east of Mareb. No European has
ever visited this town. The tradition concerning Sirwal
and Sheba is very strong in the neighbourhood. Many
of the Sheikhs of the district vouched for the tradition to
Craufurd, and called it a fact.

Can Sirwal have any connection with Siwah, said to
be the earliest capital of the Sabaeans? If so, an expedition
to the present site of the town would be of doubled
importance.

The Imam of the Yemen is becoming more friendly
to the British, but at present, exploration by anyone,
even Moslems themselves, is rigidly discouraged. The
historic part of the Yemen is one of the most shuttered
districts in the world, and entry is rigidly barred.

PARENTS AND ANTECEDENTS

Commander Craufurd bases his information, definitely
naming Sheba's father and mother, and contributing new
knowledge to the scanty details hitherto possessed on this
subject, to researches carried out with the court historian
at Sana. This official showed Craufurd a prized book in

manuscript form, written on parchment, called *Al Ikleel* or *The Devil of Stars*, another name apparently for *Orion's Belt*. It is a classic of Arabian literature and one of their lost books. Unfortunately the flyleaf of this rare and remarkable book was missing, thus Craufurd could no more than guess at its exact date.

He was also shown other volumes written before the days of printing and giving mention of Sheba and Saba. The Yemen authorities are convinced that the Queen of Sheba was an Arab princess, and that she lived and died in their country.

The *British Museum* translate *Al Ikleel* to mean "*The Crown*." One of their authorities states that this book was written by Hamdani, who died at Sana near the middle of the tenth century. Copies of the writings of this Arab chronicler were made in manuscript form, but they are rare.

MEETING BETWEEN SOLOMON AND THE QUEEN OF SHEBA

The Bible account of this meeting is very short. The most beautiful account is to be found in the Kebra Negast of Abyssinia which has been translated from the Ethiopic by the late Sir Wallis Budge and called "the Queen of Sheba and her only son Menyelek." The descriptions are full and varied, and though sometimes in a semi-mystical form are nevertheless clear and for the most part reasonable.

The Koran version is not so credible as the others, being confused frequently by mention of genii and magical lapwings, and other somewhat mythical utterances.

It is narrated in Sale's unabridged edition of the Koran that the Queen's ambassadors brought to Solomon the following things:

"Five hundred young slaves of each sex, habited in the same manner, five hundred gold bricks, a crown enriched with precious stones, besides a large quantity of musk, amber and other things. Some authorities add that Balkis, to test whether Solomon was a prophet or no, dressed the boys like girls, and the girls like boys, and sent him in a casket a pearl not drilled. Solomon distinguished the boys from the girls by the different manner of their drinking water. He ordered a worm to bore the pearl."

DIFFICULTIES OF THE KEBRA NEGAST

Much of the Sheba material is built up from legends and tradition. The earliest written sources are Coptic. The Kebra Negast, according to learned critics, was translated from an Arabic version which in turn had been adopted from the early Coptic. An interesting fact about the fourteenth century Ethiopian translation was that the principal part was borne by a Jew, Isaac, of whom posterity knows little or nothing. He is another of those curiously links between the Arabs, Jews and Abyssinians. A copy of the Kebra Negast did not arrive in England until the end of the eighteenth century; it was brought from Gondar by James Bruce, explorer of the Blue Nile. The Kebra Negast did not obtain fame and circulation in Abyssinia until the return of the Solomonic line of Kings in the thirteenth and fourteenth centuries.

THE SABAEANS

The most ancient Sabaean kings were called Mukrabs. Supreme authority was shared by a king and a priest. The Sabaeans were traders from the early days of their dim history.

The next period of the Sabaeans was one of Kingship alone. During these centuries, their capital and centre was at Mareb. Towards the end of this period they became mingled with, or at any rate adjacent to the Mineans and their kingdom.

The Mineans are said to have made a speciality of the worship of Athtar, or Ashtar, the Sabaeans preferred

Shams, their sun-goddess. Possibly this Shams has some connection with the Queen Shamsi mentioned as paying tribute to the Assyrians in pre-historic times.

During the third period of the Sabaeans, when they came into open contact with the Romans and their power began to decline, their rulers were called Kings of Saba and Raidan. This epoch is fairly well covered by the Axsum inscriptions.

Various inscriptions and coins, unearthed up-to-date, give the names of about fifty of the old Sabaean Kings.

Their trading enterprises undoubtedly covered a portion of Africa for several centuries.

KING SOLOMON'S MINES

Ruins of old mines and workings, found in northern Rhodesia and East Africa, testify clearly enough to the existence of prehistoric mining areas. King Solomon's mines were somewhere in this district, the old Sabaean workings being connected in fame and legend to the fabled opulence of Solomon. Their exact location and determination awaits discovery. But the probability remains that these gold mines were situated somewhere in Africa between the mountains and the equator, and that they were linked across to Arabia in the earliest times, partly by means of the Ophir traffic.

Relics of Ancient Civilisation in Southern Arabia Discovered up to Date.

Visible ruins—period doubtful :	*Sabaean ruins :*
In Wadi Libne eleven miles south of Ghabara.	At Mareb.
In Wadi Fahma.	At Sirwal.
At el Batak.	At Shabwa.
At about eight miles east of Kanina.	At Bir Thamud, in Wadi 'Ewa.
At Hadjdj bil Qabren.	At Maqashi, in Wadi Yesher.

Visible ruins—period doubtful:

At about six miles north of Shihr.

Near Terim.

A mile west of Sune in Wadi Adim.

Ghebun, near el Meshed.

Three miles (about) north-west of el Hadd (Wadi Serr?).

Two or three miles north of el Meshed.

In old water course two or three miles north of Sherdj.

By Dars.

Six miles north of Shibam.

A mile north of Henan.

Sabaean ruins:

Near el Ghartimi (Wadi Adim?).

At Nejran.

J. T. Bent found some undoubted Sabaean ruins near Dharfur.

Supplementary List of Books Dealing with Southern Arabia, Sheba, and kindred subjects.

HADHRAMAUT: some of its mysteries unveiled. Van den Meulen and Dr. von Wissman.

Colonial Report on Hadhramaut. Ingram. (Published by H. M. Stationery Office.)

The Southern Gates of Arabia. Freya Stark.

Southern Arabia. Theodore Bent and Mrs. Theodore Bent.

Land Without Shade.
Geheimnis um Schobua. } Dr. H. Helfritz.

The History of Ethiopia (2 Vols.). Sir E. A. Wallis Budge.

The Queen of Sheba and her only Son, Menyelek. Sir E. A. Wallis Budge.

The Empty Quarter. St. John Philby.

The Koran. Sale's unabridged edition (Chandos Classics).

Black tents of Arabia. Carl Raswan.

Sheba. E. Powys Mathers (Casanova Society).

The following letter was sent by Colonel Lawrence of Arabia to Mr. Norman Stone Pearn.

"Southampton.
"25-IX-33

"DEAR MR. PEARN,

"I'm twelve years away from the East, and wholly out of touch with it and its people. So I cannot advise you.

"Ibn Saud took my war-time supporting of the Hashimite family very ill: being an enthusiast, he thought only himself worth backing. So in approaching him you had best forget me! Philby is his only English friend: but Philby may not wish to encourage others to enter the southern desert. Expeditions there cost much money and effort.

"Marib used to be in the Imam's sphere . . . or just outside it . . . and he used to prefer Italians to Englishmen: but, as I said, I am wholly out of date, and very thankfully so.

"Why bother about Sheba, or Biblical maps? Yesterday I was eating some very good ripe blackberries.

"Yours sincerely,
"T. E. SHAW."

The following letter, dated September 13, 1933, was received by Mr. Norman Stone Pearn from Mr. St. John Philby.

as from N.W.6

"DEAR MR. PEARN,

" . . . Your project of wandering from Marib to Kuwait or thereabouts is an ambitious one, and I don't think that I can offer you much encouragement. In the first place there appears to be a little war of sorts going on in the neighbourhood of Najran which would block your passage from Marib even if you got as far as that, which is not particularly easy. To get there you would have to go to Hodeida and ingratiate yourself with the Yaman Government authorities. That is not my country at all and I fear that I am helpless to help you.

"As regards Ibn Saud's territory your best course would be to apply to Shaikh Hafidh Wahba, the Arabian Minister in London. I frankly don't think they will give you permission, as the policy is to keep out non-Muslim visitors from the country, but there is no harm in trying. I certainly would not advise you to attempt the venture without permission.

"Hoping that this rather discouraging letter will be useful to you and wishing you all luck.

"Yours sincerely,

"H. St. J. Philby."

INDEX